A TO Z JEHADI ORGANISATIONS OF PAKISTAN

Col.Puneet Raina (Retd.)

GAURAV BOOK CENTRE PVT LTD
DELHI

Publisher
GAURAV BOOK CENTRE PVT LTD
4832/24,Prahlad Lane,S-207 Ansari
Road, Daryaganj, Delhi-110002
Ph.: 43570976, 23278261
Email: gauravbookcentre@gmail.com

Edition: 2015

ISBN: 978-93-83316-13-7

Laser Typesetting
JEE-VEE Graphics, Delhi

Price: 1195/-

Printed
Vikas Computers, Delhi

Contents

Preface (*vii*)

1. Jihadist Organizations in Pakistan 1
2. Suicide Attacks by Terrorist Organizations 13
3. Successful Rising of Terrorist and Jihadi Organization 37
4. Global War against Terrorism 125
5. Islamic Terrorism 142
6. Homegrown Violent Jihadists 171
7. Al-Qaeda Unique among Terrorist Organizations 241
8. Lashkar-e-Taiba (Militant Islamist Organizations) 273

Bibliography 294

Index 295

Preface

The proliferation of jihadist organizations in Pakistan over the previous two decades had been the result of a militant culture espoused by radical madrasas like Darul Uloom Haqqania.

The proliferation of jihadist organizations in Pakistan over the previous two decades had been the result of a militant culture espoused by radical madrasas like Darul Uloom Haqqania. Thousands of madrasas across the country became hubs for militancy and religious extremism, having a spill-over effect and presenting a serious threat to Pakistan's internal security. Pakistani madrasas were once considered centres for basic religious learning, mostly attached to local mosques.

Suicide attacks by terrorist organizations have become more prevalent globally, and assessing the threat of future suicide attacks against the United States has gained in strategic importance. While suicide attacks have been employed internationally for centuries, the degree to which this tactic could be used to carry out operations against Americans was more widely appreciated after 9/11. The vulnerability of the U.S. homeland to suicide attacks was amplydemonstrated: virtuallyall previous such attacks by foreign actors against U.S. citizens had happened on foreign soil, leading to a mistaken belief that Americans were only vulnerable when they were abroad.

The present book seeks to explain the deep-seated complexities of jihadi organizsation in Pakistan.

—Editor

1

Jihadist Organizations in Pakistan

The proliferation of jihadist organizations in Pakistan over the previous two decades had been the result of a militant culture espoused by radical madrasas like Darul Uloom Haqqania. Thousands of madrasas across the country became hubs for militancy and religious extremism, having a spill-over effect and presenting a serious threat to Pakistan's internal security. Pakistani madrasas were once considered centres for basic religious learning, mostly attached to local mosques.

The more formal ones were used for educating clergy. The development of simple, sparse religious schools into training centres for Kalashnikov-toting religious warriors was directly linked with the rise of militant Islam. Many of the religious parties operating the madrasas turned to militancy courtesy of the US-sponsored Jihad in Afghanistan. From waging Jihad against infidels in that foreign land, taking on perceived enemies of Islam at home was just a small step away. The influx of huge sums of money and a growing sense of power transformed the mullah's image from that of a docile and humble man to a mafia thug with a four-wheel-drive Jeep and armed bodyguards.

The influence of mullahs with local Pakistani leaders had also become formidable. Successive governments ignored their activities out of political expediency and also because most of the foreigners supporting them were 'brotherly Muslim' countries. The Islamic revolution in Iran in 1979 opened up the first wave of foreign funding for madrasas in Pakistan. Fearful of growing Iranian influence and the spread of revolution, Kuwait, Saudi Arabia, Iraq and some other oil-rich Muslim countries started pumping money into hardline Pakistani Sunni religious organizations willing to counter the supposed Shia threat. Millions of dollars were poured into setting up madrasas across the country, particularly in Balochistan province, bordering Iran. The Islamization process started by General Zia ul-Haq's regime in 1979 also contributed to the mushrooming of madrasas. For the first time in Pakistani history, the state started providing financial support for the expansion of religious education from Zakat and Ushr funds. The Islamization of education and levying of Islamic taxes had a profound long-term effect.

Zakat, one of the five pillars of Islam, had been treated as a private matter in most Muslim states. General Zia's regime broke with that tradition by deducting it from bank accounts each year during the Islamic holy month of Ramadan. The substantial amount raised by Zakat was used to finance the traditional religious schools, most of them belonging to the Deobandi movement, which is akin to Saudi Wahabism. Zakat did little to improve the lot of millions of Pakistanis living in abject poverty. The only visible consequence was the transformation of the religious landscape of the nation. The foreign and government-funded madrasas also became the main centres for spreading sectarian hatred. Saudi Arabian patronage, especially of more radical Ahle Hadith madrasas, played a major role in worsening the situation.

Madrasas also had a key place in Pakistani religious and social life. Most of the seminary students came from the poorest sections of Pakistani society and were provided with free religious education, lodging and meals. The influx of the impoverished rural population to the madrasas was a major reason for their growth, with Punjab and the North West Frontier Province having the highest number of religious seminaries. Divided along sectarian and political lines, religious seminaries were largely controlled by the two main branches of Sunni Islam in South Asia – the Deobandi and the Barelvi. Ahle Hadith or Wahabi Muslims had their own schools, as did the Shias. The religious doctrinal differences among these sects were irreconcilable. Most of the madrasas were centuries apart from the outside world. Generally the students were poor, from broken homes, or were orphans. Conditions in schools were regularly condemned by human rights groups as crowded and inhumane. The students were often subjected to a regimen as harsh as any jail, and physical abuses were commonplace. In many schools, students were put in chains and iron fetters for the slightest violation of the rules. There were almost no extracurricular activities and television and radio were banned. Teaching was rudimentary and students were taught religion within a highly rigorous and traditional perspective, giving them a deeply retrograde world-view.

At the primary stage, madrasa pupils learnt to read, memorize and recite the Qur'an. Exegeses of the holy script and other branches of Islamic studies were introduced at the higher stages of learning. Though the focus was on religious learning, some institutions also taught elementary mathematics, science and English. The most dangerous consequence of the content and style of teaching in religious schools was that the people that emerged could do nothing apart from guide the faithful in rituals that demand no experts. Job opportunities for madrasa graduates were few and narrow. They could only work in mosques, madrasas, the parent religious sectarian party, or its affiliate businesses or organizations.

The education imparted by traditional madrasas often spawned factional, religious and cultural conflict. It created barriers to modern knowledge, stifled creativity and bred bigotry, thus laying the foundation on which fundamentalism – militant or otherwise – was based. Divided by sectarian identities, these institutions were, by their very nature, driven by their zeal to outnumber and dominate rival sects. Students were educated and trained to counter the arguments of opposing sects on matters of theology, jurisprudence and doctrines. Promoting a particular sect inevitably implied the rejection of other sects, sowing the seeds of extremism in the minds of the students. The literature produced by their parent religious organizations promoted sectarian hatred and was aimed at proving the rival sects as infidels and apostates. The efforts by the successive government to modernize madrasa curricula and introduce secular subjects failed because of stiff resistance from the religious organizations controlling the religious schools. The rise of Jihad culture since the 1980s gave madrasas a new sense of purpose. As a result, their numbers multiplied and the clergy emerged as a powerful political and social force. At independence in 1947, there were only 137 madrasas in Pakistan; in the next ten years their number rose to 244. After that, they doubled every ten years. A significant number remained unregistered and therefore it was hard to know precisely how many there were. Government sources put the figure at 13,000, with total enrolment close to 1.7 million. The vast majority of students were between five and 18 years old. Only those advancing into higher religious studies were older. According to the government's own estimates, ten to 15 per cent of the madrasas had links with sectarian militancy or international terrorism. The trail of international terror often led to the madrasas and mosques.

Madrasas were basically conservative institutions before they were radicalized during the 1980s Afghan Jihad. The growing army of extremists fought the anti-Soviet Afghan Jihad alongside Arabs and Afghans. They later served the cause of Jihad from Kashmir to Chechnya to Bosnia, Egypt and Yemen. At the height of the Afghan Jihad – 1982–1988 – more than 1,000 new madrasas were opened in Pakistan, mostly along the borders with Afghanistan in the North West Frontier Province and Balochistan. Almost all belonged to hardline Sunni religious parties like Jamiat-e-Ulema Islam (JUI) and Jamaat-i-Islami (JI), which were Zia's political allies as well as partners in the Afghan Jihad. Their location in the two border provinces, which had close cultural, linguistic and sectarian affinities with Afghan Pashtuns, made it easier to motivate the pupils to fight for their brethren in distress. These madrasas did not conduct military training or provide arms to students, but encouraged them to join the 'holy war'. The purpose was to ensure a continued supply of recruits for the Afghan resistance. The message was simple: all Muslims must perform the duty of Jihad in whatever capacity they could. It was the responsibility of the Pakistani military, particularly the ISI, to provide training to the recruits in camps inside Afghanistan and Pakistan's tribal region.

As the Afghan Jihad progressed, so did the influence of the jihadists coming out of these madrasas. The USA indirectly – and sometimes directly – promoted militancy, the culture of Jihad and supported the clergy in its war against communism.

Special textbooks were published in Dari and Pashto by the University of Nebraska-Omaha and funded by USAID with an aim to promote jihadist values and militant training. Millions of such books were distributed at Afghan refugee camps and Pakistani madrasas, where students learnt basic maths by counting dead Russians and Kalashnikov rifles. The same textbooks were later used by the Taliban in their madrasas.

As General Zia attempted to consolidate his authority through Islamization at home and Jihad in Afghanistan, the madrasa system was profoundly transformed. The Islamization process nurtured many, often mutually hostile, varieties of fundamentalism. In a society where many sects coexisted, the measures representing the belief of the dominant sect acted as an identity marker, heightening sectarian divisions and promoting sectarian conflicts. As a result, sectarian divisions were militarized. The zealots began to look inwards and fight a new Jihad against sectarian rivals, particularly Shias. The madrasa phenomenon drew international attention, particularly following the rise of the conservative Taliban regime in Afghanistan. The movement was largely the product of hundreds of seminaries in the Pashtun belt on the border with Afghanistan.

The link between madrasas and the Afghan Jihad is exemplified by the Darul Uloom Haqqania madrasa. Founded in 1947 by Haq's father, Maulana Abdul Haq, a well-respected Islamic scholar belonging to the Deobandi order, Darul Uloom Haqqania developed into a centre for pan-Islamism with the beginning of the Afghan war. It saw a huge expansion with the support of the government and funds from abroad. Like other Deobandi institutions, Darul Uloom was controlled by a faction of JUI, a mainstream religio-political party that was part of a six-party conservative alliance known as Muttehida Majlis Amal (MMA). The party became an important part of the Afghan Jihad. The seminary traditionally had a large number of students from Afghanistan, but they increased considerably with the influx of

Afghan refugees. By 1985, about 60 per cent of the students in the seminary were Afghans. It also attracted students from Tajikistan, Uzbekistan and Turkmenistan. From the beginning of the Afghan Jihad, the school had relaxed the rules concerning attendance, allowing the students to take time off to participate in the 'holy war'. The seminary, however, drew immense international attention in the 1990s with the emergence of the conservative Taliban movement. Thousands of Afghan, as well as Pakistani students crossed the border into Afghanistan to join the Islamic militia. In 1997 the school was closed for several months to allow the students to participate in the Taliban's war to capture Afghanistan's northern province of Mazar-i-Sharif. Such a large-scale cross-border movement would not have been possible without the collusion of Pakistani intelligence agencies.

Just months before the 11 September terrorist attacks in New York and Washington, the school hosted a conference of Islamic parties and militant groups to express solidarity with bin Laden and the Taliban regime. Masked gunmen in camouflage guerrilla outfits stood guard as Islamic leaders from Pakistan and Afghanistan congregated at the sprawling auditorium on 9 January 2001, vowing to defend bin Laden and to launch a holy war against the West. Besides the 300 leaders representing various radical Islamic groups, the meeting was also attended by a former army chief, General Aslam Beg, and a former ISI chief, General Hamid Gul. They declared it a religious duty of Muslims all over the world to protect the Saudi dissident whom they described as a 'great Muslim warrior'. One of the objectives of the assembly was to press Islamabad not to comply with UN sanctions against the Taliban. Interestingly, the military government, which had banned political parties holding public rallies, did not try to stop the conference. No action was taken against the militants for the public display of weapons. They obviously had the backing of the intelligence agencies. Islamic seminaries and clerics had never been as numerous and so powerful in Pakistan.

Islamic seminaries also became a transit point for foreign militants aspiring to join al-Qaeda and the Taliban forces in Afghanistan. Very few people had heard about the primitive fundamentalist Madrasa-i-Arabia outside the remote corner of north-west Pakistan until its name sprung on the international scene in connection with the American Taliban, John Walker Lindh. The young American was wounded in battle and captured by US-supported Northern Alliance forces in the Afghan northern province of Kunduz in December 2001.

It was in this isolated and spartan school where there were no amenities that the 19-year-old American learnt his lesson in Islamic sharia and Jihad. A new convert to Islam, he spent some six months in this austere madrasa housed in a one-storey building before leaving for Afghanistan in May 2001 to join the Taliban. Lindh, who had grown up in upper-middle-class surroundings in California, chose the school to properly understand Islam. Mufti Mohammed Iltimas, the white-bearded head of the school, remembered him as a hard-working student who was determined to memorize every word of the Qur'an. He slept on a rope bed in a place where there was no hot water and no electricity after 10 pm. Lindh's introduction to the madrasa came through a Pakistani missionary he met in California in 1998. A Pashtun, Khizar Hayat, who had travelled to America on a preaching mission, was closely linked with the local militant organizations. Even though he was much older than the other boys, Lindh was granted admission to the school. Lindh, who went by the name Suleyman al-Faris, was not in Pakistan to engage solely in scholarly pursuits. During his stay in the madrasa, he frequently met visiting Taliban activists. In May 2001, Hayat took him to the office of a pro-Taliban Islamic militant group, HuM, where he enrolled for guerrilla training.

Lindh was sent to a HuM camp near Islamabad. After learning the use of firearms, he was dispatched to Afghanistan to work with the Taliban. He was not the only American and not the only westerner to have joined al-Qaeda and the Taliban. Many western men, a lot of them Afro-American, were recruited by the Tablighi Jamaat and its front organizations and sent to Afghanistan after receiving basic religious training in Pakistani madrasas and guerrilla training at the camps run by militant groups, closely affiliated with the religious institutions. Some of the madrasas had links with international Islamist organizations like Egypt's Akhwan-ul Muslimeen (Muslim Brotherhood), Indonesia's Jemmah Islamiyah, Algeria's Islamic Salvation Front (FIS) and the Philippines' Abu Sayyaf group, all of whom extended support to alQaeda.

Radical madrasas were not restricted to the remote border region in northern Pakistan. In fact, the country's largest city and its main financial centre Karachi, became the hub of militant seminaries. According to one estimate, more than 200,000 students were enrolled in around one thousand madrasas in the city. Not all, but many of them, had links with sectarian or Islamic militant groups. The largest among them was the Jamia Ulumia Islami or Jamia Binoria. The sprawling red-brick campus, with tall minarets right in the heart of the city, served as the backbone of militant Islam and was the breeding ground for 'Islamic warriors'. The country's premier institution for Islamic learning had also become the citadel of Sunni extremist groups. The main campus and eight other affiliated madrasas enrolled more than ten thousand students from Pakistan as well as 30 other countries including China, Central Asia, Chechnya, Malaysia, the Philippines and Britain. Students were taught the concept of Jihad as a special subject to prepare them to fight for the cause of Islam. Many of the Taliban leaders were graduates and took guidance from their former teachers for running the fundamentalist Islamic state. The students were sent regularly to Afghanistan for training and orientation during Taliban rule. At the main gate stood a huge banner exhorting Muslims to join Taliban forces in Afghanistan. Over the last two decades, thousands of its students fought in Afghanistan and Kashmir.

Dozens of other smaller and relatively low-profile madrasas spread across Karachi became the base for al-Qaeda 'sleeper' cells in Pakistan. A lean and shy Ahmed Hadi was an ordinary student at Jamia Abu Bakr and the last person one would suspect of being an important cog in the international terrorist network. It was only after Pakistani security forces raided the seminary in Karachi's middle-class neighbourhood of Gulshan-e-Iqbal in September 2003 that his real identity was revealed. Gun Gun Rusman Gunawan was a leading member of Indonesia's Jemmah Islamiyah and the brother of Hambali, the mastermind of the 2002 bombing in the

Indonesian holiday resort of Bali in which more than 200 people died. The Indonesian, who was captured along with 11 other Southeast Asian students, had spent four years at the seminary under a fake identity.

Hambali, who was arrested in Thailand in 2003, had contacts with alQaeda's top leaders Ramzi bin al-Shibh and Khalid Sheikh Mohammed, both of whom were apprehended in Pakistan. It was the first indicator of a terrorist sleeper cell operating in Pakistan's main commercial hub. Gunawan was granted admission to the Jamia Abu Bakr Islamia in 1999. He was among 15,000 students from Muslim countries who came to Pakistan to study in Pakistani madrasas during the 1990s. Founded in 1978, the seminary had a large number of foreign students mainly from Thailand, Indonesia, Malaysia and African countries. The arrest of Gunawan provided some indication of the strong links between Islamic seminaries and the international terrorist network. His arrest was followed by a series of raids less than a kilometre away from the Abu Bakr seminary. Another eight Southeast Asian students were arrested from the Jamia Darasitul Islamia, a seminary run by Jamaatud Da'awa, the political wing of Lashkar-e-Taiba. This connection compelled investigators to explore Jemmah Islamiyah's links with Pakistan's militant groups. Pakistani intelligence agencies suspected that Gunawan was instrumental in channelling funds provided by al-Qaeda to the Jemmah Islamiyah. Despite the government's crackdown, many madrasas continued to provide safe haven to al-Qaeda sleeper cells.

Over the past several years, there had been a visible rise in the number of madrasa students belonging to families of the expatriate Pakistani community, particularly those living in the USA and Britain. Fired by the desire to become 'true Muslims', hundreds of second-generation expatriates joined Pakistani seminaries each year. Most of them from prosperous middle-class families, they took time off from their schools to learn about their faith. While the majority of the boys confined themselves to Islamic learning, dozens of them got involved in jihadist activities under the influence of militant groups that operated inside some of the madrasas.

It was one such radical madrasa where Shehzad Tanweer, one of the suicide bombers involved in the 7 July 2005 terror attacks in London, spent time during his last visit to Pakistan. Twenty-two-yearold Shehzad, who blew himself up on a subway train near Aldgate station in East London, was the eldest son of Mohammed Mumtaz Tanweer, who had migrated to England in the 1960s. He grew up in the Beeston area of Leeds, but remained connected with Pakistan through his extended family members who lived in a farming village in Faisalabad district. In December 2004, Shehzad went to Manzoor ul Islamia madrasa in Lahore, which was linked with JeM. He intended to stay there for nine months of religious education, but left just a week later.

There are strong suspicions that Shehzad might have met the mastermind of the London bombings during his brief stay there. The suspected Pakistani connection to the 7/7 attacks brought Musharraf under a renewed pressure to act against militant madrasas. As in the past, he responded this time by ordering a nationwide crackdown on Islamic extremist groups. The police again stormed a number of madrasas and arrested hundreds of suspected extremists.

But the entire operation appeared merely superficial; most of them were released after a few weeks. In his new role as a key ally in the US-led war on terror, Musharraf toned down many policies that had previously fostered militancy and religious extremism. But most of the measures, particularly against the home-grown jihadists, were taken under external pressure and lacked conviction. Very little was done to rein in the militant madrasas, despite their continuing involvement in jihadist politics. While talk about reform went on, fresh batches of volunteers ready to confront what they perceived as enemies of their faith continued to graduate from madrasas.

Even after the ousting of the Taliban regime, many madrasas in parts of Balochistan continued to preach Jihad to Afghan students. A major part of Musharraf's anti-extremism drive was to regulate and transform those madrasas whose role in promoting Jihad had come under increasing international scrutiny. The move was stalled because of the administration's failure to stop their funding from Pakistanis working abroad, as well as from foreign Muslim charities.

The biggest source of financing for madrasas was external – from Muslim countries as well as private donors and Pakistani expatriates. A report by the Brussels-based International Crisis Group (ICG) revealed that Pakistani madrasas and religious centres had received more than 90 billion rupees ($1.5 billion) every year through charitable donations. The amount was almost equal to the government's annual direct income tax revenue. Most of the madrasas, which had in the past received government funding, now relied solely on private charity.

Ninety-four per cent of charitable donations made by Pakistani individuals and business corporations went to the religious institutions. Though most donors did not support the politics of religious parties, they felt that Islamic education and the preservation of Islam were the most worthy choice for their donations. Many religious leaders who ran the Islamic seminaries had strong links in Arab countries that went back to the Afghan Jihad. For many it had become a 'status symbol' to receive funding from foreign sources.

Muslims in Britain had been one of the largest donors to the Pakistani Islamic institutions and Muslim militant groups, some of whom had been declared terrorists and outlawed by Pakistan's military government. UK-based charities were the main financiers for Islamic groups. Diversion of funds for educational and humanitarian projects to the Islamic militant groups had become a normal practice. 'It is difficult to separate finances for terror from those for charity,' said the ICG report. LeT and JeM, reportedly collected more than £5 million each year in mosques in Britain. Although both the groups were banned in Britain, the Kashmiri diaspora continued to make donations to them. While Islamabad had repeatedly downplayed the link between extremism and the madrasas, most religious schools continued to preach Jihad. After the failed attempts on Musharraf's life in December 2003, the administration launched raids on some extremist madrasas, but such half-hearted and piecemeal measures could hardly help improve the situation.

Pakistan's failure to curb extremism owed less to the difficulty of implementing reforms than to the administration's own unwillingness. Musharraf had promised to ban the use of mosques and madrasas for spreading religious and sectarian hatred. However, all those pledges remained largely rhetorical and seemed to have been made under international pressure. The sectarian groups continued to challenge the authority of the state in different ways. Pakistan's failure to strictly enforce laws against the preaching of religious hatred and reining in of the extremist madrasas had largely been responsible for the rise in sectarian-based violence.

The failure to deliver to any substantial degree on pledges to reform madrasas and contain the growth of jihadist networks had not only given rise to religious extremism in Pakistan, but also continued to present a threat to domestic, regional and international security. Several madrasas continued to provide recruits for Taliban insurgents in Afghanistan. Run by JUI, part of the coalition government in the western Balochistan province, the seminaries not only provided the Taliban with ideological training, but also extended material help. Pashtunabad, a congested slum district in the provincial capital, Quetta, had a large concentration of former Taliban activists. A stronghold of radical Islamic groups, it looked more like a Kandahar neighbourhood under the former Taliban regime, and several former Taliban leaders were believed to have taken refuge there. The main madrasa in the neighbourhood was run by Maulana Noor Mohammed, a MMA member of the National Assembly. He appeared convinced that the Taliban would re-establish their control over Afghanistan. 'They will ultimately triumph,' declared the 75-year-old cleric.

2

Suicide Attacks by Terrorist Organizations

TERRORISTS ORGANIZATIONS AND SUICIDE ATTACKS

Suicide attacks by terrorist organizations have become more prevalent globally, and assessing the threat of future suicide attacks against the United States has gained in strategic importance. While suicide attacks have been employed internationally for centuries, the degree to which this tactic could be used to carry out operations against Americans was more widely appreciated after 9/11. The vulnerability of the U.S. homeland to suicide attacks was amplydemonstrated: virtuallyall previous such attacks by foreign actors against U.S. citizens had happened on foreign soil, leading to a mistaken belief that Americans were only vulnerable when they were abroad.

Adding to the anxiety about suicide attacks is their potential connection to increasingly available new technologies. Although so-called "weapons of mass destruction" were not used in the September 11th attacks, the destruction was nonetheless unquestionably"massive." The prospect of combining modern weapons technology (especially chemical, biological, nuclear or radiological weapons) with an age-old willingness to die in the act of committing an attack could be unprecedentedly dangerous. The degree to which Al Qaeda and other groups have recently stepped up their public advocacy of so-called martyrdom operations, combined with captured evidence of their interest in these weapons, is also worrisome. With increasing numbers of casualties from suicide attacks occurring globally in places such as Israel, Saudi Arabia, Morocco, Russia/Chechnya, and post-conflict Iraq, a focus on the threat of future suicide attacks against Americans and their interests, in the United States and elsewhere, merits consideration. This report focuses on the following questions: What are suicide attacks? What have been the patterns and motivations for terrorist organizations using suicide attacks in the past? What terrorist groups and other organizations are most likely to launch such attacks? How great a threat are terrorist suicide attacks to the United States, at home and abroad? How can the United States counter such a threat? In short, the goal of this report is to summarize the key lessons of the international experience with suicide attacks in the modern era and examine their relevance to the United States in the current threat environment.

DEFINITIONS OF TERRORISM

A number of argue that the language used to describe terrorism plays a role in how it is perceived, so words used in describing it must be very carefully chosen. For example, there are many phrases used to describe the phenomenon. Some people use the phrase "suicide bombings," but that is too restrictive for this report, as it seems to refer only to attacks that are carried out with the use of explosives. Suicide attacks can occur with other types of weapons, including jetliners. "Genocide bombings" and "homicide attacks" are phrases frequently used by those who identify with the unwilling victims of attacks; these terms emphasize the criminal nature of the violence and de-emphasize the self-inflicted death of the perpetrator. On the other hand, "martyrdom operations" places the emphasis upon the cause of the perpetrators, implying a connection to the notions of "holy war" and/or self defence, even in the killing of civilians. Finally "suicide operations" places the emphasis on the organization's role in staging the episodes, implying a military-type character to them.

None of the at present used terms is perfect. For the purposes of this report, the phrase used will be "suicide attacks," by which is meant, in the sense used here, events where the "success" of the operation cannot occur without the death of the perpetrator, and he or she is apparently aware of this in advance. Likewise, this report concentrates on suicide attacks that are carried out by "terrorists," by which is meant nonstate actors whose goal is the threat or use of violence for political ends against noncombatant or civilian targets. These are off-the-battlefield episodes, with the attackers not integrated into units in a formal military sense. Therefore, specifically excluded are high risk military operations, where, although the perpetrator may expect his chances of survival to be virtually nil, he or she is not deliberately seeking his or her own death. And this report also does not include self-inflicted deaths that occur without any violence directed outward, like hunger strikes or cult suicides.

HISTORICAL BACKGROUND OF SUICIDE ATTACKS

The occurrence of suicide attacks cannot be fully understood without placing it within its broader historical context. Self-sacrifice in the interest of a broader cause is not unusual in human history, especially in military settings; but terrorist suicide attacks as they are defined here also have a lengthy pedigree. Members of premodern groups without access to dynamite did not have the immediacy and certainty of their own demise that is currently the case, nor could they expect the publicity for their attacks that is seen today; but they did engage in deliberate, calculated self-sacrifice in the act of killing civilian targets for symbolic effect.

For example, among the earliest groups that have been thoroughly studied, the Muslim Assassins (also known as Ismailis-Nazari) operated from 1090-1275, C.E. They prepared their members to die in the execution of an attack, deliberately seeking martyrdom as they used daggers to kill their victims. The Assassins assured themselves publicity by attacking prominent officials in public places, usually on holy days when there were many witnesses. The group's description of the assailants as "fedayeen" (meaning consecrated ones or dedicated ones) and their admiration for martyrdom in the course of killing is an often-cited historical precursor for some of the suicide attacks by Islamic terrorist organizations seen today.

Another historical instance of the use of suicide attacks is found among Muslim communities in Asia during the eighteenth, nineteenth and early twentieth centuries, particularly on the Malabar coast of Southwestern India, in Atjeh in Northern Sumatra, and in Mindanao and Sulu in the Southern Philippines. Muslims in these regions engaged in suicidal jihads aimed at inflicting punishment and instilling fear among the European colonial powers. In all of these places, the perpetrators engaged in religious rituals prior to carrying out the attacks, aspired to a perceived heroic status of martyrdom, and carried out their killings as religious acts intended to serve the interests of their own community. In each case, a shift to the use of suicide attacks followed a period of unsuccessful open warfare against the militarily much stronger Europeans. The suicidal jihad against civilians was seen as a means of desperate counterattack and even a means of keeping awareness of the cause alive.

The service of suicide attacks as a terrorist technique is not exclusive to one culture or religion: with the invention of dynamite in the late 19 century, the use of bombs in terrorist attacks became a generally favored method, and this also applied to suicide tactics. For example, the Russian radicals of the late 19th century, in putting themselves close enough to the target to assure success, usually also consciously sought their own demise. Proximity was important to the successful targeting of the crude explosions. In those instances where the terrorists survived and were captured, they often refused offers of clemency and were executed. Dying for the cause was a highly valued fate, a source of legitimacy for the cause, and a rallying point for future recruits. It was not, on the other hand, an effective long-term strategy in this case: the Russian regime successfully rooted out such well-known groups as *Narodnaya Volya* (People's Will) well before the Russian revolution, and they were not admired by the Bosheviks.

Ironically, with the development of better explosives and means of detonating them, suicide attacks became less common in the twentieth century. More advanced technological means meant that it was not necessary to sacrifice a member of the organization. Favored methods in the mid-twentieth century included pre-placed or remotely detonated explosives, hostage-taking, and attacks on airliners. As counterterrorist methods began to improve, however, methods of terrorist attack began to evolve as well. Faced with metal detectors at airports, increased security perimeters around valuable targets, and many other antiterrorism measures, terrorist organizations began to innovate tactically. The reintroduction of the use of suicide attacks, especially by ethno-nationalist groups or religiously-motivated groups, was one of the results.

Although it was not the first such attack, many people date the initiation of a wave of contemporary suicide attacks to the October 1983 destruction of the U.S. Marine barracks in Beirut by a truck bomb, a watershed particularly for Americans. The explosion lifted the entire building off its foundation and caused it to implode upon itself, killing 241 off-duty U.S. soldiers and injuring more than 100 others. At almost precisely the same time, a similar truck bomb exploded at the French peacekeeping compound nearby, killing 58 soldiers and wounding 15 others. The 1983 Beirut attacks resulted in the withdrawal of U.S. and French forces from Lebanon. These withdrawals have subsequently been pointed to by Al Qaeda andother groups as important signs that suicide attacks can be extremelyeffective against Western democratic powers.

Between 1983 and 1986, the obvious success of the Beirut suicide attacks against the U.S. and France was followed by a redirection of targeting toward the Israeli Defence Forces in Lebanon and then South Lebanese Army posts. The 1983 Marine barracks bombing also led at least indirectly to the initiation of perhaps the most ruthless and bloody suicide campaign in modern history by the Tamil Tigers (LTTE). Their first attack occurred in Sri Lanka in May 1987. The Tamil Tigers, whose leader Velupillai Prabhakaran later claimed that he was inspired by the 1983 attacks, have since been responsible for more than half of all suicide attacks carried out worldwide.

While the method was by no means historically unprecedented, the 1983 attacks signaled the beginning of a growing use of suicide attacks in the late 20 and early 21st centuries. In modern times, suicide attacks have been employed by a large varietyof groups, including Muslim (both Shi'ite and Sunni), Christian, Hindu, Sikh, Jewish and secular organizations, especially in the Middle East but also many other regions of the world. A partial list of terrorist groups that actively use suicide attacks includes Hamas, the Palestinian Islamic Jihad, the al-Aqsa Martyrs Brigades of Yassir Arafat's Fatah movement, Al-Ansar Mujahidin in Chechnya, the Egyptian Islamic Jihad (EIJ), Hezbollah, Lashkar-e-taiba of Pakistan/ Kashmir, the Armed Islamic Group (GIA) of Algeria, Barbar Khalsa International(BKI) of India, the Liberation Tigers of Tamil Eelam (LTTE or Tamil Tigers) of Sri Lanka, the Kurdistan Worker's Party (PKK) of Turkey, and Al Qaeda. It is the apparently growing use of suicide attacks internationally and the increased targeting against Americans that concerns counterterrorism experts. The trend may have important implications for future U.S. security.

Individual Motivations for Suicide Attacks

One insight about suicide attacks is that they are carried out by individual deranged fanatics but this is almost never the case. Research on suicide attacks indicates that most terrorist operatives are psychologically normal, in the sense that psychological pathology does not seem to be present, and the attacks are virtually always premeditated. There have been instances of coercion or deception in recruiting suicide attackers and/or executing the attacks, but most perpetrators are as aware of their imminent fate as they are of the fate of their victims. Why would anyone choose to engage in such an attack? The answer to this question requires an insight into the psychological and cultural aspects of terrorism. The motivations for suicide attacks are not so different in many ways from the motivations for other types of terrorism, including attention to a cause, personal notoriety, anger, revenge and retribution against a perceived injustice. From the perspective of the individual attacker, the act of "martyrdom" may offer an opportunity to impress an audience and be remembered, an act that may be a powerful incentive for individuals who perceive their lives as having little significance otherwise. Suicide attackers are sometimes widows or bereaved siblings who wish to take vengeance for their loved one's violent death. In the case of widows, for example, the death of the spouse may cut the woman off from productive society and/or leave her with a sense of hopelessness, especially in very traditional societies.

A longing for religious cleanliness and/or a strong commitment to the welfare of the group may drive individuals to engage in suicide attacks. The role of the central religious, political, or ethnic culture or ideology is important. Suicide attacks among Palestinian groups, for example, seem to have inspired a self-perpetuating subculture of martyrdom. Children who grow up in such settings may be subtly indoctrinated in a culture glorifying ultimate sacrifice in the service of the Palestinian cause and against the Israeli people. There are social, cultural, religious, and material incentives presented in such a context, sometimes including spiritual rewards in the after life, vast celebrity, cash bonuses, free apartments and/ or the guarantee of a place with God for the attackers' families.

Other attackers seem to be driven apparently by a sense of humiliation or injustice, a worrisome development that has appeared for example among young Egyptians. Some argue, for example, that perceptions regarding the plight of the Palestinian people may have had an influence upon the willingness of young Egyptians to participate in suicide attacks, especially among those who are unemployed and frustrated for other reasons. Indeed, desperation is often mentioned in press reports: Palestinians in particular are quoted as saying that suicide attacks are the "weapon of last resort." In some conflicts, rising use of suicide attacks is seen widely as a potential sign that the struggle is being "Islamicized." The historical connection to the Muslim Assassins groups is often mentioned. Al Qaeda's use of suicide attacks is well-known, and growing links between that organization and many other, more local indigenous groups are sometimes demonstrated at least in part by a shift in the local group's tactics. For example, the recent use of suicide attacks by Chechen militants is seen by some as a worrisome indicator of growing influence of radical Islamist factions within Chechnya and/or links with radical groups like Al Qaeda. Recent suicide attacks in Morocco are likewise viewed this way. The August 2003 suicide attacks on the Jordanian Embassy and the UN Headquarters in Iraq may also reflect a shift from local nationalistic resistance to the more active involvement of outside Islamist fighters.

So-called "martyrdom" is not just a religious concept, however. The tradition of heroic martyrdom, where the hero sacrifices to save the life of his community, nation, or people, is a powerful element in many secular traditions. Among Palestinian groups non-religious nationalist motivations are sometimes dominant, especially with respect to groups such as the al-Aqsa Martyrs' Brigades, which is an offshoot of militant elements of the essèntially secular PLO's Fatah faction. Indeed, globally, an apparently larger proportion overall of the suicide attacks of the last twenty years has been carried out by secular groups like the Tamil Tigers and the PKK, who both appeal primarily to traditional concepts of nationhood and sacrifice, than by religiously-motivated groups.

Following the September 11th attacks, one of the important developments among those who study terrorism has been the reexamination of the concept of a "profile" or typical characteristics of suicide attackers. Some people had argued on the basis of research done especially on Hamas members, that suicide terrorists were typically male, aged 18-27 years, unmarried, relatively uneducated, and highly susceptible to suggestion. This description proved to be inadequate, however, especially after the 9/11 attacks in which older, well-educated operatives like Mohammed Atta participated. In the Palestinian intifada, as well, previous assumptions are being reexamined, with suicide attacks being carried out by operatives as diverse as a college student, a middle-aged married men with children, and the son of a wealthy businessman, not to mention increasing numbers of women and children. Some have argued that there is no pattern to these "profiles" at all. In any case, as we move into the twenty-first century, stereotypes about who is likely to carry out terrorist suicide attacks are evaporating. Although research indicates that individual suicide attackers make choices and are not technically "crazy," according to experts they are often manipulated by the pressures and belief structures of the group. Because of this, it is important to study the role of the organization in the phenomenon.

EXECUTION OF SUICIDE ATTACKS

The organization is crucial in the execution of most suicide attacks, in planning, acquiring weaponry, choosing operatives, targeting, and carrying them out. Indeed, most terrorism experts argue that the role of the organization is a much more powerful factor than is the nature of the individual, since the individual has often yielded his or her identity to the group. With very few exceptions, suicide attacks in the modern era have involved a fairlywell developed organization, and historically they have been employed by terrorist groups when they are both strong and weak. There is a chilling logic in the choice of suicide operations by terrorist organizations. From an organizational perspective, there are arguably numerous advantages in using such attacks as part of a terrorist campaign.

First, suicide attacks generally result in a larger number of casualties on average than do other types of terrorist attacks. From 1980 to 2001, suicide attacks reportedly represented only 3% of all terrorist attacks but accounted for 48% of total deaths due to terrorism. Looking just at Palestinian attacks between 2000 and 2002, suicide attacks represented only 1% of the total number of attacks but they caused about 44% of the Israeli casualties. The larger number of casualties causes more physical and psychological damage to the targeted state or community and, especially in a democracy, arguably increases the likelihood that the government will be compelled to respond.

Whether that reply takes the form of concessions or retaliations, it can potentially serve the interests of the terrorist campaign. Concessions may advance the terrorist organization's goals and increase its psychological leverage against a militarily stronger foe; retaliations may draw international condemnation and increase the pool of recruits from which the organization may draw. If an organization is at a significant military disadvantage, this may be a calculation it is willing to make. Or the organization may engender a more specific reaction such as disrupting negotiations in the Israeli-Palestinian peace process, for example.

Second, suicide attacks usually attract more publicity than do other types of attacks. The fate of the bomber him- or herself is part of the story, and the large number of victims, again, ensures public attention. Sometimes the goal of an organization is simply to draw attention to itself and to its cause: in an age of ubiquitous media, suicide attacks are more likely to be noticed. Since the main effect of the violence is intended to be impressed upon an audience, the shocking nature of the attack is part of the calculation. From the perspective of the victims and their sympathizers, on the other hand, the media coverage that is a natural part of the terrible tragedy does help to publicize the terrorists' cause.

A related aspect is the symbolic value of martyrdom for a cause, not only in Islamic cultures but in other cultures as well. Even in secular groups, the death of a member contributes to the sense of legitimacy and dramatic community investment in a cause. The message is that there is no going back. Some groups engage in glorification of the act, deliberatelyhyping a "culture of martyrdom" that mayinclude posters, songs, legends, etc., lionizing the attacker. This celebrity can be powerfully attractive to potential recruits, and with the suicide often comes greater general attention as well to the motivation for the act.

Third, suicide attackers are sometimes seen by sponsoring organizations as assets whose loss generates a net gain. The gains can be political or monetary. As for political gain, in situations where groups are competing for power, there is evidence that suicide attacks are seen as a means of gaining relative advantage vis-avis rival groups; according to one report, this may have been the case for Palestinian groups such as Hamas and the Islamic Jihad. The organization's role in the attack is made obvious in the style and content of the videotapes that attackers usually make on the eve of their operation: typically, the so-called "living martyr" is standing in front of the terrorist group's flag, holding an assault rifle and perhaps also a copy of the Koran, as he or she explains the motivation behind his or her attack. The image of the now-deceased becomes a powerful tool for winning adherents. Suicide attacks are also used to boost morale, engendering greater cohesion among members of a group; the PKK and the Tamil Tigers apparently used suicide attacks in this way. Indeed, the Tamil Tigers have even filmed some of the suicide attacks themselves and used them for recruitment and motivation.

In cost/advantage terms, suicide attacks are financially inexpensive: according to one expert, the price of materials used in a suicide attack in Israel is about $150. Monetary rewards for terrorist organizations, on the other hand, can be large. Suicide attackers sometimes draw sympathy from sources distant from the location of the attacks, especially donors who are willing to enable *others* to die in the service of a cause. For example, following a supermarket bombing byan 18-year-old Palestinian girl, a Saudi telethon reportedly raised more than $100 million for the Palestinians. Support from the diaspora is also common: the Tamil Tigers have been funded by 800,000 Tamils living abroad, in Canada, Australia, and elsewhere, who have sent back as much as $150 million annually, according to one estimate. Payments and other benefits are given to the individual families of the dead Palestinian attackers. In cold cost/benefit terms, the organizational incentives seem to be far more compelling than the personal ones.

Fourth, the use of suicide operatives helps to control the timing and placement of attacks. If there is no need to provide an escape route for the attacker, the complexity of the plan is greatly reduced. Suicide attackers can often get closer to the target at the desired time than can other terrorist methods. The human being is in control until the moment of detonation. The human being is the delivery system, and the attacker together with his weapon is the ultimate "smart bomb." The suicide attack may be less dangerous to an organization's viability, as there is no risk that intelligence will be leaked. Likewise, for his or her part, the attacker does not need to fear capture, interrogation, trial, imprisonment and the accompanying humiliation–fates that, in some settings and some cultures, may seem worse than death.

Finally, suicide attacks can be particularly intimidating for the target population. There is a perception that suicide attacks are unstoppable, an impression perpetuated not only by the logistical challenges of detecting and repulsing the threat but also by the impression that the attacker is driven by a desperate determination. While many suicide attackers may be normal psychologically, there is benefit to be gained on the part of the terrorist organization in perpetuating the stereotype that they are fanatics. Likewise, the message (true or not) that there are dozens more recruits waiting to take the dead attacker's place serves the organization's interests and is often difficult to verify, one way or another. There is often a sense of extreme anxiety or almost inhuman determination on the part of a suicide attacker. The rituals in which the prospective attacker typically engages are designed to make it virtually impossible to back out of an attack without losing honour and a place in society. Sometimes prospective attackers are encouraged to lie down in graves to have the feeling of peace that they are told they will experience after death. The relationship with other recruits can be very close, with the "living dead" competing to be the first to be sent on a mission. They often write letters or make video tapes for relatives left behind. Secular groups use such techniques as well. Members of the LTTE typically enjoy a meal with their leader and are photographed on their last night before the attack. With nowhere to turn, captured operatives who have failed to carry out their mission have consigned themselves to ignominy as "half martyrs" and may consider themselves as good as dead. After such elaborate psychological preparation, the attack is meant to seem almost an afterthought.

Another aspect to the intimidating natural world of suicide attacks, particularly among Palestinian groups, is the deliberate effort to maximize human suffering not only in the immediate explosion but also in the minutes, days, and even years following it. Planners of suicide attacks in Israel have often packed explosives with foreign objects. Long after the attack, victims can have imbedded in their bodies pieces of shrapnel, nails, bolts, screws, ball bearings and other projectiles that were built into the bombs. Another recent innovation is the addition of chemicals such as rat poison, which is an anticoagulant and makes it much more difficult for rescue workers to stem the bleeding from injured victims. Over time, suicide attacks that incorporate such elements can be psychologically more punishing, not only to the victims but to the population at large. Finally, trying to stop a suicide attack can result in a premature detonation of the explosive that kills the defenders and the attacker. This can lead to increased wariness on the part of police or soldiers, who then may be more inclined to shoot otherwise innocent-looking civilians who could conceivably be carrying explosives. This is a particular problem if the suicide attackers are identifiable as members of a different race or ethnicity than the target population. The result can be deep polarization and a cycle of violence that may destabilize the target society and perpetuate the goals of the terrorist group.

ROLE OF WOMEN IN SUICIDE ATTACKS

The role of women in carrying out suicide attacks has been the focus of increasing concern. The use of women in suicide attacks may point to a broadening to include members of society not usually recruited by contemporary terrorist organizations for this type of mission. Although female participation in terrorism is not historically unusual (notably among left-wing groups), participation in suicide attacks is less common. Growing numbers of female suicide attackers may reflect a number of different factors.

The most famous examples of female suicide attackers have been among the members of the Tamil Tigers (LTTE). In the conservative societies of the Middle East and South Asia, there is more reluctance to search a woman, which gives such attackers an advantage over men. They are also assumed to be potentially less dangerous and may be able to approach the target with greater ease. Among the Black Tigers, as the Tamil suicide attack squad is known, both male and female children as young as 10 years old are chosen to be prepared to carry out missions. About a third of the suicide operations carried out by the LTTE have been conducted by women. Most famously, a female suicide bomber killed Indian Prime Minister Rajiv Gandhi in 1991 while he was campaigning for reelection. The attacker was wearing an explosive device under her robes that made it appear that she was pregnant. In December 1999 another woman blew herself up at a rally for Sri Lankan

President Chandrika Kumaratunga; the blast killed 23 people and wounded the president, who lost the sight in her right eye. In the Middle East, it is often forgotten in the focus on the very recent past that women engaged in suicide missions years earlier, during the 1980s. In southern Lebanon, women who were fighting as part of the National Resistance Front engaged in suicide attacks against Israelis. On 9 April 1985, for example, San Mheidleh, a 16-year-old Shi'a school girl, drove a car packed with 450 pounds of dynamite into an Israeli check point, killing herself and two Israeli soldiers. Just before the attack, she made a video tape explaining her mission which was later shown on Lebanese television. A number of other women followed her example. Since these attacks were technically against military targets, they do not fit our definition exactly; however, the form of the attack and the organizational planning are directly reflective of the phenomenon occurring among Palestinian groups attacking Israeli civilians today.

The use of womanly suicide bombers in the Israeli-Palestinian conflict has been seen by some as an act of desperation on the part of Palestinian women. Others consider it a result of calculated evolution in the terrorist organization's tactics; as the Israelis began to frisk young Palestinian men, for example, reportedly older men and then women began to step forward. The first confirmed use of a Palestinian female suicide attacker in Israel occurred in January 2002. Wafa Idrees, 28-year-old Palestinian woman, blew herself to pieces outside a shoe shop in Jerusalem on 28 January 2002, killing an 81-year-old Israeli man and injuring more than 100 people. Among the injured was an American lawyer from New York who had survived the September 11th attacks. Following that incident, other attacks by women have occurred, including by Daria Abu Aysha, a Palestinian student who killed herself and wounded three soldiers at a West Bank checkpoint in February 2002; and 18-year-old Ayat Akhras, who killed herself and two Israelis near a Jerusalem supermarket in March 2002. All of these women were prepared and armed by the al-Aqsa Martyrs' Brigades, which, according to one source, has set up a special unit for female suicide bombers.

Another group with a history of using women for suicide attacks is the PKK, whose campaign of suicide attacks began on 30 June 1995 and ended on 5 July 1999. About two-thirds of the attacks—eleven of fourteen—were undertaken by women. The large majority of attackers did not volunteer but were chosen by the leadership for their missions, a distinguishing feature of the PKK. Much coercion was reportedly used in forcing PKK members to participate: one of those selected who then refused the 'honour' was said to have been killed in front of another who had been chosen; a different person who tried to escape was turned over to the police. According to interviews, the PKK's preference for using female suicide attackers reflected a number of causes, including the belief among the leadership that the presence of the women was burdening the men in their hit-and-run operations, and the general perception in the group that the women were more expendable than the men.

Although the act of commit suicide and the participation of women in combat are both contrary to Chechen social tradition, increasing numbers of Chechen women are participating in suicide attacks against Russian targets. There have been numerous attacks involving women perpetrators, including two apparently Chechen female suicide attackers who detonated themselves outside a rock concert in July 2003 on the outskirts of Moscow, killing more than a dozen young people. The motivations for female Chechen suicide attackers are reported to be often related to the deaths of husbands, brothers, fathers and sons at the hands of Russian forces; indeed, the Kremlin calls them "black widows." Some argue that the traditional nature of Chechen society pushes women into suicide missions because they are excluded from joining regular guerrilla units. The unprecedented prominence of women suicide attackers among Chechen fighters is also seen as a sign of desperation in the struggle, and a transition to a "Palestinization" of the so-called war of independence from Russia.

Over the long term, terrorist organizations would not use women or children if the population at large did not actively or at least passively support it. There is polling data that clearly indicates support on the part of most Palestinians for the terrorist organizations carrying out these operations, support that seemed to grow immediately after the increase in suicide attacks using both male and female perpetrators, although enthusiasm for the violence then later declined. Longer term acquiescence of the broader population, particularly in Chechnya and among the Palestinians, would be most concerning and could be indicative of the staying power of this phenomenon.

GROUPS ENGAGING IN SUICIDE ATTACKS AND THREAT TO THE UNITED STATES

Until very freshly, most of the groups engaging in suicide attacks have been interested in pursuing a cause that is geographically distant from the United States, usually limited to territory that is connected somehow to the origin of the group. The groups that were most likely to use suicide attacks, including Hamas, Islamic Jihad, the PKK, the Tamil Tigers and others described here, had no interest in directly targeting a suicide attack against U.S. citizens or interests at home or abroad. But suicide attacks are no longer primarily a local phenomenon. Looking at the evolution of the use of suicide attacks globally, the geographical distribution of the phenomenon seems to be widening, as is the targeting of the attacks. In recent years, suicide attacks have been perpetuated across borders and even continents, for example in Croatia, Argentina, Algeria, Panama, and now the United States.

The most effective globalized network of terrorist organizations is associated with Al Qaeda—the only organization that has successfully used suicide attacks on U.S. soil. Indeed, the most likely future use of suicide attacks against Americans would come from Al Qaeda and its many associated groups. Al Qaeda's global networking of militant Islamic groups derives from its genesis in the struggle against the Soviet Union in Afghanistan and the subsequent development under the Taliban regime there of numerous training camps, where attendees were schooled in many different techniques of fighting, including the use of explosives and suicide attacks. Al Qaeda has relied upon suicide attacks frequently, especially as the organization has evolved from a primary focus on supporting Islamist insurgencies throughout the world to an increasingly widespread and direct role in attacking American and other Western targets through any available means. Notable suicide attacks include the 1998 truck bombings of the U.S. Embassies in Dar es Salaam, Tanzania, and Nairobi, Kenya. (Twelve Americans died and 7 were wounded in those attacks, while 291 Africans were killed and about 5100 wounded.) The October 2000 attack on the U.S.S. Cole in Yemen was a suicide operation, albeit clearly directed against a military not civilian target. (Seventeen American sailors died and thirty-nine were wounded.) And finally, the September 11th attacks, in which more than 3,000 people were killed, were carried out by nineteen Al Qaeda suicide operatives. There have been numerous other planned but thwarted apparent suicide attacks directly or indirectly attributable to Al Qaeda. And suicide assaults in Saudi Arabia and Morocco in May 2003 also appear to have had ties to Al Qaeda. Suicide tactics seem to be gaining importance in the organization's arsenal.

At this summit there is no evidence that Palestinian groups like Hamas and Islamic Jihad have developed ties with Al Qaeda. There is clear evidence, however, of Al Qaeda connections with Chechen militant groups, the increasing use of suicide attacks in Russia and Chechnya is seen as a worrisome sign of potentially growing influence on the part of radical Islamist elements among the Chechens. Al Qaeda has also provided support for Pakistani groups like Lashkar-e-taiba of Pakistan/Kashmir. And there are worrisome indications of outside fighters possibly being responsible for major suicide attacks in Iraq, including the Jordanian Embassy and the UN Headquarters in Baghdad. While a transition to the use of suicide techniques among groups with Muslim members is often seen as a reflection of Islamist militancy, the role of Al Qaeda in these attacks is becoming blurred by their increasing globalization. The knowledge needed to carry them out is increasingly available and being disseminated internationally through means such as the Internet. Al Qaeda's *Jihad Manual* and its thirteen volume *Encyclopedia of Jihad,* for example, are both available on the world wide web and can be downloaded easily to discs, sent as attachments via e-mail, and transferred to CD-Rom. The increasing globalization of terrorism also means increasing globalization of suicide tactics, because, for all the reasons described above, they are sometimes perceived as being uniquely effective.

There has been no specific evidence in open literature thus far that Al Qaeda is preparing to use women to engage in suicide attacks. Given Al Qaeda's ideology, some might argue that the organization would consider it difficult to use women in its so-called "jihad." However, a number of factors have led the FBI to warn that female suicide attackers could be used by Al Qaeda against the United States in the future. First, an interview published in an Arabic-language newspaper in mid-March 2003 quotes a woman who claims that Al Qaeda is setting up training camps to prepare women for "martyrdom operations," and specifically cites the successful use of female suicide attackers by Palestinian and Chechen organizations. Apparently as a result, the FBI has issued notices to law enforcement agencies to be alert to the possibility of a growing role for women in Al Qaeda. Second, at least in theory, it is possible that the capture of senior leaders and other members of Al Qaeda could increase the likelihood of women operatives being used to carry out missions. Other terrorist organizations have innovated in this waywhen advances in counterterrorism have forced them to adapt.

Suicide Attacks in Iraq

There are two types of suicide attacks that have been in evidence in Iraq: those specifically directed against U.S. military forces, and those specifically directed against noncombatant targets. These will be dealt with in turn. Technically suicide operations alongside military targets such as U.S. soldiers in Iraq do not qualify as "terrorist" operations because the victims are not civilians or noncombatants. Nonetheless, some of the techniques that have been described here have appeared in both wartime and postwar Iraq, includin suicide attacks carried out by Iraqi women. Techniques for suicide attacks are regularlycopied between groups, and this can make it difficult to distinguish between perpetrators, especially in the early hours after an attack. Al Qaeda has called for attacks on U.S. forces in Iraq, and at one point an unknown group calling itself the Armed Islamic Movement for Al Qaeda, the Fallujah Branch, claimed responsibility for attacks on U.S. military targets. (A connection to Al Qaeda has not been independently verified.) There have also been uncorroborated reports, attributed to the Arab television network al-Jazeera, of training camps for Arab volunteers willing to carryout suicide bombings against U.S. forces. In April, the British reportedly found a stash of weapons in Basra that was believed to be meant for suicide bombers, and Americans reportedly found a cache of about fiftyexplosives vests in a school in Baghdad. Some apparentlyregular Iraqi soldiers used suicide explosives vests to try to kill more American soldiers, particularly when the Iraqis were ostensibly surrendering.

From the end of major hostilities to August 2003, much of the postwar violence in Iraq seemed to have been carried out by Saddam Hussein loyalists, particularly members of the Ba'ath party, and perhaps also members of the disbanded Iraqi army. According to U.S. military commanders, most attacks on U.S. forces displayed characteristics of traditional guerrilla or insurgency campaigns, involving weapons such as rocket propelled grenades, remotely detonated explosives, and gunfire. There were also attacks on elements of the Iraqi infrastructure, including the water and power systems, ostensibly designed to disrupt postwar rebuilding and stabilization efforts. These types of attacks had not generally involved suicide tactics, although such operations by quasi-military groups are not uncommon in situations of occupation.

But the August 2003 suicide attacks on civilian soft targets such as the Jordanian Embassy and the U.N. Headquarters building in Baghdad seemed to bring an added dimension to the threat. They were classic terrorist suicide attacks using a car bomb and a truck bomb. Many terrorism experts point to the change in targeting and the style of attack as evidence of a possible broadening of the strategy from mainly a guerrilla insurgency against U.S. forces to include a coordinated terrorist campaign that could involve foreign elements. How the threat will evolve is hard to predict.

COUNTER SUICIDE ATTACKS

As mention on top of, it is difficult to prevent or counter suicide attacks. Nonetheless, there are both offensive and defensive measures that may reduce the number and/or severity of attacks. Among the offensive measures are preemptive strikes against the organizations that orchestrate suicide attacks (especially their leaders), vigorous intelligence collection, and efforts to reduce the ability of terrorist organizations to recruit suicide candidates.

Since the organization is a crucial element in orchestrating suicide attacks, preemptive attacks are most promising if they undermine the ability of the organization to operate. This can mean, for example, military operations to destroy the physical infrastructure of the group, efforts to cut off funding, and/or preemptive strikes designed to capture or kill leaders. These types of measures are often employed by the Israeli Defence Forces, for example, especially the very controversial policy of targeted killings (also called targeted assassinations). Sometimes preemptive attacks are employed in order to intimidate, harass, or disable a group: the goal can be to keep the organization so worried about staying ahead of potential military or police action that carefully indoctrinating future suicide attackers becomes difficult. According to this strategy, targeting known operatives or training camps disrupts imminent operations and/or reduces the ability of the group to indoctrinate people toward being prepared to kill themselves and others.

Others assert that although capturing or killing a leader can undermine the organization, it can also energize the followers into acting in the name of the "martyr." Likewise, operations that enrage the surrounding population can result in an increase in recruitment and rapid reconstruction of the group's capabilities. But this can also work the opposite way: when indigenous civilians are victimized by terrorist attacks, the organization can be marginalized by the local population. It depends upon the group and the political context.

In this regard, the second offensive measure, vigorous human and technical intelligence gathering, is vital. Good intelligence can provide critical information on a terrorist group's dynamics. Successful intelligence gathering can occur at many points along the process, from the initial contact with individuals, to the indoctrination, targeting, equipping, training and launching of the attackers. These terrorist group activities require such acts as purchases of equipment, reconnaissance of possible target areas, and other potentially observable activities. It is important to have international cooperation in intelligence gathering, especially in regions of the world where Americans are unfamiliar with the culture and language, or may not know the local population well. Intelligence can be crucial to prevent attacks before they occur, and to retaliate effectively in the aftermath, if necessary.

Suicide attacks cannot occur in a population that does not provide individuals who are willing to die for the cause. The last of the offensive measures therefore relates to efforts to reducing the potential recruitment ability of terrorist groups. These measures are the most controversial and can be frustrating to those who are primarily concerned with preventing imminent attacks: they would include policies that alter the political, cultural and socio-economic contexts that perpetuate suicide attacks, such as improving quality of life, increasing social stability, providing opportunities for productive political expression, employment, education, and so on.

Other important means of reducing recruitment include methods to undermine the ideology of the individual attacker, especially his or her dedication and faith in the meaningful nature of his or her death. Historical experience demonstrates that terrorist organizations can not continue to employ methods that alienate actual or potential constituents. The ultimate active measure over time is to remove the constituencies.

Defensive measures against suicide attacks include preventing perpetrators from physically getting at the target. The goal is to make it much more difficult for an organization to achieve a successful attack, increasing the costs in relation to the benefits gained through the attackers' death.

These include the full range of measures in homeland defence, from physical barriers to security screening to strict border controls. Some also suggest decreasing the quantity or profile of potentially symbolic targets, by measures such as restricting unnecessary travel in dangerous areas abroad or controlling the availability of sensitive information on the Internet, for example.

Preparing the public to respond calmly in the face of an attack is another way to reduce the potential attractiveness of the attack in advance.

Such anti-terrorism means are often greatly underrated in the general discussion of how to stop suicide attackers, but their role can be crucial. The purpose is to deny the terrorist organization its most attractive targets. The cost/benefit calculations undertaken by the organization as well as the individuals must be manipulated to the point where achieving a spectacular symbolic strike with its attendant publicity becomes increasingly difficult and unattractive.

THREAT OF SUICIDE ATTACKS AGAINST THE UNITED STATES

The question of how to reduce the threat of suicide attacks against the United States and its interests at home and abroad is extremely important to Congress. Most central to Congress's interests is determining the appropriate future funding levels for homeland security, the Department of Defence, and foreign operations, especially the balance between measures like homeland security and force protection, and more pro-active measures like targeted foreign aid programs, public diplomacy, multilateral cooperation, military/law enforcement operations, and intelligence for counterterrorism.

The competing requirements to spend for the operations in Iraq and Afghanistan, for example, as well as on domestic homeland security, are likely to continue to be an area of concern. Additional suicide attacks at home or in the field will affect these calculations, especially if they result in increasing numbers of casualties.

Another area of concern is the question of instituting better and more comprehensive threat assessments with respect to suicide attacks on U.S. interests in advance of potentially painful episodes, placing such assessments within the historical context of the considerable international experience with this phenomenon. Spending on counterterrorism and antiterrorism measures to deal with the evolving threat will be increasingly difficult to gauge in the absence of better analysis of the threat.

This includes not just concentrating upon potential imminent attacks, but also longer-term rigorous, focused and dispassionate evaluation of the terrorist organizations and their constituencies, informed byan indepth understanding of their political, social, and cultural context. Spending on intelligence for counterterrorism will continue to be a serious concern, both in the domestic and international arenas, as will having a sufficient quantity of well-qualified people to fill counterterrorism positions in the relevant U.S. agencies.

In this respect, the number of people well-trained to analyse terrorist organizations in depth is currently quite small in the United States, especially compared to other major powers who have in the past faced a serious terrorist threat. The suicide attacks usually depend upon an organization to be successful. Traditional academic institutions do not, on the whole, support terrorism studies as a discipline and are wary of devoting resources to a policy-relevant field that has in the past waxed and waned with the perception of the threat. In an age of globalization, good analysis comes not only from access to classified sources, but also from thorough analysis of open source literature that is often not fully exploited.

This approach could involve providing support for additional civilian and/or military training programs, possibly associated with academic institutions or government agencies, to be devoted to the study of terrorist organizations, similar to those that were implemented to face the Soviet threat. In addition to vigorous military responses, longer-term measures for reducing the constituencies for terrorist organizations and the number of candidates for suicide attacks will continue to be important. Nonmilitary measures can involve both "carrots" and "sticks." Funding for initiatives such as the recently-created Middle East Partnership Initiative, or other such programs devoted to promoting political, economic and educational development in regions where terrorist organizations recruit, may provide effective alternatives to those who would otherwise engage in terrorism. Efforts at better public diplomacy may also help.

Other measures to deter or reduce the attractiveness to individuals and their families of suicide attacks might lessen the organizations' ability to find candidates. Some have suggested that payments to families of suicide attackers be specifically outlawed, or that all states from which such payments emerge be held specifically accountable for supporting terrorist activity. Another suggestion is to deny family members of suicide attackers visas to the United States. Other measures may attempt to undercut the ideology of the potential recruit, for example byincreasing the profile of moderate Islamic clerics who condemn suicide attacks.

Finally, Congressional oversight of Defence Department activities in Iraq, including funding of reconstruction and stability operations in future months and years, will almost inevitably be affected by the future evolution of the resistance forces there. Continued suicide attacks in Iraq will not only victimize American soldiers, as well as international, U.S., and Iraqi civilians, but could potentially have important larger effects on perceptions of the postwar effort as well. Developing the best possible countermeasures to potential suicide attacks in Iraq and elsewhere may be central to the success of U.S. policy there in future months and years.

3

Successful Rising of Terrorist and Jihadi Organization

INTRODUCTION

Al Qaeda is the most successful terrorist organization in history. By destroying the World Trade Centre in New York on 9/11 it provoked the US into launching wars damaging to itself in Afghanistan and Iraq. Al Qaeda aimed to destroy the status quo in the Middle East and it succeeded beyond its wildest dreams.

Its success has not been all its own doing. Ayman al-Zawahiri, al-Qaeda's number two and chief strategist, wrote at the time of 9/11 that the aim of the group was to lure the US into an over-reaction in which it would "wage battle against the Muslims." Once the US was committed to a ground war, and no longer exercised its power primarily through local surrogates, the way would be open for Muslims to launch a jihad against America. By over-reacting, President Bush, aided by Tony Blair, responded to 9/11 very much as al-Qaeda would have wished.

In the decade since the attack on the Twin Towers "terrorist experts" and governments have frequently portrayed al-Qaeda as a tightly organized group located in north-west Pakistan. From some secret headquarters its tentacles reach out across the world, feeding recruits, expertise and money to different battlefronts.

Al-Qaeda has never operated like that. The closest it ever came to being a sort of Islamic Comintern was when it had several hundred militants based in the Tora Bora mountains of Afghanistan in 1996-2001. Even at that time, when it could operate more or less freely in the Afghan mountains, its numbers were so small that it would hire local tribesmen by the day to be filmed for al-Qaeda propaganda videos, showing its men marching and training.

Many of the most important al-Qaeda leaders from that era have since been detained or killed. But al-Qaeda has proved so hard to eradicate because it exists primarily as a set of ideas and methods for fighting holy war. Osama bin Laden's target was primarily the US and its western allies, though this has not always been true of local franchises. Civilians were fair game because they had chosen or tolerated evil rulers. In its fundamentalist religious beliefs al-Qaeda is little different from Wahhabism, the puritanical and intolerant version of Sunni Islam that is dominant in Saudi Arabia.

Suicide bombing became the preferred method for al-Qaeda to wage war. It was tactically effective because it meant that untrained but fanatical recruits willing to die could be deployed as a lethal weapon capable of killing many enemies. Moreover, the public-self sacrifice of the bomber as a demonstration of Islamic faith was an important part of a successful operation.

The CIA and other intelligence agencies were criticized after 9/11 for failing to pick up on the threat posed by al-Qaeda early in the 1990s. But in practice it barely existed before 1996 when bin Laden moved to Afghanistan from Sudan and, even then, he was only one among several players leading Islamic Jihadi groups.

Since 2001 al-Qaeda has continued to exist organizationally mainly as a series of local franchises. In Iraq, for instance, al ?Qaeda in Mesopotamia was led by a Jordanian Abu Musab al-Zarqawi who had previously opposed Osama bin Laden in Afghanistan. Expanding rapidly among the defeated Iraqi Sunni after the overthrow of Saddam Hussein in 2003, it launched a ferocious war of suicide bombings, though these were primarily directed against the newly dominant Shia Iraqis rather than Americans.

The US itself played a role in the expansion of al-Qaeda. In Iraq the US army spokesman in Baghdad attributed all armed attacks to al-Qaeda regardless of who carried them out. He hoped thereby to discredit the insurgents in the eyes of Shia Iraqis and the outside world. But within Iraq this only added to the high profile of the organization among those hostile to the new order of things, while abroad it made it much easier for al-Qaeda to raise money. The wave of anti-Americanism that swept the Muslim world after the invasion of Iraq also benefited the group.

One vicious aspect of al-Qaeda activities is always under-reported in the western media: It has always killed more Shia Muslims than it ever did Americans. The US occupation of Iraq benefited the group, but it was sectarian before it was nationalist. The Shia were seen as heretics as worthy of death as an American or British soldier.

Again and again its suicide bombers would target Shia day labourers as they waited for work in public squares in the early morning in Baghdad or massive bombs would be detonated as Shia worshippers left their mosques. Likewise in Pakistan the Pakistan Taliban, ideologically linked to al-Qaeda, has shown equal enthusiasm for slaughtering Shia where ever they can be targeted.

Al-Qaeda had the advantage post 9/11 that it did not have to do much to have an impact in the US. It had entered US demonology to a degree that any action by it, however ineffectual or trivial, had an effect out of all proportion to its size or success: a Nigerian student, who had received training from al-Qaeda in Yemen, failed to blow up a plane over Detroit using explosives hidden in his underpants; a Pakistani man living in the US was unable to detonate explosives in a car in Times Square in New York. But as al-Qaeda in Yemen gleefully pointed out in a statement such failures had almost the same effect as a successful bombing in terms of the disruption and dismay caused.

No US government can afford to have another 9/11 take place without devastating retaliation from the voters. Washington had to be seen to be doing something successful to restore American confidence in its own strength. One of the reasons why George Bush's administration had invaded Afghanistan and Iraq rather than devoting all efforts to hunting down bin Laden, was that the first two options seemed easy and the third was not.

Saddam Hussein was easy to puff up as a threat and eliminate in a way that was not true of the leader of al-Qaeda. Bush set up a special cell to find bin Laden and Zawahiri. At his morning briefings during his final months in office he would ask plaintively: "How are you getting on getting number one and number two?" In the presidential election of 2008 the Democrats made the damaging, though somewhat spurious charge, that the White House had taken its eye off the ball in the pursuit of bin Laden in Afghanistan in order to invade Iraq.

Some US foreign policy specialists argued that bin Laden no longer mattered and, if he was alive, was cut off in a cave somewhere in the mountains on Pakistan's northwest frontier. The argument was always dubious since it was not known where he was or how far, if at all, he was in operational control. In the event it turned out that bin Laden, at least in recent years, had moved far into the interior of Pakistan and was living in a house in Abbottabad, an hour's drive north of the capital Islamabad.

The claim that bin Laden was operationally ineffective also missed the point that he remained a potent symbol. This had been true ever since 9/11 and all he had to do was to go on surviving for his survival to be a further sign that the US will could be frustrated. This is why bin Laden's killing by US forces has importance, regardless of how far he master-minded different plots or was behind more recent attacks on the US.

His demise will have some impact on al-Qaeda itself, in so far as it exists as an organization but its main impact will be on American self-confidence. Of course, there will be Jihadi groups who will want to restore the balance of terror by making new attacks, but none are likely to have the same impact as 9/11. The psychological effect was so great not just because so many were killed but because of the uniquely public nature of the attack: the planes crashing into the World Trade Centre and the crumbling of the two towers.

Will al-Qaeda attacks be easier to carry out this year than in the past because of the fall or disruption of so many police states such as Egypt, Tunisia and Libya? The "strongmen" in the Arab world, like Hosni Mubarak or Ali Abdullah Saleh of Yemen, had post 9/11 been swift to manipulate Washington to support their despotic regimes in return for them clamping down on Islamic fundamentalists. Sometimes the repression, as in Yemen, was less effective than it looked, but in Pakistan the authorities were prepared to locate and hand-over al-Qaeda members to the US while being careful to shield the Afghan Taliban.

But the collapse of the old order in the Arab world may play against al-Qaeda: it will no longer be the beneficiary to the extent it was in the past of the hatred felt towards local dictators allied to or tolerated by the US. Other ways of ending an intolerable political and social status quo have been demonstrated. Mr Mubarak effectively allied himself with Israel and the US during Israel's war in Lebanon in 2006 and in Gaza in 2006. This created anger among many Egyptians which benefited fundamentalist Islamic groups but it is difficult to envisage future more democratic Egyptian governments being on such friendly terms with Israel. Al-Qaeda's appeal will be diluted. But already its significance was mainly confined to the world of perceptions rather than real threats. This is why it is of such real importance that bin Laden, the symbol of so many American fears, is dead.

THE RISE OF ISLAMIST TERRORIST GROUPS

Despite Islamic teachings against suicide and killing innocent people in battle, terrorist groups like Al Qaeda have used a fundamentalist form of Islam to justify an unholy war of terrorism.

In recent years, the terrorist group Al Qaeda has committed terrorist acts killing many innocent men, women, and children. It was responsible for the September 11, 2001, suicide terrorist attacks on New York's World Trade Center and the Pentagon, which murdered close to 3,000 people. On August 7, 1998, Al Qaeda terrorists almost simultaneously set off bombs 150 miles apart at U.S. Embassies in the East African countries of Kenya and Tanzania. The blasts killed 12 Americans and about 250 Africans, most of them Muslims. On May 12, 2003, Al Qaeda suicide terrorists set off bombs in three housing compounds in the capital of Saudi Arabia. The bombs killed 35 people, including 12 Americans. Al Qaeda has been linked to many other attacks and continues to be a threat.

In a 1998 interview, Al Qaeda's leader, Osama bin Laden, called Americans "the worst thieves in the world today and the worst terrorists . . . ." He went on to say that, "We do not have to differentiate between military or civilian. As far as we are concerned, they are all targets." He justified targeting Americans in the name of Islam. He said: "The terrorism we practice is of the commendable kind for it is directed at the tyrants and the aggressors and the enemies of God . . . ."

Other groups also commit terrorism in the name of Islam. The U.S. Department of State lists, to name a few, Lebanon's Hizbollah, Algeria's Armed Islamic Group, Egypt's Islamic Jihad, Palestine's Islamic Jihad and Hamas, Uzbekistan's Islamic Movement, the Philippines' Abu Sayyaf, and Pakistan's Jaish-e-Muhammad (Army of Muhammad) as foreign terrorist groups. Unlike Al Qaeda, most of these groups do not commit terrorism internationally. Instead, they use terrorism to help overthrow the regimes in control of their countries. Although their goals differ, they all want to set up Islamist states, based on Islamic fundamentalism. (The political form of Islamic fundamentalism is sometimes called Islamism.) The vast majority of Islamic fundamentalists are not terrorists, but their teachings have been adopted by terrorist groups to justify their actions.

Islamic fundamentalism calls for a society ruled by Islamic law. It rejects most things Western (except technology). Islamists believe their culture has been infected by Western ideas and practices, which must be rooted out. They want a more equal society with less division between the rich and poor. They want women to return to their traditional role and dress. This can mean women taking care of the family, staying out of the political and business worlds, wearing a veil, and even dressing in garments that cover them completely. Fundamentalists call for a return to a strict, "pure" Islam as practiced in the seventh century by the Prophet Muhammad and his immediate successors, the first four caliphs.

But the Encyclopaedia of the Orient states that:

. . . there are no Muslim sources indicating that the Islam of the Golden Age was as strict and conservative as the Islamists believe. All indications show that it was the liberal Islam that paved the ground for cultural, social and military achievements of those days--values foreign to all major Islamist groups. Hence, there is reason to say that the Islamist idea of the Golden Age is a dramatic falsification of history.

Islamist terrorists, like Al Qaeda, view themselves as following Muhammad's example. Muhammad in A.D. 622 had to flee from Mecca with a small band of followers. Yet in 630, he returned with an army of followers to conquer Mecca and then spread Islam throughout the Arabian Peninsula. The terrorist groups see themselves as small bands that will lead Islam to victory.

But terrorist tactics run against the basic teachings of Islam. The Koran, the holy scripture of Islam, set strict rules against suicide and killing women, children, and old people in battle.

The overwhelming majority of Muslims deplore terrorist attacks and view them as violating the Koran. Even many fundamentalist Muslims believe terrorism violates Islamic law. Nonetheless, Al Qaeda and other Islamist terrorist groups draw their supporters from the ranks of Islamic fundamentalists.

Secular States After World War II

Islam is the religion of more than 80 percent of the people in North Africa, the Middle East, and Central Asia. Islamic empires controlled these areas for more than a thousand years. The last great Islamic empire--the Ottoman Empire --finally collapsed after World War I. During the 200 years it was crumbling, European nations were busy adding most of the predominantly Islamic areas of North Africa, the Middle East, and Central Asia to their empires. Following World War I, they carved up most of the remaining parts of the old Ottoman Empire.

European control ended state by state. Most countries in this heavily Islamic area gained their independence shortly after World War II. Almost all the new leaders who emerged in countries like Iraq, Syria, and Egypt chose to follow a secular model of government pioneered by Turkey after World War I. Many adopted European or American legal systems and other Western ways, forcing Islamic law and culture into the background.

The most significant leader of the era was Egypt's Gamal Abdel Nasser . In 1952, he led a group of Egyptian military officers in overthrowing Egypt's weak monarchy, which was supported by the British. Nasser set Egypt on a secular path and tried to unify his people by promoting loyalty to the nation. Islam would remain important, but no longer dominate government, the law, and education.

Egypt under Nasser adopted a socialist economic system and an authoritarian government with close links to the military. For a while, Nasser was an inspiration and hero to many Egyptians and others in the region. But poor management and corruption in the Egyptian government resulted in massive unemployment, increased poverty, and political repression. The same was true most of the other newly independent states.

The Jewish State and the PLO

In 1948, the United Nations, with the strong support of the United States, partitioned the land then called Palestine into Jewish and Arab states. The surrounding Arab countries, however, rejected this partition and attacked Israel. They viewed the partition as another case of European colonialism, with Jews displacing Arabs and taking land that they had occupied for more than a thousand years. But Israel defended its new borders and even gained territory.

In 1967, Nasser asked the U.N. to remove its troops along the Egypt-Israel border, and he blockaded the Straits of Tiran to prevent goods from reaching Israel. When Egypt and Syria mobilized their troops in preparation for war, Israel attacked. This war lasted a mere six days and resulted in Israel occupying Egyptian land all the way to the Suez Canal as well as Jordan's West Bank, Syria's Golan Heights, and East Jerusalem. In 1973, Egypt and Syria attempted to defeat Israel in yet another war, but failed again.

The failures showed that the Arab states were too weak to overcome Israel, which was far more advanced economically and militarily. A new entity, the nationalistic Palestinian Liberation Organization (PLO), stepped in to take up the war against Israel. Founded in 1964 by Arab states, the PLO was set up as an umbrella organization to bring together the many Palestinian groups that had formed in Arab lands. The PLO set two goals: destroying Israel and establishing a secular, democratic state in its place. It never favored an Islamist state. Initially, the PLO launched guerilla attacks on Israeli military targets. But then factions of it started using terrorism--kidnappings, shootings, bombings, and hijackings. The two most notorious attacks were probably the hostage-taking and murder of 11 Israeli athletes during the 1972 Munich Olympics and the 1985 hijacking of the Italian cruise ship Achille Lauro and murder of a disabled American tourist on board. In 1988, the PLO renounced its goal of destroying Israel. (The PLO has consistently denied it was ever involved in terrorism.)

THE RISE AND SPREAD OF ISLAMIC FUNDAMENTALISM

For many years, two main forces have worked to spread Islamic fundamentalism. One is a grassroots, non-governmental effort. The other is sponsored by the government of Saudi Arabia.

One of the primary grassroots efforts has been through the Muslim Brotherhood (the Society of Muslim Brothers). Today, this organization exists in more than 70 nations in the world. It was founded in 1928 in Egypt, during British colonial rule. An Egyptian named Hasan al-Banna wanted to create an ideal government, based on Islamic law and society of the seventh century. Before this ideal Islamist state could be achieved, he argued, the Muslim masses would have to be gradually brought back to a fundamentalist Islam that was unpolluted by Western ideas.

Al-Banna's Muslim Brotherhood preached self-help, generosity, family values, and restricting women to their traditional role in the home. The Brotherhood also worked to provide hospitals, schools, and other services for the poor that the secular government was failing to provide. In the 1940s, Al-Banna created a secret organization within the Brotherhood that took part in attacks on police and British officials. In December 1948, a member of this group assassinated Egypt's prime minister. Al-Banna had not known about the plan and quickly denounced the killing. But the government retaliated by murdering Al-Banna two months later.

The Brotherhood splintered between those who advocated violence and those who wanted to work non-violently for an

Islamist society. The same process has repeated itself in other countries, with the Brotherhood starting as a peaceful organization and sometimes splitting into more radical factions.

A second powerful force pushing fundamentalism has been the Saudi Arabian government. The home to about one-fourth of the world's known oil reserves, Saudi Arabia produces great wealth. The Saudi government supports a fundamentalist Islam called Wahhabism, named after a Muslim named Muhammad bin Abd al-Wahhab who lived in the 1700s. Wahhab led a religious movement to restore the purity of Islam in Arabia, the Muslim holy land where the Prophet Muhammad lived and died. Wahhab believed in the strict literal reading of the Koran. His movement became the model for many Islamic fundamentalists today.

Wahhab joined with the Saudi family of Arabia to violently suppress all Arab Muslims who resisted his fundamentalist version of Islam. After about two centuries of conflict, the Saudis and their Wahhabi allies established the Kingdom of Saudi Arabia in 1932.

Since the founding of the kingdom, the Saudi royal family has handed over control of religious, moral, educational, and legal matters to the Wahhabi clergy. Wahhabi Saudi Arabia has no elected government, and it allows no other religion and few human rights. The hands of thieves are still cut off as they were in Muhammad's time. Women have virtually no public life. They are even forbidden to drive automobiles.

Wahhabism is the basis for the Saudi education system. The curriculum and textbooks refer to infidels (unbelievers in Islam) as the enemy and promote the hatred of Jews, Christians, and Muslims who reject Wahhabi beliefs. (In 2002, the Saudi government promised to remove these passages and promote tolerance in its schools.) The Saudi government has used money from its oil revenues to fund Wahhabi missionaries, mosques, and schools and to promote Wahhabism in dozens of countries, including the United States.

The Revolution in Iran

Two events beginning in 1979 promoted the spread of radical Islamism. The first took place in Iran. That year's Iranian Revolution, which overthrew the shah (king), electrified the Muslim world. Many Muslims viewed the shah as a despot who had been put in power by the United States and Great Britain. Fundamentalists saw him as a Westernizer and traitor to Islam. During the turmoil that took place during the revolution, radical Muslim students seized the U.S. embassy and held American diplomats hostage for more than a year.

The galvanizing leader of the Iranian Revolution was a Shi'ite Muslim, Ayatollah (a religious title) Ruhollah Khomeini. (Shi'ite Muslims are a small minority--about 15 percent of all Muslims--but they constitute the majority in Iran, Iraq, and Bahrayn and are about 40 percent of the population in Lebanon.) A fundamentalist, Khomeini seized power over other factions and created an Islamist state headed by a "Supreme Religious Leader." Rejecting Western culture, he installed a political system with him as leader for life surrounded by other religious leaders. The new government did hold popular elections for other positions and even allowed women to vote and hold public office. But Shi'ite religious leaders control the military, law-making power, courts, education system, and all matters of public morality, which are enforced by a "morals police."

Iran has also become a central source for arming and financing radical Islamist groups like Lebanon's Hizbollah (Party of God). In the 1980s in Lebanon, Hizbollah kidnapped a number of Westerners and was also responsible for the bombing that killed 241 U.S. Marines, sailors, and soldiers. Hizbollah also led an 18-year guerilla campaign against Israeli occupation of southern Lebanon, which caused Israel to remove its troops in 2000.

But the Iranian Revolution has not improved the lives of many Iranians. Iranians are increasingly demanding democratic reforms. They have elected new members of government who are attempting to modify the religious state. The final word, however, still rests with religious officials.

The Soviet War in Afghanistan

The second event in 1979 that promoted Islamist radicalism was the Soviet invasion of Afghanistan, a remote, mountainous, landlocked country with Muslim inhabitants. The Soviets invaded to help Afghan communists who had seized power. Muslims from around the world called for a jihad, or holy war in defense of Islam, to free the Muslim country from the invaders. Thousands from many countries volunteered to be mujahedeen, holy warriors. Saudi-funded religious schools (known as madrasas) in neighboring Pakistan produced many volunteers for the jihad.

Money poured in. The Muslim Brotherhood contributed heavily. But the two biggest backers of the jihad were Saudi Arabia and the U.S. Central Intelligence Agency. The Saudis sent many volunteer fighters and spent untold millions of dollars. The CIA contributed more than $3 billion, supplied more than 1,000 small, portable Stinger missiles (for shooting down helicopters and low-flying airplanes), and trained the mujahedeen. Afghanistan had become a battleground in the Cold War between the Soviet Union and the United States.

One of the Saudi volunteers was 25-year-old Osama bin Laden, a member of a wealthy Saudi family. He had attended Wahhabi schools and completed college studying engineering and public administration. In college, he had grown increasingly religious and had come in contact with radical elements of the Muslim Brotherhood. For the Afghan jihad, he raised money through his family connections, set up training camps, and commanded mujahedeen in battle against the Soviets. He also created a computer database to organize his fighters. This became known as Al Qaeda ("the base"). After the Soviet Union withdrew its troops from Afghanistan in 1989, bin Laden returned home to Saudi Arabia as a Muslim hero.

But in 1990, Iraq (led by Saddam Hussein) invaded Kuwait. Fearing that Iraq would next invade Saudi Arabia next, Bin Laden offered to bring mujahedeen from Afghanistan to Saudi Arabia to help defend it from attack. Instead, Saudi King Fahd decided to rely on American military forces to defeat Iraq, and he allowed them to set up bases in the Muslim holy land.

The stationing of non-Muslim troops on Saudi Arabia's holy soil transformed bin Laden. He viewed King Fahd as a traitor against Islam. From this point, bin Laden became an outspoken enemy of the Saudi ruling family and its American defenders. Saudi Arabia expelled him in 1991. Bin Laden went to Sudan, a country south of Egypt with a strict Islamist government. He took with him an estimated $250 million, part of which he spent to fund terrorist training camps. Outraged with what he was doing, the Saudi government revoked his citizenship, froze his assets remaining in Saudi Arabia, and reportedly even tried to assassinate him in Sudan.

Back in Afghanistan, civil war raged among Muslim warlords, producing chaos and great loss of life. Then, in 1996, a group of former madrasa students, the Taliban, seized power and imposed a strict Wahhabi Islamist regime. (In Arabic, talib means "student.")

Bin Laden had become an international outlaw, and Sudan, under pressure from the United States and Saudi Arabia, expelled him in 1996. The Taliban offered him sanctuary in Afghanistan where he provided the regime with financial aid and fighters. He also created training camps for his growing Al Qaeda terrorist network.

In 1998, bin Laden proclaimed his jihad against Americans and Jews. He declared that since the Gulf War against Iraq in 1991, "the United States is occupying the lands of Islam in the holiest of its territories, Arabia, plundering its riches, overwhelming its rulers, humiliating its people, threatening its neighbors." He also charged that the United States was destroying the Iraqi people with crippling economic sanctions and supporting Israel's occupation of Arab Palestine.

All of these acts, bin Laden argued, added up to a "clear declaration of war by the Americans against God, His Prophet, and the Muslims." Therefore, he concluded, "Jihad becomes a personal duty of every Muslim."

A short time later, bin Laden issued a "fatwa." This a legal opinion issued by a religious authority. Since bin Laden is not a religious authority, only his followers would take his fatwa seriously. Nonetheless, bin Laden decreed that it was the duty of every Muslim "to kill Americans." After bin Laden issued his fatwa, Islamist terrorists began to strike American targets. In 1998, two U.S. embassies were bombed in Africa. In 2000, suicide bombers attacked the U.S.S. Cole warship off the coast of Yemen. In 2001, terrorist airplane hijackers killed almost 3,000 people in the United States.

The United States responded to the September 11, 2001, attacks by declaring a war on terrorism. U.S. troops invaded Afghanistan and overthrew the Taliban. In 2003, the United States and allies invaded Iraq and toppled the regime of Saddam Hussein, a brutal secular dictator. A large force of U.S. troops remains in Iraq and a smaller contingent is in Afghanistan. Bin Laden remains at large, probably in the mountains of Afghanistan or Pakistan.

The overwhelming majority of Muslims today reject terrorism, bin Laden, and his call for a war on America. They view his beliefs as a perversion of Islam.

Bin Laden appeals to those who believe the United States is the enemy. In the last 25 years, Islamic fundamentalism had gained more adherents. It has attracted the poor, the unemployed and underemployed, and frustrated young people. Most of the states in the Middle East, North Africa, and Central Asia have failed to improve the lives of their citizens. Some are brutally oppressive, and Islamist groups sometimes offer opposition to the rulers. Some Islamists have joined terrorist groups linked to Al Qaeda's international network and its jihad against the United States.

RELIGION, POLITICS AND TERRORISM IN PAKISTAN

During the 1950s, if one were to attempt to predict which of the new Muslim states that emerged during the 20th century would pose a major threat to global peace and security, Pakistan would be very much at the bottom of the list. Pakistan was then widely regarded as a beacon of moderation: a highly tolerant secular state and a strong ally of the West in its conflict with the Soviet Union. Since the attacks on the United States on 11 September 2001, however, Pakistan has come to be regarded as the world's epicentre of terrorist activity committed in the name of Islam. Currently, the Pakistan state is waging a bitter war with terrorist groups many of whom are also actively supporting the Taliban in fighting the US and its allies in neighbouring Afghanistan. Pakistani nationals have been involved in terrorist attacks on India, Britain and the United States. In Pakistan itself, sectarian violence between extremists from the majority Sunnis perpetrated against the minority Shia sect has involved assassinations, attacks on religious processions and places of worship, and, most deadly of all, suicide bombings.

The major precondition for the emergence of terrorism during the 1980s has been the ongoing structural weaknesses of Pakistan. Ever since its formation in 1947, Pakistan has been ruled either by weak ineffectual civilian governments or military dictators both of whom have failed to address Pakistan's problems particularly relating to good governance and the maintenance of law and order. Weak governments, both civilian and military, have had a poor record in combating terrorism. Indeed, some politicians and elements within the armed forces have supported extremists for political advantage.

In addition, three specific major political developments provide an explanation for the terrorist phenomenon. The first is the long-standing bitter dispute between India and Pakistan over control of the Kashmir Valley that had been partitioned between India and Pakistan in 1947. Ever since, Pakistan has felt threatened by its much more powerful neighbor India and the countries have waged two major and one localized war over Kashmir. Pakistan governments – both civilian and military – have trained, financed and used terrorist groups to fight a proxy war in Indian–ruled Kashmir. This policy backfired after Pakistan was coerced by the United States into supporting the disastrous highly unpopular invasion of Afghanistan in October 2001 which is regarded throughout the Islamic world as an attack on Islam itself. As a consequence, many of the jihadi groups turned on the Pakistani government and security forces which previously had nurtured them.

The second major development was the military dictatorship of General Zia ul-Haq who ruthlessly governed Pakistan from 1977 to 1988. In part because of his religious zealotry but also to build his legitimacy and power, Zia attempted to Islamize Pakistan according to his own narrow interpretation of Sunni Islam. Under Zia the tolerance so long characteristic of Pakistani Islam began to break down. The most damaging consequence of Zia's Islamization policy was the outbreak of on-going sectarian violence between the majority Sunnis and the minority Shias, who had been threatened by Zia's attempts to impose Sunni law on the country. These sectarian terrorist organisations were the forerunners of many other terrorist groups that have plagued Pakistani society since the 1980s.

The final, and, in many ways, the most critical factor was the impact of the Soviet invasion of Afghanistan in 1979. The spontaneous uprising of the Afghans assumed the form of a holy war or jihad which was strongly supported by Pakistan. The Pakistan military, particularly its intelligence service, the Inter-Services Intelligence (ISI), channeled lavish funds and weapons, supplied largely by the United States and Saudi Arabia, to the most extremist groups of the mujahedin or holy warriors who fought the Soviets. After the Soviets had left Afghanistan in 1989, the numerous well trained and well armed jihadists were recruited, with the tacit support of Pakistani governments, by the many terrorist groups active in Pakistan and in Indian-ruled Kashmir. In addition, Saudi Arabia used the Afghanistan jihad to promote its narrow Wahhabi ideology within Afghanistan and Pakistan itself. Wahhabism is implacably hostile both to Shias and to Sufism, the mystical more tolerant form of Islam that is widely practised in Pakistan. Many of the Sunni extremists engaged in anti-Shia and anti-Sufi acts of terrorism have drawn upon Wahhabi doctrines to justify violence whose roots lie in political, economic and social rivalries.

The historical analysis demonstrates clearly that Islam as a belief system played little or no role in the rise of terrorism in Pakistan. Although dubious interpretations of Islamic teachings, which have been rejected by mainstream Islamic scholars, have been used to justify terrorist actions, the history of terrorism in Pakistan refutes the belief held by many Western political leaders, the media and a great many Western academics that 'Islamic extremism' is one of the primary drivers of contemporary terrorism and that Islam is a prime security threat facing Western countries. Unfortunately, the mainstream Western media continues to report and explain acts of terrorism largely in terms of their roots in religious extremism without reference to the political and historical contexts. Researchers also need to challenge the assumption held by many Western politicians and the media that Muslims engaged in terrorist actions are irrational religious fanatics whose repression justifies the abuse of human rights through torture, extrajudicial killings and other violent forms of counter-terrorism. Finally, contrary to the popular view held in non-Muslim countries, the major victims of terrorism in Pakistan committed in the name of Islam have been other Muslims – not outsiders. The major struggle today is not between Islam and the West but rather within Islam itself between the majority of Muslims who desire to live at peace with their neighbors and the small but powerful minority who want to impose their extremist forms of Islam on their fellow Muslims and non-Muslims alike. More in-depth studies of Pakistan and other Islamic states are needed in order to understand the complex social, economic and political problems that have nurtured violence that has been committed in the name, if not the essential spirit, of Islam.

ISLAMIC TERRORIST ORGANIZATIONS

ABU NIDAL ORGANIZATION (ANO)

a.k.a. Fatah Revolutionary Council, Arab Revolutionary Brigades, Black September, and Revolutionary Organization of Socialist Muslims.

Description

International terrorist organization led by Sabri al-Banna. Split from PLO in 1974. Made up of various functional committees, including political, military, and financial.

Activities

Has carried out terrorist attacks in 20 countries, killing or injuring almost 900 persons. Targets include the United States, the United Kingdom, France, Israel, moderate Palestinians, the PLO, and various Arab countries. Major attacks included the Rome and Vienna airports in December 1985, the Neve Shalom synagogue in Istanbul and the Pan Am flight 73 hijacking in Karachi in

September 1986, and the City of Poros day-excursion ship attack in Greece in July 1988. Suspected of assassinating. PLO deputy chief Abu Iyad and PLO security chief Abu Hul in Tunis in January 1991. ANO assassinated a Jordanian diplomat in Lebanon in January 1994 and has been linked to the killing of the PLO representative there. Has not attacked Western targets since the late 1980s.

Strength

A few hundred plus limited overseas support structure.

Location/Area of Operation

Al-Banna relocated to Iraq in December 1998, where the group maintains a presence. Has an operational presence in Lebanon, including in several Palestinian refugee camps. Financial problems and internal disorganization have reduced the group's activities and capabilities. Authorities shut down the ANO's operations in Libya and Egypt in 1999. Has demonstrated ability to operate over wide area, including the Middle East, Asia, and Europe.

External Aid

Has received considerable support, including safehaven, training, logistic assistance, and financial aid from Iraq, Libya, and Syria (until 1987), in addition to close support for selected operations.

ABU SAYYAF GROUP (ASG)

Description

The ASG is the smallest and most radical of the Islamic separatist groups operating in the southern Philippines. Some ASG members have studied or worked in the Middle East and developed ties to mjuahidin while fighting and training in Afghanistan. The group split from the Moro National Liberation Front in 1991 under the leadership of Abdurajik Abubakar Janjalani, who was killed in a clash with Philippine police on 18 December 1998. Press reports place his younger brother, Khadafi Janjalani, as the nominal leader of the group, which is composed of several factions.

Activities

Engages in bombings, assassinations, kidnappings, and extortion to promote an independent Islamic state in western Mindanao and the Sulu Archipelago, areas in the southern Philippines heavily populated by Muslims. Raided the town of Ipil in Mindanao in April 1995—the group's first large-scale action—and kidnapped more than 30 foreigners, including a US citizen, in 2000.

Strength

Believed to have about 200 core fighters, but more than 2,000 individuals motivated by the prospect of receiving ransom payments for foreign hostages allegedly joined the group in August.

Location/Area of Operation

The ASG primarily operates in the southern Philippines with members occasionally traveling to Manila, but the group expanded its operations to Malaysia this year when it abducted foreigners from two different resorts.

External Aid

Receives support from Islamic extremists in the Middle East and South Asia. Is partnered with Jemaah Islamiyah and Al-Qaeda.

Abu Sayyaf (1991-present; Islamic separatists; the Philippines) Based in the southern islands of Jolo, Basilan, and Mindanao. Branched off of the Moro National Liberation Front.

AL-AQSA MARTYRS BRIGADE (AAMB)

Description: Designated as a Foreign Terrorist Organization on March 27, 2002, the al-Aqsa Martyrs Brigade (AAMB) is composed of an unknown number of small cells of Fatah-affiliated activists that emerged at the outset of the al-Aqsa Intifada, in September 2000. Al-Aqsa's goal is to drive the Israeli military and West Bank settlers from the West Bank in order to establish a Palestinian state loyal to the Fatah.

Activities: Al-Aqsa employed primarily small-arms attacks against Israeli military personnel and settlers as the intifada spread in 2000, but by 2002 they turned increasingly to suicide bombings against Israeli civilians inside Israel. In January 2002, the group claimed responsibility for the first female suicide bombing inside Israel. In 2010, AAMB launched numerous rocket attacks on communities in Israel, including the city of Sederot and areas of the Negev desert. AAMB has not pursued a policy of targeting U.S. interests, although its anti-Israeli attacks have killed dual U.S.-Israeli citizens. In December 2011, AAMB launched rockets aimed at communities in the Negev. The attack caused no injuries or damage.

Strength: A few hundred members .

Location/Area of Operation: Most of al-Aqsa's operational activity is in Gaza but the group also planned and conducted attacks inside Israel and the West Bank. The group also has members in Palestinian refugee camps in Lebanon.

External Aid: Iran has exploited al-Aqsa's lack of resources and formal leadership by providing funds and guidance, mostly through Hizballah facilitators.

ANSAR AL-ISLAM (AAI)

aka Ansar al-Sunna; Ansar al-Sunna Army; Devotees of Islam; Followers of Islam in Kurdistan; Helpers of Islam; Jaish Ansar al-Sunna; Jund al-Islam; Kurdish Taliban; Kurdistan Supporters of Islam; Partisans of Islam; Soldiers of God; Soldiers of Islam; Supporters of Islam in Kurdistan

Description: Designated as a Foreign Terrorist Organization on March 22, 2004, Ansar al-Islam's (AI's) goals include expelling the western interests from Iraq and establishing an independent Iraqi state based on Sharia law. AI was established in 2001 in Iraqi Kurdistan with the merger of two Kurdish extremist factions that traced their roots to the Islamic Movement of Kurdistan.

On May 4, 2010 Abu Abdullah al-Shafi'i, Ansar al-Islam's leader was captured by U.S. forces in Baghdad and remains in prison. On December 15, 2011 AI announced a new emir, Sheikh Abu Hashim Muhammad bin Abdul Rahman al Ibrahim.

Activities: AI has conducted attacks against a wide range of targets including the Iraqi government and security forces, and

U.S. and Coalition forces. AI has conducted numerous kidnappings, executions, and assassinations of Iraqi citizens and politicians. The group has either claimed responsibility or is believed to be responsible for attacks in 2011 that killed 24 and wounded 147 people. On February 7, AI posted leaflets in Kirkuk warning of an attack on a Kurdish militia in retaliation for the arrest of Muslim women in the city. Two days later, a series of car bombs exploded in Kirkuk, destroying the militia's headquarters and injuring two nearby police patrols. The attack killed ten and wounded 90. On October 13, 16 civilians and two police officers were killed and 43 others wounded in a double improvised explosive device attack in Baghdad. The group was also responsible for kidnappings in February and December.

Strength: Although precise numbers are unknown, AI is considered one of the largest Sunni terrorist groups in Iraq.

Location/Area of Operation: Primarily northern Iraq but maintained a presence in western and central Iraq.

External Aid: AI received assistance from a loose network of associates in Europe and the Middle East.

ARMY OF ISLAM (AOI)

aka Jaysh al-Islam; Jaish al-Islam

Description: Designated a Foreign Terrorist Organization on May 19, 2011, the Army of Islam (AOI) is a Gaza-based terrorist organization founded in late 2005 that has been responsible for numerous terrorist acts against the Governments of Israel and Egypt, as well as American, British, and New Zealander citizens. AOI is led by Mumtaz Dughmush, and operates in Gaza. It subscribes to a Salafist ideology together with the traditional model of armed Palestinian resistance. AOI has previously worked with Hamas and is attempting to develop closer al-Qa'ida contacts.

Activities: AOI's terrorist acts include a number of rocket attacks on Israel, the 2006 kidnapping of two journalists in Gaza (an American and a New Zealander), and the 2007 kidnapping of a British citizen, journalist Alan Johnston, in Gaza. AOI is also responsible for early 2009 attacks on Egyptian civilians in Cairo and Heliopolis, Egypt. AOI is alleged to have planned the January

1, 2011 Alexandria attack on a Coptic Christian church that killed 25 and wounded 100 . On May 7, 2011, the group released a eulogy for Usama bin Ladin via its Al Nur Media Foundation.

Strength: Membership estimates range in the low hundreds.

Location/Area of Operation: Gaza, with attacks in Egypt and Israel.

External Aid: AOI receives the bulk of its funding from a variety of criminal activities in Gaza.

ASBAT AL-ANSAR (AAA)

aka Asbat al-Ansar; Band of Helpers; Band of Partisans; League of Partisans; League of the Followers; God's Partisans; Gathering of Supporters; Partisan's League; AAA; Esbat al-Ansar; Isbat al-Ansar; Osbat al-Ansar; Usbat al-Ansar; Usbat ul-Ansar

Description: Designated as a Foreign Terrorist Organization on March 27, 2002, Asbat al-Ansar is a Lebanon-based Sunni extremist group composed primarily of Palestinians with links to al-Qa'ida (AQ) and other Sunni extremist groups. Some of the group's stated goals include thwarting perceived anti-Islamic and pro-Western influences in the country, although the group remains largely confined to Lebanon's refugee camps.

Activities: Asbat al-Ansar first emerged in the early 1990s. In the mid-1990s, the group assassinated Lebanese religious leaders and bombed nightclubs, theaters, and liquor stores. The group has also plotted against foreign diplomatic targets. In October 2004, Mahir al-Sa'di, a member of Asbat al-Ansar, was sentenced, in absentia, to life imprisonment for his 2000 plot to assassinate then-U.S. Ambassador to Lebanon David Satterfield. Asbat al-Ansar has no formal ties to the AQ network, but the group shares AQ's ideology and has publicly proclaimed its support for al-Qa'ida in Iraq. Members of the group have traveled to Iraq since 2005 to fight Coalition Forces. Asbat al-Ansar has been reluctant to involve itself in operations in Lebanon due in part to concerns over losing its safe haven in Ain al-Hilwah. AAA did not stage any successful attacks in 2011.

Strength: The group has fewer than 2,000 members, mostly of Palestinian descent.

Location/Area of Operation: The group's primary base of operations is the Ain al-Hilwah Palestinian refugee camp near Sidon in southern Lebanon. The group is also in Iraq, where it has engaged in fighting U.S. and Coalition Forces.

External Aid: It is likely that the group receives money through international Sunni extremist networks.

AL-GAMA'A AL-ISLAMIYYA (ISLAMIC GROUP, IG)

Description

Egypt's largest militant group, active since the late 1970s; appears to be loosely organized. Has an external wing with a worldwide presence. The group issued a cease-fire in March 1999, but its spiritual leader, Shaykh Umar Abd al-Rahman, incarcerated in the United States, rescinded his support for the cease-fire in June 2000. The Gama'a has not conducted an attack inside Egypt since August 1998. Rifa'i Taha Musa-a hardline former senior member of the group-signed Usama Bin Ladin's February 1998 fatwa calling for attacks against US civilians. The IG since has publicly denied that it supports Bin Ladin and frequently differs with public statements made by Taha Musa. Taha Musa has in the last year sought to push the group toward a return to armed operations, but the group, which still is led by Mustafa Hamza, has yet to break the unilaterally declared cease-fire. In late 2000, Taha Musa appeared in an undated video with Bin Ladin and Ayman al-Zawahiri threatening retaliation against the United States for Abd al-Rahman's continued incarceration. The IG's primary goal is to overthrow the Egyptian Government and replace it with an Islamic state, but Taha Musa also may be interested in attacking US and Israeli interests.

Activities

Group specialized in armed attacks against Egyptian security and other government officials, Coptic Christians, and Egyptian opponents of Islamic extremism before the cease-fire. From 1993 until the cease-fire, al-Gama'a launched attacks on tourists in Egypt, most notably the attack in November 1997 at Luxor that killed 58 foreign tourists. Also claimed responsibility for the attempt in

June 1995 to assassinate Egyptian President Hosni Mubarak in Addis Ababa, Ethiopia. The Gama'a has never specifically attacked a US citizen or facility but has threatened US interests.

Strength

Unknown. At its peak the IG probably commanded several thousand hard-core members and a like number of sympathizers. The 1998 cease-fire and security crackdowns following the attack in Luxor in 1997 probably have resulted in a substantial decrease in the group's numbers.

Location/Area of Operation

Operates mainly in the Al-Minya, Asyu't, Qina, and Sohaj Governorates of southern Egypt. Also appears to have support in Cairo, Alexandria, and other urban locations, particularly among unemployed graduates and students. Has a worldwide presence, including Sudan, the United Kingdom, Afghanistan, Austria, and Yemen.

External Aid

Unknown. The Egyptian Government believes that Iran, Bin Ladin, and Afghan militant groups support the organization. Also may obtain some funding through various Islamic nongovernmental organizations.

AL-JIHAD

a.k.a. Egyptian Islamic Jihad, Jihad Group, Islamic Jihad

Description

Egyptian Islamic extremist group active since the late 1970s. Close partner of Bin Ladin's al-Qaida organization. Suffered setbacks as a result of numerous arrests of operatives worldwide, most recently in Lebanon and Yemen. Primary goals are to overthrow the Egyptian Government and replace it with an Islamic state and attack US and Israeli interests in Egypt and abroad.

Activities

Specializes in armed attacks against high-level Egyptian

Government personnel, including cabinet ministers, and car-bombings against official US and Egyptian facilities. The original Jihad was responsible for the assassination in 1981 of Egyptian President Anwar Sadat. Claimed responsibility for the attempted assassinations of Interior Minister Hassan al-Alfi in August 1993 and Prime Minister Atef Sedky in November 1993. Has not conducted an attack inside Egypt since 1993 and has never targeted foreign tourists there. Responsible for Egyptian Embassy bombing in Islamabad in 1995; in 1998, planned attack against US Embassy in Albania was thwarted.

Strength

Not known but probably has several hundred hard-core members.

Location/Area of Operation

Operates in the Cairo area. Has a network outside Egypt, including Yemen, Afghanistan, Pakistan, Sudan, Lebanon, and the United Kingdom.

External Aid

Not known. The Egyptian Government claims that both Iran and Bin Ladin support the Jihad. Also may obtain some funding through various Islamic nongovernmental organizations, cover businesses, and criminal acts.

AL-QAIDA

Description

Established by Usama Bin Ladin in the late 1980s to bring together Arabs who fought in Afghanistan against the Soviet invasion. Helped finance, recruit, transport, and train Sunni Islamic extremists for the Afghan resistance. Current goal is to establish a pan-Islamic Caliphate throughout the world by working with allied Islamic extremist groups to overthrow regimes it deems "non-Islamic" and expelling Westerners and non-Muslims from Muslim countries. Issued statement under banner of "the World Islamic Front for Jihad Against the Jews and Crusaders" in February

1998, saying it was the duty of all Muslims to kill US citizens—civilian or military—and their allies everywhere.

Activities

Plotted to carry out terrorist operations against US and Israeli tourists visiting Jordan for millennial celebrations. (Jordanian authorities thwarted the planned attacks and put 28 suspects on trial.) Conducted the bombings in August 1998 of the US Embassies in Nairobi, Kenya, and Dar es Salaam, Tanzania, that killed at least 301 persons and injured more than 5,000 others. Claims to have shot down US helicopters and killed US servicemen in Somalia in 1993 and to have conducted three bombings that targeted US troops in Aden, Yemen, in December 1992. Linked to the following plans that were not carried out: to assassinate Pope John Paul II during his visit to Manila in late 1994, simultaneous bombings of the US and Israeli Embassies in Manila and other Asian capitals in late 1994, the midair bombing of a dozen US trans-Pacific flights in 1995, and to kill President Clinton during a visit to the Philippines in early 1995. Continues to train, finance, and provide logistic support to terrorist groups in support of these goals.

Strength

May have several hundred to several thousand members. Also serves as a focal point or umbrella organization for a worldwide network that includes many Sunni Islamic extremist groups such as Egyptian Islamic Jihad, some members of al-Gama'at al-Islamiyya, the Islamic Movement of Uzbekistan, and the Harakat ul-Mujahidin.

Location/Area of Operation

Al-Qaida has a worldwide reach, has cells in a number of countries, and is reinforced by its ties to Sunni extremist networks. Bin Ladin and his key lieutenants reside in Afghanistan, and the group maintains terrorist training camps there.

External Aid

Bin Ladin, son of a billionaire Saudi family, is said to have inherited approximately $300 million that he uses to finance the group. Al-Qaida also maintains moneymaking front organizations, solicits donations from like-minded supporters, and illicitly siphons funds from donations to Muslim charitable organizations.

Also known as Qa'idat al-Jihad, Islamic Army for the Liberation of the Holy Places, World Islamic Front for Jihad Against Jews and Crusaders, Islamic Salvation Foundation, and the Osama bin Laden Network.

AL-QA'IDA (AQ)

Variant spelling of al-Qa'ida, including al Qaeda; translation "The Base"; Qa'idat al-Jihad (The Base for Jihad) ; formerly Qa'idat Ansar Allah (The Base of the Supporters of God); the Islamic Army; Islamic Salvation Foundation; the Base; The Group for the Preservation of the Holy Sites; The Islamic Army for the Liberation of the Holy Places; the World Islamic Front for Jihad Against Jews and Crusaders; the Usama Bin Ladin Network; the Usama Bin Ladin Organization; al-Jihad; the Jihad Group; Egyptian al-Jihad; Egyptian Islamic Jihad; New Jihad

Description: Designated as a Foreign Terrorist Organization on October 8, 1999, al-Qa'ida (AQ) was established by Usama bin Ladin in 1988. The group helped finance, recruit, transport, and train Sunni Islamist extremists for the Afghan resistance. AQ's strategic objectives are to remove Western influence and presence from the Muslim world, topple "apostate" governments of Muslim countries, and establish a pan-Islamic caliphate governed by its own interpretation of Sharia law that ultimately would be at the center of a new international order.

These goals remain essentially unchanged since the group's public declaration of war against the United States in 1996. AQ leaders issued a statement in February 1998 under the banner of "The World Islamic Front for Jihad against the Jews and Crusaders," saying it was the duty of all Muslims to kill U.S. citizens, civilian and military, and their allies everywhere. AQ merged with al-Jihad (Egyptian Islamic Jihad) in June 2001. Many AQ leaders were killed in 2011, including Usama bin Ladin and then second in command Atiyah Abd al-Rahman in May and August, respectively.

Activities: AQ and its supporters conducted three bombings that targeted U.S. troops in Aden in December 1992, and claim to have shot down U.S. helicopters and killed U.S. servicemen in Somalia in 1993. AQ also carried out the August 1998 bombings of the U.S. Embassies in Nairobi and Dar es Salaam, killing up to 300 individuals and injuring more than 5,000. In October 2000, AQ conducted a suicide attack on the USS Cole in the port of Aden, Yemen, with an explosive-laden boat, killing 17 U.S. Navy sailors and injuring 39.

On September 11, 2001, 19 AQ members hijacked and crashed four U.S. commercial jets – two into the World Trade Center in New York City, one into the Pentagon near Washington, DC; and the last into a field in Shanksville, Pennsylvania – leaving over 3,000 individuals dead or missing.

In November 2002, AQ carried out a suicide bombing of a hotel in Mombasa, Kenya that killed 15. In 2003 and 2004, Saudi-based AQ operatives and associated extremists launched more than a dozen attacks, killing at least 90 people, including 14 Americans in Saudi Arabia. Ayman al-Zawahiri claimed responsibility on behalf of AQ for the July 7, 2005 attacks against the London public transportation system. AQ likely played a role in the unsuccessful 2006 plot to destroy several commercial aircraft flying from the United Kingdom to the United States using liquid explosives. AQ claimed responsibility for a suicide car bomb attack on the Danish embassy in 2008 that killed five, as retaliation for a Danish newspaper re-publishing cartoons depicting the Prophet Muhammad and for Denmark's involvement in Afghanistan.

In January 2009, Bryant Neal Vinas – a U.S. citizen who traveled to Pakistan, allegedly trained in explosives at AQ camps, was captured in Pakistan and extradited to the United States – was charged with providing material support to a terrorist organization and conspiracy to commit murder. Vinas later admitted his role in helping AQ plan an attack against the Long Island Rail Road in New York and confessed to having fired missiles at a U.S. base in Afghanistan. In September 2009, Najibullah Zazi, an Afghan immigrant and U.S. lawful permanent resident, was charged with conspiracy to use weapons of mass destruction, to commit murder in a foreign country, and with providing material support to a terrorist organization as part of an AQ plot to attack the New York subway system. Zazi later admitted to contacts with AQ senior leadership, suggesting they had knowledge of his plans. In February 2010, Zazi pled guilty to charges in the United States District Court for the Eastern District of New York.

In a December 2011 video, new AQ leader al-Zawahiri claimed AQ was behind the August kidnapping of American aid worker Warren Weinstein in Pakistan. As conditions for his release, al-Zawahiri demanded the end of U.S. air strikes and the release of all terrorist suspects in U.S. custody.

Strength: AQ's organizational strength is difficult to determine precisely in the aftermath of extensive counterterrorism efforts since 9/11. The death or arrest of mid- and senior-level AQ operatives—including the group's long-time leader Usama Bin Ladin in May 2011— have disrupted communication, financial, facilitation nodes, and a number of terrorist plots. Additionally, supporters and associates worldwide who are "inspired" by the group's ideology may be operating without direction from AQ central leadership; it is impossible to estimate their numbers. AQ serves as a focal point of "inspiration" for a worldwide network of affiliated groups – al-Qa'ida in the Arabian Peninsula, al-Qa'ida in Iraq, al-Qa'ida in the Lands of the Islamic Maghreb – and other Sunni Islamic extremist groups, including the Islamic Movement of Uzbekistan, the Islamic Jihad Union, Lashkar i Jhangvi, Harakat ul-Mujahadin, and Jemaah Islamiya. TTP also has strengthened its ties to AQ.

Location/Area of Operation: AQ was based in Afghanistan until Coalition Forces removed the Taliban from power in late 2001. Since then, they have resided in Pakistan's Federally Administered Tribal Areas. AQ has a number of regional affiliates, including al-Qa'ida in Iraq (AQI), al-Qa'ida in the Arabian Peninsula (AQAP), al-Qa'ida in the Islamic Maghreb (AQIM), and al-Shabaab.

External Aid: AQ primarily depends on donations from like-minded supporters as well as from individuals who believe that their money is supporting a humanitarian cause. Some funds are diverted from Islamic charitable organizations.

AL-QA'IDA IN THE ARABIAN PENINSULA (AQAP)

aka al-Qa'ida in the South Arabian Peninsula; al-Qa'ida in Yemen; al-Qa'ida of Jihad Organization in the Arabian Peninsula; al-Qa'ida Organization in the Arabian Peninsula; Tanzim Qa'idat al-Jihad fi Jazirat al-Arab; AQAP; AQY

Description: Al-Qa'ida in the Arabian Peninsula (AQAP) was designated as a Foreign Terrorist Organization on January 19, 2010. In January 2009, the leader of al-Qa'ida in Yemen (AQY), Nasir al-Wahishi, publicly announced that Yemeni and Saudi al-Qa'ida (AQ) operatives were working together under the banner of AQAP. This announcement signaled the rebirth of an AQ franchise that previously carried out attacks in Saudi Arabia. AQAP's self-stated goals include establishing a caliphate in the Arabian Peninsula and the wider Middle East, as well as implementing Sharia law.

On September 30, 2011, AQAP cleric and head of external operations Anwar al-Aulaqi, as well as Samir Khan, the publisher of AQAP's online magazine, Inspire, were killed in Yemen.

Activities: AQAP has claimed responsibility for numerous terrorist acts against both internal and foreign targets since its inception in January 2009. Attempted attacks against foreign targets include a March 2009 suicide bombing against South Korean tourists in Yemen, the August 2009 attempt to assassinate Saudi Prince Muhammad bin Nayif, and the December 25, 2009 attempted attack on Northwest Airlines Flight 253 from Amsterdam to Detroit, Michigan. AQAP was responsible for an unsuccessful attempt to assassinate the British Ambassador in April 2010, and a failed attempt to target a British embassy vehicle with a rocket in October of that year. Also in October 2010, AQAP claimed responsibility for a foiled plot to send explosive-laden packages to the United States via cargo plane. The parcels were intercepted in the United Kingdom and in the United Arab Emirates.

AQAP took advantage of the pro-democracy demonstrations that swept the Middle East in 2011 when similar demonstrations took place in Yemen. The demonstrations quickly turned violent in Sanaa; and as a result, the Yemeni government focused its attention away from AQAP and towards suppressing the upheaval in the capital. This allowed AQAP to carry out numerous attacks, including multiple attempts to disrupt oil pipelines, attacks on police and government personnel that killed approximately 60 people, and the October assassination of the head of the counterterrorism police force for Abyan Governorate. AQAP was also able to seize small amounts of territory in southern Yemen.

Strength: AQAP has a few thousand members.

Location/Area of Operation: Yemen

External Aid: AQAP's funding primarily comes from robberies and kidnap for ransom operations, and to a lesser degree donations from like-minded supporters.

AL-QA'IDA IN IRAQ (AQI)

aka al-Qa'ida Group of Jihad in Iraq; al-Qa'ida Group of Jihad in the Land of the Two Rivers; al-Qa'ida in Mesopotamia; al-Qa'ida in the Land of the Two Rivers; al-Qa'ida of Jihad in Iraq; al-Qa'ida of Jihad Organization in the Land of The Two Rivers; al-Qa'ida of the Jihad in the Land of the Two Rivers; al-Tawhid; Jam'at al-Tawhid Wa'al-Jihad; Tanzeem Qa'idat al Jihad/Bilad al Raafidaini; Tanzim Qa'idat al-Jihad fi Bilad al-Rafidayn; The Monotheism and Jihad Group; The Organization Base of Jihad/Country of the Two Rivers; The Organization Base of Jihad/Mesopotamia; The Organization of al-Jihad's Base in Iraq; The Organization of al-Jihad's Base in the Land of the Two Rivers; The Organization of al-Jihad's Base of Operations in Iraq; The Organization of al-Jihad's Base of Operations in the Land of the Two Rivers; The Organization of Jihad's Base in the Country of the Two Rivers; al-Zarqawi Network

Description: Al-Qa'ida in Iraq (AQI) was designated as a Foreign Terrorist Organization on December 17, 2004. In the 1990s, Abu Mus'ab al-Zarqawi, a Jordanian-born militant, organized a terrorist group called al-Tawhid wal-Jihad to oppose the presence of U.S. and Western military forces in the Islamic world and the West's support for and the existence of Israel. In late 2004, he joined al-Qa'ida (AQ) and pledged allegiance to Usama bin Ladin. After this al-Tawhid wal-Jihad became known as al-Qa'ida in Iraq

(AQI). Zarqawi traveled to Iraq during Operation Iraqi Freedom and led his group against U.S. and Coalition Forces until his death in June 2006. In October 2006, AQI publicly re-named itself the Islamic State of Iraq and has since used that name in its public statements. In 2011, AQI was led by Ibrahim Awwad Ibrahim Ali al-Badri, aka Abu Du'a, who was designated under Executive Order 13224 on October 4 .

Activities: Since its founding, AQI has conducted high profile attacks, including improvised explosive device (IED) attacks against U.S. military personnel and Iraqi infrastructure, videotaped beheadings of Americans Nicholas Berg (May 11, 2004), Jack Armstrong (September 22, 2004), and Jack Hensley (September 21, 2004), suicide bomber attacks against both military and civilian targets, and rocket attacks. AQI perpètrates the majority of suicide and mass casualty bombings in Iraq, using foreign and Iraqi operatives.

Examples of high profile AQI attacks in 2011 included a series of bombings that spanned January 18-20 that killed 139 people in Tikrit. In August, AQI vowed to carry out "100 attacks" across Iraq, starting in the middle of the Ramadan, to exact revenge for the May 2011 death of Usama bin Ladin. On November 28, AQI killed 20 police officers, government employees, civilians, and children, and wounded 28 others in a suicide vehicle-borne IED attack in At Taji, Baghdad, Iraq. On December 27, n ine car bombs, six roadside bombs, and a mortar round all went off in a two-hour period, targeting residential, commercial, and government districts in Baghdad. AQI later claimed responsibility for the attacks, which killed 70 and wounded almost 200.

Strength: Membership is estimated at 1,000-2,000, making it the largest Sunni extremist group in Iraq.

Location/Area of Operation: AQI's operations are predominately Iraq-based, but it has perpetrated attacks in Jordan. The group maintains a logistical network throughout the Middle East, North Africa, Iran, South Asia, and Europe, and is believed to be responsible for attacks in Syria as well. In Iraq, AQI conducted the majority of its operations in Ninawa, Diyala, Salah ad Din, and Baghdad provinces in 2011.

External Aid: AQI receives most of its funding from a variety of businesses and criminal activities within Iraq.

AL-QA'IDA IN THE ISLAMIC MAGHREB (AQIM)

aka AQIM; Group for Call and Combat; GSPC; Le Groupe Salafiste Pour La Predication Et Le Combat; Salafist Group for Preaching and Combat

Description: The Salafist Group for Call and Combat (GSPC) was designated as a Foreign Terrorist Organization on March 27, 2002. After the GSPC officially merged with al-Qa'ida (AQ) in September 2006 and became known as al-Qa'ida in the Islamic Maghreb (AQIM), the Department of State amended the GSPC designation to reflect the change on February 20, 2008. AQIM remains largely a regionally-focused terrorist group. It has adopted a more anti-Western rhetoric and ideology and has aspirations of overthrowing "apostate" African regimes and creating an Islamic Caliphate. Abdelmalek Droukdel, aka Abu Mus'ab Abd al-Wadoud, is the group's leader.

AQIM factions in the northern Sahel (northern Mali, Niger, and Mauritania) conducted kidnap for ransom operations and conducted small-scale attacks and ambushes on security forces. The targets for kidnap for ransom are usually Western citizens from governments or third parties that have established a pattern of making concessions in the form of ransom payments for the release of individuals in custody.

In September 2010, AQIM claimed responsibility for the kidnapping of seven people working at a mine in Niger. AQIM released three of the hostages in February 2011, but at year's end, four French citizens remained in captivity. AQIM continued kidnapping operations throughout 2011. In January, AQIM kidnapped two French civilians in Niamey, Niger. The kidnappers later killed both hostages during a failed rescue attempt. In February, AQIM conducted its first abduction of a foreigner in Algeria since 2003 when it kidnapped an Italian tourist in Alidena. In October, AQIM kidnapped two Spanish and one Italian aid worker from a refugee camp near Tindouf, Algeria. In November, AQIM was responsible for the November 26 killing of a German

man in Mali and the abduction of three men from the Netherlands, South Africa, and Sweden in Mali.

Strength: AQIM has under a thousand fighters operating in Algeria with a smaller number in the Sahel. AQIM is significantly constrained by its poor finances and lack of broad general appeal in the region. It is attempting to take advantage of the volatile political situation in the Sahel to expand its membership, resources, and operations.

Location/Area of Operation: Northeastern Algeria (including but not limited to the Kabylie region) and northern Mali, Niger, and Mauritania.

External Aid: AQIM members engage in kidnapping for ransom and criminal activitities to finance their operations. Algerian expatriates and AQIM supporters abroad, many residing in Western Europe, provide limited financial and logistical support.

ARMED ISLAMIC GROUP (GIA)

Description

An Islamic extremist group, the GIA aims to overthrow the secular Algerian regime and replace it with an Islamic state. The GIA began its violent activities in 1992 after Algiers voided the victory of the Islamic Salvation Front (FIS)—the largest Islamic opposition party—in the first round of legislative elections in December 1991.

Activities

Frequent attacks against civilians and government workers. Between 1992 and 1998 the GIA conducted a terrorist campaign of civilian massacres, sometimes wiping out entire villages in its area of operation. Since announcing its campaign against foreigners living in Algeria in 1993, the GIA has killed more than 100 expatriate men and women—mostly Europeans—in the country. The group uses assassinations and bombings, including car bombs, and it is known to favour kidnapping victims and slitting their throats. The GIA hijacked an Air France flight to Algiers in December 1994. In late 1999 several GIA members were convicted by a French court for conducting a series of bombings in France in 1995.

The Salafi Group for Call and Combat (GSPC) splinter faction appears to have eclipsed the GIA since approximately 1998 and is currently assessed to be the most effective remaining armed group inside Algeria. Both the GIA and GSPC leadership continue to proclaim their rejection of President Bouteflika's amnesty, but in contrast to the GIA, the GSPC has stated that it limits attacks on civilians. The GSPC's planned attack against the Paris-Dakar Road Rally in January 2000 demonstrates, however, that the group has not entirely renounced attacks against high-profile civilian targets.

Strength

Unkown; probably several hundred to several thousand.

Location/Area of Operation

Algeria.

AUM SHINRIKYO (AUM)

aka A.I.C. Comprehensive Research Institute; A.I.C. Sogo Kenkyusho; Aleph; Aum Supreme Truth

Description: Aum Shinrikyo (Aum) was designated as a Foreign Terrorist Organization on October 8, 1997. Jailed leader Shoko Asahara established Aum in 1987, and the organization received legal status in Japan as a religious entity in 1989. The Japanese government revoked its recognition of Aum as a religious organization following Aum's deadly sarin gas attack in Tokyo in March 1995. Despite claims of renunciation of violence and Asahara's teachings, members of the group continue to adhere to the violent and apocalyptic teachings of its founder.

Activities: In March 1995, Aum members simultaneously released the chemical nerve agent sarin on several Tokyo subway trains, killing 12 people and causing up to 6,000 to seek medical treatment. Subsequent investigations by the Japanese government revealed the group was responsible for other mysterious chemical incidents in Japan in 1994, including a sarin gas attack on a residential neighborhood in Matsumoto that killed seven and hospitalized approximately 500. Japanese police arrested Asahara in May 1995; in February 2004, authorities sentenced him to death for his role in the 1995 attacks. In September 2006, Asahara lost his final appeal against the death penalty and the Japanese Supreme Court upheld the decision in October 2007. In February 2010, the death sentence for senior Aum member Tomomitsu Miimi was finalized by Japan's Supreme Court . In 2011, the death sentences of Masami Tsuchiya, Tomomasa Nakagawa, and Seiichi Endo were affirmed by Japanese courts, bringing the number of Aum members on death row to 13.

Since 1997, the group has recruited new members, engaged in commercial enterprises, and acquired property, although it scaled back these activities significantly in 2001 in response to a public outcry. In July 2001, Russian authorities arrested a group of Russian Aum followers who had planned to detonate bombs near the Imperial Palace in Tokyo as part of an operation to free Asahara from jail and smuggle him to Russia.

Although Aum has not conducted a terrorist attack since 1995, concerns remain regarding its continued adherence to the violent teachings of founder Asahara that led AUM to carry out the 1995 sarin gas attack.

Strength: According to a study by the Japanese government issued in December 2009, Aum Shinrikyo/Aleph membership in Japan is approximately 1,500 with another 200 in Russia. As of November 2011, Aum continues to maintain 32 facilities in 15 Prefectures in Japan and may continue to possess a few facilities in Russia. At the time of the Tokyo subway attack, the group claimed to have as many as 40,000 members worldwide, including 9,000 in Japan and 30,000 members in Russia.

Location/Area of Operation: Aum's principal membership is located in Japan; a residual branch of about 200 followers live in Russia.

External Aid: Funding primarily comes from member contributions.

BASQUE FATHERLAND AND LIBERTY (ETA)

aka ETA, Askatasuna; Batasuna; Ekin; Euskal Herritarrok; Euzkadi Ta Askatasuna; Herri Batasuna; Jarrai-Haika-Segi; K.A.S.; XAKI

Description: Designated as a Foreign Terrorist Organization on October 8, 1997, Basque Fatherland and Liberty (ETA) was founded in 1959 with the aim of establishing an independent homeland based on Marxist principles encompassing the Spanish Basque provinces of Vizcaya, Guipuzcoa, and Alava; the autonomous region of Navarra; and the southwestern French territories of Labourd, Basse-Navarre, and Soule. Spain and the European Union have listed ETA as a terrorist organization. In 2002, the Spanish Parliament banned the political party Batasuna, ETA's political wing, charging its members with providing material support to the terrorist group. The European Court of Human Rights in June 2009 upheld the ban on Batasuna. In September 2008, Spanish courts also banned two other Basque independence parties with reported links to Batasuna. In 2010, Batasuna continued to try to participate in regional politics and splits between parts of ETA became publicly apparent in deciding a way forward.

Activities: ETA primarily has conducted bombings and assassinations. Targets typically have included Spanish government officials, businessmen, politicians, judicial figures, and security and military forces, but the group has also targeted journalists and tourist areas. The group is responsible for killing 829 civilians and members of the armed forces or police and injuring thousands since it formally began a campaign of violence in 1968.

ETA has committed numerous attacks in the last four decades. Some of the group's high profile attacks include the February 2005 ETA car bombing in Madrid at a convention center where Spanish King Juan Carlos and then Mexican President Vicente Fox were scheduled to appear, wounding more than 20 people. In December 2006, ETA exploded a massive car bomb that destroyed much of the covered parking garage at Madrid's Barajas International Airport. ETA marked its 50 th anniversary in 2009 with a series of high profile and deadly bombings including the July attack on a Civil Guard Barracks that injured more than 60 people including children.

In March 2010, a Spanish judge charged ETA and Revolutionary Armed Forces of Colombia members of terrorist plots, including a plan to assassinate Colombian President Alvaro Uribe. Spanish authorities arrested more than 400 ETA members between 2007 and 2010 and have arrested an additional 52 in 2011. In 2011, in cooperation with international partners, Spanish security services arrested an additional 52 ETA member or associates. In April 2011, Spanish authorities seized 1,600 kilos of bomb-making material while arresting three ETA members. In the same month, French police arrested two ETA members in Creuse, France, after they fired shots from their car and wounded a police officer while speeding through a police checkpoint. On July 7, 2011, Eneko Gogeaskoetxea, one of the alleged attempted assassins of King Juan Carlos I in 1997, was apprehended in the United Kingdom and is being held there pending extradition to Spain on several arrest warrants.

The militarily weakened and politically isolated ETA, in October 2011, publicly announced a "definitive cessation" of armed activity. As the group has made and broken several past cease-fires, Madrid rejected the latest announcement and continues to demand that ETA disarm and disband.

Strength: Estimates put ETA membership of those who have not been captured by authorities at fewer than 100. Spanish and French prisons together hold approximately 750 ETA members.

Location/Area of Operation: ETA operates primarily in the Basque autonomous regions of northern Spain and southwestern France, but has attacked Spanish and French interests elsewhere. In previous years, ETA safe houses were identified and raided in Portugal. The group also maintains a low profile presence in Cuba and Venezuela.

External Aid: ETA is probably experiencing financial shortages given that the group announced publicly in September 2011 that it had ceased collecting "revolutionary taxes" from Basque businesses. This extortion program was a major source of ETA's income.

COMMUNIST PARTY OF PHILIPPINES/NEW PEOPLE'S ARMY (CPP/NPA)

aka CPP/NPA; Communist Party of the Philippines; the CPP; New People's Army; the NPA

Description: The Communist Party of the Philippines/New People's Army (CPP/NPA) was designated as a Foreign Terrorist Organization on August 9, 2002. The military wing of the Communist Party of the Philippines (CPP), the New People's Army (NPA), is a Maoist group formed in March 1969 with the aim of overthrowing the government through protracted guerrilla warfare. Jose Maria Sison, the Chairman of the CPP's Central Committee and the NPA's founder, reportedly directs CPP and NPA activity from the Netherlands, where he lives in self-imposed exile. Luis Jalandoni, a fellow Central Committee member and director of the CPP's overt political wing, the National Democratic Front (NDF), also lives in the Netherlands and has become a Dutch citizen. Although primarily a rural-based guerrilla group, the NPA had an active urban infrastructure to support its terrorist activities and, at times, used city-based assassination squads.

Activities: The CPP/NPA primarily targeted Philippine security forces, government officials, local infrastructure, and businesses that refused to pay extortion, or "revolutionary taxes." The CPP/NPA charged politicians running for office in CPP/NPA-influenced areas for "campaign permits." Despite its focus on Philippine governmental targets, the CPP/NPA has a history of attacking U.S. interests in the Philippines. In 1987, the CPP/NPA conducted direct action against U.S. personnel and facilities killing three American soldiers in four separate attacks in Angeles City. In 1989, the CPP/NPA issued a press statement taking credit for the ambush and murder of Colonel James Nicholas Rowe, chief of the Ground Forces Division of the Joint U.S.-Military Advisory Group.

For many years, the CPP/NPA carried out killings, raids, acts of extortion, and other forms of violence. In May 2010, 40 CPP/NPA guerillas ambushed an army convoy escorting election officials in the Compostela Valley, an attack that culminated in five deaths; and 40 CPP/NPA assailants launched a synchronized landmine improvised explosive device and light arms attack against a police vehicle on August 21 that resulted in nine deaths in Cataman, Philippines.

In 2011, the CPP/NPA's attacks and kidnappings continued unabated. In January, the CPP/NPA was responsable for detonating a landmine IED in Illuro Sur, Philippines that killed five and injured two police officers. In February, two civilians were killed when 50 CPP/NPA assailants fired upon a police checkpoint in Trento, Philippines. In August, the CPP/NPA kidnapped the Mayor of Lingig, Phillippines, and two of his bodyguards. The group demanded a prisoner swap before releasing the hostages in October.

Strength: The Philippines government estimates there are 5,000 members.

Location/Area of Operations: The CPP/NPA o perates in rural Luzon, Visayas, and parts of northern and eastern Mindanao. There are also cells in Manila and other metropolitan centers.

External Aid: The CPP raises funds through extortion.

CONTINUITY IRISH REPUBLICAN ARMY (CIRA)

aka Continuity Army Council; Continuity IRA; Republican Sinn Fein

Description: Designated as a Foreign Terrorist Organization on July 13, 2004, the Continuity Irish Republican Army (CIRA) is a terrorist splinter group formed in 1994 as the clandestine armed wing of Republican Sinn Fein; it split from Sinn Fein in 1986. "Continuity" refers to the group's belief that it is carrying on the original Irish Republican Army's (IRA) goal of forcing the British out of Northern Ireland. CIRA cooperates with the larger Real IRA (RIRA).

Activities: CIRA has been active in Belfast and the border areas of Northern Ireland, where it has carried out bombings, assassinations, kidnappings, hijackings, extortion, and robberies. On occasion, it provided advance warning to police of its attacks. Targets have included the British military, Northern Ireland security forces, and Loyalist paramilitary groups. CIRA did not join the Provisional IRA in the September 2005 decommissioning and remained capable of effective, if sporadic, terrorist attacks. On April 21, 2011, authorities defused an explosive device planted by CIRA near a statue of the Duke of Wellington in Trim, Meath, Ireland.

Strength: Membership is small, with possibly fewer than 50

hard-core activists. Police counterterrorist operations have reduced the group's strength. In June, the CIRA may have experienced further splintering when hard-liners made an apparently unsuccessful attempt to take over the leadership of the group.

Location/Area of Operation: Northern Ireland and the Irish Republic.

External Aid: CIRA supported its activities through criminal activities, including smuggling. CIRA may have acquired arms and materiel from the Balkans, in cooperation with the RIRA.

GAMA'A AL-ISLAMIYYA (IG)

aka al-Gama'at; Egyptian al-Gama'at al-Islamiyya; GI; Islamic Gama'at; IG; Islamic Group

Description: Gama'a al-Islamiyya (IG) was designated as a Foreign Terrorist Organization on October 8, 1997. Once Egypt's largest militant group, IG was active in the late 1970s, but is now a loosely organized network and formed the Building and Development political party that competed in the 2011 parliamentary elections, winning 13 seats. Egypt-based members of IG released from prison prior to the revolution have renounced terrorism, although some members located overseas have worked with or joined al-Qa'ida (AQ). Hundreds of members who may not have renounced violence were released from prison in 2011. The external wing, composed of mainly exiled members in several countries, maintained that its primary goal was to replace the Egyptian government with an Islamic state. IG's spiritual leader, Sheik Umar Abd al-Rahman, is serving a life sentence in a U.S. prison for his involvement in the 1993 World Trade Center bombing. Supporters of Sheikh Abd al-Rahman still remain a possible threat to U.S. interests and have called for reprisal attacks in the event of his death in prison.

Activities: In the 1990s, IG conducted armed attacks against Egyptian security and other government officials and Coptic Christians. IG claimed responsibility for the June 1995 assassination attempt on Egyptian President Hosni Mubarak in Addis Ababa, Ethiopia. The group also launched attacks on tourists in Egypt, most notably the 1997 Luxor attack. In 1999, part of the group publicly renounced violence. There were no known terrorist attacks by the IG in 2011.

Strength: At its peak, IG likely commanded several thousand hardcore members and a similar number of supporters. Security crackdowns following the 1997 attack in Luxor and the 1999 cease-fire, along with post-September 11 security measures and defections to AQ, have probably resulted in a substantial decrease in what is left of an organized group.

Location/Area of Operation: The IG maintained an external presence in Afghanistan, Yemen, Iran, the United Kingdom, Germany, and France. IG terrorist presence in Egypt was minimal due to the reconciliation efforts of former local members.

External Aid: Unknown.

HAMAS (ISLAMIC RESISTANCE MOVEMENT)

Description

Formed in late 1987 as an outgrowth of the Palestinian branch of the Muslim Brotherhood. Various HAMAS elements have used both political and violent means, including terrorism, to pursue the goal of establishing an Islamic Palestinian state in place of Israel.

Loosely structured, with some elements working clandestinely and others working openly through mosques and social service institutions to recruit members, raise money, organize activities, and distribute propaganda. HAMAS's strength is concentrated in the Gaza Strip and a few areas of the West Bank. Also has engaged in peaceful political activity, such as running candidates in West Bank Chamber of Commerce elections.

Activities

HAMAS activists, especially those in the Izz el-Din al-Qassam Brigades, have conducted many attacks—including large-scale suicide bombings—against Israeli civilian and military targets. In the early 1990s, they also targeted suspected Palestinian collaborators and Fatah rivals. Claimed several attacks during the unrest in late 2000.

Strength

Unknown number of hard-core members; tens of thousands of supporters and sympathizers.

Location/Area of Operation

Primarily the occupied territories, Israel. In August 1999, Jordanian authorities closed the group's Political Bureau offices in Amman, arrested its leaders, and prohibited the group from operating on Jordanian territory.

External Aid

Receives funding from Palestinian expatriates, Iran, and private benefactors in Saudi Arabia and other moderate Arab states. Some fundraising and propaganda activities take place in Western Europe and North America.

HARAKAT-UL JIHAD ISLAMI (HUJI)

aka HUJI, Movement of Islamic Holy War; Harkat-ul-Jihad-al Islami; Harkat-al-Jihad-ul Islami; Harkat-ul-Jehad-al-Islami; Harakat ul Jihad-e- Islami; Harakat-ul Jihad Islami

Description: Designated as a Foreign Terrorist Organization on August 6, 2010, Harakat-ul Jihad Islami (HUJI) was founded in 1980 in Afghanistan to fight against the Soviet Union. Following the Soviet withdrawal from Afghanistan in 1989, the organization re-focused its efforts on India. HUJI seeks the annexation of Indian Kashmir and expulsion of Coalition Forces from Afghanistan. It also has supplied fighters for the Taliban in Afghanistan. In addition, some factions of HUJI espouse a more global agenda and conduct attacks in Pakistan as well. HUJI is composed of militant Pakistanis and veterans of the Soviet-Afghan war. HUJI has experienced a number of internal splits and a portion of the group has aligned with al-Qa'ida (AQ) in recent years, including training its members in AQ training camps. Mohammad Ilyas Kashmiri, one of HUJI's top leaders who also served as an AQ military commander and strategist, was killed on June 3, 2011.

Activities: HUJI has been involved in a number of terrorist attacks in recent years. On March 2, 2006, a HUJI leader was the mastermind behind the suicide bombing of the U.S. Consulate in Karachi, Pakistan, which killed four people, including U.S. diplomat David Foy, and injured 48 others. HUJI was also responsible for terrorist attacks in India including the May 2007 Hyderabad mosque attack, which killed 16 and injured 40, and the March 2007 Varanasi attack, which killed 25 and injured 100. HUJI claimed credit for the September 7, 2011 bombing of the New Delhi High Court, which left at least 11 dead and an estimated 76 wounded. HUJI sent an email to the press stating that the bomb was intended to force India to repeal a death sentence of a HUJI member.

Strength: HUJI has an estimated strength of several hundred members.

Location/Area of Operations: HUJI's area of operation extends throughout South Asia, with its terrorist operations focused primarily in India and Afghanistan. Some factions of HUJI conduct attacks within Pakistan.

External Aid: Unknown.

HARAKAT UL-JIHAD-I-ISLAMI/BANGLADESH (HUJI-B)

aka HUJI-B, Harakat ul Jihad e Islami Bangladesh; Harkatul Jihad al Islam; Harkatul Jihad; Harakat ul Jihad al Islami; Harkat ul Jihad al Islami; Harkat-ul-Jehad-al-Islami; Harakat ul Jihad Islami Bangladesh; Islami Dawat-e-Kafela; IDEK

Description: Designated as a Foreign Terrorist Organization on March 5, 2008, Harakat ul-Jihad-i-Islami/Bangladesh (HUJI-B) was formed in April 1992 by a group of former Bangladeshi Afghan veterans to establish Islamic rule in Bangladesh. In October 2005, Bangladeshi authorities banned the group. HUJI-B has connections to Pakistani militant groups such as Lashkar e-Tayyiba (LeT) and the Indian Mujahedeen (IM), which advocate similar objectives. The leaders of HUJI-B signed the February 1998 fatwa sponsored by Usama bin Ladin that declared American civilians legitimate targets.

Activities: In December 2008, three HUJI-B members were convicted for the May 2004 grenade attack that wounded the British High Commissioner in Sylhet, Bangladesh. In 2011, Bangladeshi authorities formally charged multiple suspects, including HUJI-B leader Mufti Abdul Hannan, with the killing of former Finance Minister Shah AMS Kibria of Awami League (AL) in a grenade attack on January 27, 2005. Bangladeshi police also arrested many top HUJI-B leaders in 2011, including Amir Rahmatullah (aka Sheikh Farid) in April, and chief Moulana Yahiya in August. Bangladeshi police recovered arms, explosives and bomb making materials following the arrest of HUJI-B operative Abdul Alim in May.

Strength: HUJI-B leaders claim that up to 400 of its members are Afghan war veterans, but its total membership is unknown.

Location/Area of Operation: The group operates primarily in Bangladesh and India. HUJI-B trains and has a network of madrassas in Bangladesh.

External Aid: HUJI-B funding comes from a variety of sources. Several international Islamic non-governmental organizations may have funneled money to HUJI-B and other Bangladeshi militant groups.

HIZBALLAH (PARTY OF GOD)

a.k.a. Islamic Jihad, Revolutionary Justice Organization, Organization of the Oppressed on Earth, and Islamic Jihad for the Liberation of Palestine

Description

Radical Shia group formed in Lebanon; dedicated to increasing its political power in Lebanon and opposing Israel and the Middle East peace negotiations. Strongly anti-West and anti-Israel. Closely allied with, and often directed by, Iran but may have conducted operations that were not approved by Tehran.

Activities

Known or suspected to have been involved in numerous anti-US terrorist attacks, including the suicide truck bombing of the US Embassy and US Marine barracks in Beirut in October 1983 and the US Embassy annex in Beirut in September 1984. Elements of the group were responsible for the kidnapping and detention of US and other Western hostages in Lebanon. The group also attacked the Israeli Embassy in Argentina in 1992 and is a suspect in the 1994 bombing of the Israeli cultural centre in Buenos Aires. In fall 2000, it captured three Israeli soldiers in the Shabaa Farms and kidnapped an Israeli noncombatant whom it may have lured to Lebanon under false pretenses.

Strength

Several thousand supporters and a few hundred terrrorist operatives.

Location/Area of Operation

Operates in the Bekaa Valley, the southern suburbs of Beirut, and southern Lebanon. Has established cells in Europe, Africa, South America, North America, and Asia.

External Aid

Receives substantial amounts of financial, training, weapons, explosives, political, diplomatic, and organizational aid from Iran and Syria.

HARAKAT UL-MUJAHIDIN (HUM)

Description

Formerly known as the Harakat al-Ansar, the HUM is an Islamic militant group based in Pakistan that operates primarily in Kashmir.

Long-time leader of the group, Fazlur Rehman Khalil, in mid-February stepped down as HUM emir, turning the reins over to the popular Kashmiri commander and his second-in-command, Farooq Kashmiri. Khalil, who has been linked to Bin Ladin and signed his fatwa in February 1998 calling for attacks on US and Western interests, assumed the position of HUM Secretary General. Continued to operate terrorist training camps in eastern Afghanistan.

Activities

Has conducted a number of operations against Indian troops and civilian targets in Kashmir. Linked to the Kashmiri militant group al-Faran that kidnapped five Western tourists in Kashmir in July 1995; one was killed in August 1995 and the other four reportedly were killed in December of the same year. The new millennium brought significant developments for Pakistani militant groups, particularly the HUM. Most of these sprang from the hijacking of an Indian airliner on 24 December by militants believed to be associated with the HUM.

The hijackers negotiated the release of Masood Azhar, an important leader in the former Harakat ul-Ansar imprisoned by the Indians in 1994. Azhar did not, however, return to the HUM, choosing instead to form the Jaish-e-Mohammed (JEM), a rival militant group expressing a more radical line than the HUM.

Strength

Has several thousand armed supporters located in Azad Kashmir, Pakistan, and India's southern Kashmir and Doda regions. Supporters are mostly Pakistanis and Kashmiris and also include Afghans and Arab veterans of the Afghan war. Uses light and heavy machineguns, assault rifles, mortars, explosives, and rockets. HUM lost some of its membership in defections to the JEM.

Location/Area of Operation

Based in Muzaffarabad, Rawalpindi, and several other towns in Pakistan and Afghanistan, but members conduct insurgent and terrorist activities primarily in Kashmir. The HUM trains its militants in Afghanistan and Pakistan.

External Aid

Collects donations from Saudi Arabia and other Gulf and Islamic states and from Pakistanis and Kashmiris. The sources and amount of HUM's military funding are unknown.

Islamic Front for the Liberation of Bahrain - Bahrain

Islamic Movement of Central Asia -Central Asia

INDIAN MUJAHEDEEN (IM)

aka Indian Mujahidin; Islamic Security Force-Indian Mujahideen (ISF-IM)

Description: The Indian Mujahideen (IM) was designated as a Foreign Terrorist Organization on September 19, 2011.

An India-based terrorist group with significant links to Pakistan, IM has been responsible for dozens of bomb attacks throughout India since 2005, and has caused the deaths of hundreds of innocent civilians.

IM maintains close ties to other U.S.-designated terrorist entities including Pakistan-based Lashkar e-Tayyiba (LeT), Jaish-e-Mohammed (JEM), and Harakat ul-Jihad-i-Islami (HUJI). IM's stated goal is to carry out terrorist actions against non-Muslims in furtherance of its ultimate objective, an Islamic Caliphate across South Asia.

Activities: IM's primary method of attack is multiple coordinated bombings in crowded areas against economic and civilian targets to maximize terror and casualties. In 2008, an IM attack in Delhi killed 30 people; that same year, IM was responsible for 16 synchronized bomb blasts in crowded urban centers and a local hospital in Ahmedabad that killed 38 and injured more than 100.

IM also played a facilitative role in the 2008 Mumbai attack carried out by LeT that killed 163 people, including six Americans. In 2010, IM carried out the bombing of a popular German bakery in Pune, India, frequented by tourists, killing 17 and injuring over 60 people.

In 2011, IM conducted multiple bombings killing dozens of innocent civilians and injuring hundreds more. On May 25, IM was suspected of an improvised explosive device (IED) attack in New Delhi. On July 13, 25 civilians were killed and 137 wounded in an IED attack in Mumbai. On September 7, 15 civilians were killed, and 91 others injured in a bombing in New Delhi.

Strength: Estimated to have several thousand supporters and members.

Location/Area of Operation: India

External Aid: Suspected to obtain funding and support from other terrorist organizations, such as LeT and HUJI, and from sources in the Middle East.

ISLAMIC JIHAD UNION (IJU)

aka Islamic Jihad Group; Islomiy Jihod Ittihodi; al-Djihad al-Islami; Dzhamaat Modzhakhedov; Islamic Jihad Group of Uzbekistan; Jamiat al-Jihad al-Islami; Jamiyat; The Jamaat Mojahedin; The Kazakh Jama'at; The Libyan Society

Description: Designated as a Foreign Terrorist Organization on June 17, 2005, the Islamic Jihad Union (IJU) is a Sunni extremist organization that splintered from the Islamic Movement of Uzbekistan (IMU).

Activities: The IJU, based in Pakistan, primarily operates against Coalition Forces in Afghanistan and continues to pose a threat of attacks in Central Asia. The group claimed responsibility for attacks in March and April 2004, targeting police at several roadway checkpoints and at a popular bazaar, killing approximately 47 people, including 33 IJU members, some of whom were suicide bombers. In July 2004, the group carried out near-simultaneous suicide bombings of the Uzbek Prosecutor General's office and the U.S. and Israeli Embassies in Tashkent. In September 2007, German authorities disrupted an IJU plot by detaining three IJU operatives, including two German citizens. Foreign fighters from Germany, Turkey, and elsewhere in Europe continued to travel to the Afghan-Pakistan border area to join the IJU to fight against U.S. and Coalition Forces.

Strength: 100-200 members .

Location/Area of Operation: IJU members are scattered throughout Central Asia, Europe, Pakistan, and Afghanistan.

External Aid: Unknown.

ISLAMIC MOVEMENT OF UZBEKISTAN (IMU)

Description

Coalition of Islamic militants from Uzbekistan and other Central Asian states opposed to Uzbekistani President Islom Karimov's secular regime. Goal is the establishment of an Islamic state in Uzbekistan. The group's propaganda also includes anti-Western and anti-Israeli rhetoric.

Activities

Believed to be responsible for five car bombs in Tashkent in February 1999. Took hostages on several occasions in 1999 and 2000, including four US citizens who were mountain climbing in August 2000, and four Japanese geologists and eight Kyrgyzstani soldiers in August 1999.

Strength

Militants probably number in the thousands.

Location/Area of Operation

Militants are based in Afghanistan and Tajikistan. Area of operations includes Uzbekistan, Tajikistan, Kyrgyzstan, and Afghanistan.

External Aid

Support from other Islamic extremist groups in Central and South Asia. IMU leadership broadcasts statements over Iranian radio.

JAISH-E-MOHAMMED (JEM) (ARMY OF MOHAMMED)

Description

The Jaish-e-Mohammed (JEM) is an Islamist group based in Pakistan that has rapidly expanded in size and capability since Maulana Masood Azhar, a former ultrafundamentalist Harakat ul-Ansar (HUA) leader, announced its formation in February. The group's aim is to unite Kashmir with Pakistan. It is politically aligned with the radical, pro-Taliban, political party, Jamiat-i Ulema-i Islam (JUI-F).

Activities

The JEM's leader, Masood Azhar, was released from Indian imprisonment in December 1999 in exchange for 155 hijacked Indian Airlines hostages in Afghanistan. The 1994 HUA kidnappings of US and British nationals in New Delhi and the July 1995 HUA/Al Faran kidnappings of Westerners in Kashmir were two of several previous HUA efforts to free Azhar.

Azhar organized large rallies and recruitment drives across Pakistan throughout 2000. In July, a JEM rocket-grenade attack failed to injure the Chief Minister at his office in Srinagar, India, but wounded four other persons. In December, JEM militants launched grenade attacks at a bus stop in Kupwara, India, injuring 24 persons, and at a marketplace in Chadoura, India, injuring 16 persons.

JEM militants also planted two bombs that killed 21 persons in Qamarwari and Srinagar.

Strength

Has several hundred armed supporters located in Azad Kashmir, Pakistan, and in India's southern Kashmir and Doda regions.

Following Maulana Masood Azhar's release from detention in India, a reported three quarters of Harakat ul-Mujahedin (HUM) members defected to the new organization, which has managed to attract a large number of urban Kashmiri youth.

Supporters are mostly Pakistanis and Kashmiris and also include Afghans and Arab veterans of the Afghan war. Uses light and heavy machineguns, assault rifles, mortars, improvised explosive devices, and rocket grenades.

Location/Area of Operation

Based in Peshawar and Muzaffarabad, but members conduct terrorist activities primarily in Kashmir. The JEM maintains training camps in Afghanistan.

External Aid

Most of the JEM's cadre and material resources have been drawn from the militant groups Harakat ul-Jihad al-Islami (HUJI) and the Harakat ul-Mujahedin (HUM). The JEM has close ties to Afghan Arabs and the Taliban. Usama Bin Ladin is suspected of giving funding to the JEM.

Jama'at al-Tawhid wa'al - Jihad-Abu Musab al-Zarqawi's network, operating in Iraq on U.S. State Department list of Foreign Terrorist Organizations

Jemaah Islamiyah -Southeast Asia

JKLF Jammu and Kashmir Liberation Front -Pakistan and Kashmir

JEMAAH ISLAMIYA (JI)

aka Jemaa Islamiyah; Jema'a Islamiyah; Jemaa Islamiyya; Jema'a Islamiyya; Jemaa

Islamiyyah; Jema'a Islamiyyah; Jemaah Islamiah; Jemaah Islamiyah; Jema'ah Islamiyah; Jemaah Islamiyyah; Jema'ah Islamiyyah; JI

Description: Designated as a Foreign Terrorist Organization on October 23, 2002, Jemaah Islamiya (JI) is a Southeast Asia-based terrorist group co-founded by Abu Bakar Ba'asyir and Abdullah Sungkar that seeks the establishment of an Islamic caliphate spanning Indonesia, Malaysia, southern Thailand, Singapore, Brunei, and the southern Philippines. More than 400 JI operatives have been captured since 2002, including operations chief and al-Qa'ida (AQ) associate Hambali. In 2006, several members connected to JI's 2005 suicide attack in Bali were arrested; in 2007, JI emir Muhammad Naim (a.k.a. Zarkasih) and JI military commander Abu Dujana were arrested; and in 2008, two senior JI operatives were arrested in Malaysia and a JI-linked cell was broken up in Sumatra. In September 2009, JI-splinter group leader Noordin Mohammad Top was killed in a police raid. Progress against JI continued in February 2010, when Indonesian National Police discovered and disbanded an extremist training base in Aceh in which members of JI and other Indonesian extremist groups participated. The police raid resulted in the capture of over 60 militants, including some JI operatives, and led authorities to former JI leader Dulmatin, one of the planners of the 2002 Bali bombing. In March 2010, Dulmatin was killed outside of Jakarta. In June 2010, wanted JI commander Abdullah Sunata was captured while planning to bomb the Danish Embassy in Jakarta. In January 2011, JI member Umar Patek was captured in Abbottabad, Pakistan, and transferred to Indonesia for trial.

Activities: In December 2001, Singaporean authorities uncovered a JI plot to attack U.S., Israeli, British, and Australian diplomatic facilities in Singapore. Other significant JI attacks include the 2002 Bali bombings, which killed more than 200, including seven U.S. citizens; the August 2003 bombing of the J. W. Marriott Hotel in Jakarta, the September 2004 bombing outside the Australian Embassy in Jakarta, and JI's October 2005 suicide bombing in Bali, which killed 26, including the three suicide bombers.

A JI faction led by Noordin Mohammad Top conducted the most recent high-profile attack associated with the group July 17, 2009 at the J.W. Marriott and Ritz-Carlton hotels in Jakarta when two suicide bombers detonated explosive devices, killing seven and injuring more than 50, including seven Americans.

Strength: Estimates of total JI members vary from 500 to several thousand.

Location/Area of Operation: JI is based in Indonesia and is believed to have elements in Malaysia and the Philippines.

External Aid: Investigations have indicated that JI is fully capable of its own fundraising through membership donations and criminal and business activities. It has received financial, ideological, and logistical support from Middle Eastern contacts and non-governmental organizations.

JUNDALLAH

aka People's Resistance Movement of Iran (PMRI); Jonbesh-i Moqavemat-i-Mardom-i Iran; Popular Resistance Movement of Iran; Soldiers of God; Fedayeen-e-Islam; Former Jundallah of Iran; Jundullah; Jondullah; Jundollah; Jondollah; Jondallah; Army of God (God's Army); Baloch Peoples Resistance Movement (BPRM)

Description: Jundallah was designated as a Foreign Terrorist Organization on November 4, 2010. Since its 2003 inception, Jundallah, a violent extremist organization that operates primarily in the province of Sistan va Balochistan of Iran, has engaged in numerous attacks, killing and maiming scores of Iranian civilians and government officials. Jundallah's stated goals are to secure recognition of Balochi cultural, economic, and political rights from the Government of Iran and to spread awareness of the plight of the Baloch situation through violent and nonviolent means.

Activities : In March 2006, Jundallah attacked a motorcade in eastern Iran, which included the deputy head of the Iranian Red Crescent Security Department, who was then taken hostage. The Governor of Zahedan, his deputy, and five other officials were wounded; seven others were kidnapped; and more than 20 were killed in the attack. An October 2009 suicide bomb attack in a marketplace in the city of Pishin in the Sistan va Balochistan province, which killed more than 40 people, was reportedly the deadliest terrorist attack in Iran since the 1980s. In a statement on its website, Jundallah claimed responsibility for the December 15, 2010 suicide bomb attack inside the Iman Hussein Mosque in Chabahar, which killed an estimated 35 to 40 civilians and wounded 60 to 100. In July 2010, Jundallah attacked the Grand Mosque in Zahedan, killing approximately 30 and injuring an estimated 300. There were no reported attacks attributed to Jundallah in 2011.

Strength: Reports of Jundallah membership vary from 500 to 2,000.

Location/Area of Operation: Throughout Sistan va Balochistan province in southeastern Iran and the greater Balochistan area of Afghanistan and Pakistan.

External Aid: Unknown.

KAHANE CHAI

aka American Friends of the United Yeshiva; American Friends of Yeshivat Rav Meir; Committee for the Safety of the Roads; Dikuy Bogdim; DOV; Forefront of the Idea; Friends of the Jewish Idea Yeshiva; Jewish Legion; Judea Police; Judean Congress; Kach; Kahane; Kahane Lives; Kahane Tzadak; Kahane.org; Kahanetzadak.com; Kfar Tapuah Fund; Koach; Meir's Youth; New Kach Movement; Newkach.org; No'ar Meir; Repression of Traitors; State of Judea; Sword of David; The Committee Against Racism and Discrimination (CARD); The Hatikva Jewish Identity Center; The International Kahane Movement; The Jewish Idea Yeshiva; The Judean Legion; The Judean Voice; The Qomemiyut Movement; The Rabbi Meir David Kahane Memorial Fund; The Voice of Judea; The Way of the Torah; The Yeshiva of the Jewish Idea; Yeshivat Harav Meir

Description: Kach – the precursor to Kahane Chai – was founded by radical Israeli-American Rabbi Meir Kahane with the goal of restoring Greater Israel, which is generally used to refer to Israel, the West Bank, and Gaza.

Its offshoot, Kahane Chai, (translation: "Kahane Lives") was founded by Meir Kahane's son Binyamin following his father's 1990 assassination in the United States. Both organizations were designated as Foreign Terrorist Organizations on October 8, 1997. The group has attempted to gain seats in the Israeli Knesset over the past several decades but has won only one seat in 1984.

Activities: Kahane Chai has harassed and threatened Arabs, Palestinians, and Israeli government officials, and has vowed revenge for the death of Binyamin Kahane and his wife.

The group is suspected of involvement in a number of low-level attacks since the start of the First Palestinian Intifada in 2000. Since 2003, Kahane Chai activists have called for the execution of former Israeli Prime Minister Ariel Sharon, and physically intimidated other Israeli and Palestinian government officials who favored the dismantlement of Israeli settlements.

Although they have not explicitly claimed responsibility for a series of mosque burnings in the West Bank, individuals affiliated with Kahane Chai are widely suspected of being the perpetrators.

Strength: Kahane Chai's core membership is believed to be fewer than 100. The group's membership and support networks are overwhelmingly composed of Israeli citizens, most of whom live in West Bank settlements.

Location/Area of Operation: Israel and West Bank settlements, particularly Qiryat Arba' in Hebron.

External Aid: Receives support from sympathizers in the United States and Europe.

KATA'IB HIZBALLAH (KH)

aka Hizballah Brigades; Hizballah Brigades In Iraq; Hizballah Brigades-Iraq; Kata'ib Hezbollah; Khata'ib Hezbollah; Khata'ib Hizballah; Khattab Hezballah; Hizballah Brigades-Iraq Of The

Islamic Resistance In Iraq; Islamic Resistance In Iraq; Kata'ib Hizballah Fi Al-Iraq; Katibat Abu Fathel Al A'abas; Katibat Zayd Ebin Ali; Katibut Karbalah

Description: Designated as a Foreign Terrorist Organization on July 2, 2009, Kata'ib Hizballah (KH) was formed in 2006 and is a radical Shia Islamist group with an anti-Western outlook and extremist ideology that has conducted attacks against Iraqi, U.S., and Coalition targets in Iraq. KH has threatened the lives of Iraqi politicians and civilians that support the legitimate political process in Iraq.

The group is notable for its extensive use of media operations and propaganda by filming and releasing videos of attacks. KH has ideological ties to Lebanese Hizballah and may have received support from that group and its sponsor, Iran.

Activities: KH has been responsible for numerous violent terrorist attacks since 2007, including improvised explosive device bombings, rocket propelled grenade attacks, and sniper operations. In 2007, KH gained notoriety with attacks on U.S. and Coalition Forces in Iraq. KH was particularly active in summer 2008, recording and distributing video footage of its attacks against U.S. and Coalition soldiers. Using the alias "Hizballah Brigades in Iraq," KH filmed attacks on U.S. Stryker vehicles, Abrams tanks, and Bradley armored personnel carriers. In 2009, KH continued to release videos of attacks ranging in date from 2006 to 2008 on the Internet.

In June 2011, five U.S. soldiers were killed in a rocket attack in Baghdad, Iraq, when KH assailants fired between three and five rockets at the United States military base Camp Victory, which surrounds Baghdad's International airport.

Strength: Membership is estimated at 400 individuals.

Location/Area of Operation: KH's operations are predominately Iraq-based. In 2011, KH conducted the majority of its operations in Baghdad but was active in other areas of Iraq, including Kurdish areas such as Mosul.

External Aid: KH is almost entirely dependent on support from Iran and Lebanese Hizballah.

KURDISTAN WORKERS' PARTY (PKK)

aka the Kurdistan Freedom and Democracy Congress; the Freedom and Democracy Congress of Kurdistan; KADEK; Partiya Karkeran Kurdistan; the People's Defense Force; Halu Mesru Savunma Kuvveti; Kurdistan People's Congress; People's Congress of Kurdistan; KONGRA-GEL

Description: Founded by Abdullah Ocalan in 1978 as a Marxist-Leninist separatist organization, the Kurdistan Workers' Party (PKK) or Kongra-Gel (KGK) was designated as a Foreign Terrorist Organization on October 8, 1997. The group, composed primarily of Turkish Kurds, launched a campaign of violence in 1984. The PKK's original goal was to establish an independent Kurdish state in southeastern Turkey, but in recent years it has spoken more often about autonomy within a Turkish state that guarantees Kurdish cultural and linguistic rights.

In the early 1990s, the PKK moved beyond rural-based insurgent activities to include urban terrorism. In the 1990s, southeastern Anatolia was the scene of significant violence; some estimates place casualties at approximately 30,000 persons. Following his capture in 1999, Ocalan announced a "peace initiative," ordering members to refrain from violence and requesting dialogue with Ankara on Kurdish issues.

Ocalan's death sentence was commuted to life imprisonment; he remains the symbolic leader of the group. The group foreswore violence until June 2004, when the group's hard-line militant wing took control and renounced the self-imposed cease-fire of the previous five years. Striking over the border from bases within Iraq, the PKK has engaged in terrorist attacks in eastern and western Turkey.

Activities: Primary targets have been Turkish government security forces, local Turkish officials, and villagers who oppose the organization in Turkey. In 2006, 2007, and 2008, PKK violence killed or injured hundreds of Turks.

The PKK remained active in 2011, with approximately 61 credited attacks. At least 88 people were killed in the attacks and 216 wounded. Although the majority of the attacks took place in

Turkey, suspected PKK members have carried out multiple attacks on the offices of a Turkish newspaper in Paris, France.

Strength: Approximately 4,000 to 5,000; 3,000 to 3,500 are located in northern Iraq.

Location/Area of Operation: The PKK o perate primarily in Turkey, Iraq, and Europe.

External Aid: In the past, the PKK received safe haven and modest aid from Syria, Iraq, and Iran. Since 1999, Iran has also cooperated in a limited fashion with Turkey against the PKK. The PKK receives substantial financial support from the large Kurdish diaspora in Europe and from criminal activity there.

LASHKAR-E-TAYYIBA (LT) (ARMY OF THE RIGHTEOUS)

Description

The LT is the armed wing of the Pakistan-based religious organization, Markaz-ud-Dawa-wal-Irshad (MDI)—a Sunni anti-US missionary organization formed in 1989. One of the three largest and best-trained groups fighting in Kashmir against India, it is not connected to a political party. The LT leader is MDI chief, Professor Hafiz Mohammed Saeed.

Activities

Has conducted a number of operations against Indian troops and civilian targets in Kashmir since 1993. The LT is suspected of eight separate attacks in August that killed nearly 100, mostly Hindu Indians. LT militants are suspected of kidnapping six persons in Akhala, India, in November 2000 and killing five of them. The group also operates a chain of religious schools in the Punjab.

Strength

Has several hundred members in Azad Kashmir, Pakistan, and in India's southern Kashmir and Doda regions. Almost all LT cadres are foreigners—mostly Pakistanis from seminaries across the country and Afghan veterans of the Afghan wars. Uses assault rifles, light and heavy machineguns, mortars, explosives, and rocket propelled grenades.

Location/Area of Operation

Based in Muridke (near Lahore) and Muzaffarabad. The LT trains its militants in mobile training camps across Pakistan-administered Kashmir and Afghanistan.

Maktab al-Khadamat -Afghanistan

Moroccan Islamic Combatant Group -Morocco and Spain

Muslim Brotherhood -international

LASHKAR I JHANGVI (LJ)

aka Army of Jhangvi; Lashkar e Jhangvi; Lashkar-i-Jhangvi

Description: Designated as a Foreign Terrorist Organization on January 30, 2003, Lashkar I Jhangvi (LJ) is the militant offshoot of the Sunni Deobandi sectarian group Sipah-i-Sahaba Pakistan. LJ focuses primarily on anti-Shia attacks and other attacks in Pakistan and Afghanistan, and was banned by Pakistan in August 2001 as part of an effort to rein in sectarian violence. Many of its members then sought refuge in Afghanistan with the Taliban, with whom they had existing ties. After the collapse of the Taliban as the ruling government in Afghanistan, LJ members became active in aiding other terrorists, providing safe houses, false identities, and protection in Pakistani cities, including Karachi, Peshawar, and Rawalpindi. LJ works closely with Tehrik-e-Taliban Pakistan (TTP).

Activities: LJ specializes in armed attacks and bombings and has admitted responsibility for numerous killings of Shia religious and community leaders in Pakistan. In January 1999, the group attempted to assassinate former Prime Minister Nawaz Sharif and his brother Shabaz Sharif, Chief Minister of Punjab Province. Media reports linked LJ to attacks on Christian targets in Pakistan, including a March 2002 grenade assault on the Protestant International Church in Islamabad that killed two U.S. citizens. Pakistani authorities believe LJ was responsible for the July 2003 bombing of a Shia mosque in Quetta, Pakistan. Authorities also implicated LJ in several sectarian incidents in 2004, including the May and June bombings of two Shia mosques in Karachi, which killed more than 40 people.

LJ was very active in 2011. The most notable attack occurred on December 6, in Kabul, Afghanistan, when a suicide bomber detonated an improvised explosive device in a crowd of Shia mourners, killing 48 civilians – including 12 children – and wounding 193.

LJ claimed responsibility. In another attack on September 29, in Balochistan, LJ operatives ordered Shia pilgrims off a bus and shot dead 29 victims. An hour after the initial attack, gunmen killed family members travelling to retrieve the victims of the first attack. Additional 2011 attacks included: a January firebombing attack that injured four police officers, and six civilians, including three children; a May attack that killed eight civilians and wounded 15; another May attack that killed two police officers and wounded three; and a July 30 attack that killed 11 civilians and wounded three.

Strength: Assessed in the low hundreds.

Location/Area of Operation: LJ is active primarily in Punjab, FATA, Karachi, and Baluchistan. Some members travel between Pakistan and Afghanistan.

External Aid: Funding comes from wealthy donors in Pakistan as well as the Middle East, particularly Saudi Arabia. The group also engages in criminal activity to fund its activities, including extortion and protection money.

LIBERATION TIGERS OF TAMIL EELAM (LTTE)

Description: Founded in 1976 and d esignated as a Foreign Terrorist Organization on October 8, 1997, the Liberation Tigers of Tamil Eelam (LTTE) became a powerful Tamil secessionist group in Sri Lanka. Despite its military defeat at the hands of the Sri Lankan government in 2009, the LTTE's international network of sympathizers and financial support persists. LTTE remnants continued to collect contributions from the Tamil diaspora in North America, Europe, and Australia, where there were reports that some of these contributions were coerced by locally-based LTTE sympathizers. The LTTE also used Tamil charitable organizations as fronts for its fundraising.

Activities: Although the LTTE has been largely inactive since its military defeat in Sri Lanka in 2009, in the past the LTTE was responsible for an integrated battlefield insurgent strategy that targeted key installations and senior Sri Lankan political and military leaders. It conducted a sustained campaign targeting rival Tamil groups, and assassinated Prime Minister Rajiv Gandhi of India in 1991 and President Ranasinghe Premadasa of Sri Lanka in 1993. Although most notorious for its cadre of suicide bombers, the Black Tigers, the organization included an amphibious force, the Sea Tigers, and a nascent air wing, the Air Tigers. Fighting between the LTTE and the Sri Lanka government escalated in 2006 and continued through 2008.

In early 2009, Sri Lankan forces recaptured the LTTE's key strongholds, including their capital of Kilinochchi. In May 2009, government forces defeated the last LTTE fighting forces and killed LTTE leader Prahbakaran and other members of the LTTE leadership and military command. As a result, the Sri Lankan government declared military victory over LTTE. In 2010, some LTTE members reportedly fled Sri Lanka and have since attempted to reorganize in India. In June 2010, assailants claiming LTTE membership may have been responsible for an attack against a railway in Tamil Nadu, India. No one was injured when the targeted train was able to stop in time to prevent derailment. There have been no known attacks in Sri Lanka that could verifiably be attributed to the LTTE since the end of the war. In March 2010, German police arrested six Tamil migrants living in Germany for supposedly using blackmail and extortion to raise funds for the LTTE. LTTE's financial network of support continued to operate throughout 2011.

Strength: Exact strength is unknown.

Location/Area of Operations: Sri Lanka and India.

External Aid: The LTTE used its international contacts and the large Tamil diaspora in North America, Europe, and Asia to procure weapons, communications, funding, and other needed supplies. The group employed charities as fronts to collect and divert funds for their activities.

LIBYAN ISLAMIC FIGHTING GROUP (LIFG)

Description: The Libyan Islamic Fighting Group (LIFG) was designated as a Foreign Terrorist Organization on December 17, 2004. In the early 1990s, LIFG emerged from the group of Libyans who had fought Soviet forces in Afghanistan and pledged to overthrow Libyan leader Muammar al-Qadhafi. In the years following, some members maintained an anti-Qadhafi focus and targeted Libyan government interests. Others, such as Abu al-Faraj al-Libi, who was arrested in Pakistan in 2005, have aligned with Usama bin Ladin and are believed to be part of the al-Qa'ida (AQ) leadership structure. On November 3, 2007, AQ leader Ayman al-Zawahiri announced a formal merger between AQ and LIFG. However, on July 3, 2009, LIFG members in the United Kingdom released a statement formally disavowing any association with AQ. In September 2009, six imprisoned LIFG members issued a 417-page document that renounced violence. More than 100 LIFG members pledged to adhere to this revised doctrine and have been pardoned and released from prison in Libya since September 2009.

Activities: LIFG has been largely inactive operationally in Libya since the late 1990s when members fled predominately to Europe and the Middle East because of tightened Libyan security measures. In early 2011, in the wake of the Libyan revolution and the fall of Qadhafi, LIFG members created the LIFG successor group, the Libyan Islamic Movement for Change (LIMC), and became one of many rebel groups united under the umbrella of the opposition leadership known as the Transitional National Council. Former LIFG emir and LIMC leader Abdel Hakim Bil-Hajj was appointed the Libyan Transitional Council's Tripoli military commander during the Libyan uprisings and has denied any link between his group and AQ.

Strength: Unknown.

Location/Area of Operation: Since the late 1990s, many members have fled to southwest Asia, and European countries, particularly the UK.

External Aid: Unknown.

MOROCCAN ISLAMIC COMBATANT GROUP (GICM)

aka Groupe Islamique Combattant Marocain; GICM

Description: Designated as a Foreign Terrorist Organization on October 11, 2005, the Moroccan Islamic Combatant Group (GICM) is a transnational terrorist group centered in the Moroccan diaspora communities of Western Europe. Its goals include establishing an Islamic state in Morocco. The group emerged in the 1990s and is composed of Moroccan recruits who trained in armed camps in Afghanistan, including some who fought in the Soviet war in Afghanistan. GICM members interact with other North African extremists, particularly in Europe.

Activities: GICM members are believed to be among those responsible for the 2004 Madrid train bombings, which killed 191 people. GICM members were also implicated in the recruitment network for Iraq, and at least one GICM member carried out a suicide attack against Coalition Forces in Iraq. According to open source reports, GICM individuals are believed to have participated in the 2003 Casablanca attacks. However, the group has largely been inactive since these attacks, and has not claimed responsibility for or had attacks attributed to them since the Madrid train bombings.

Strength: Much of GICM's leadership in Morocco and Europe has been killed, imprisoned, or is awaiting trial. Alleged leader Mohamed al-Guerbouzi was convicted in absentia by the Moroccan government for his role in the Casablanca attacks but remains free in exile in London.

Location/Area of Operation: Morocco, Western Europe, and Afghanistan.

External Aid: In the past, GICM has been involved in narcotics trafficking in North Africa and Europe to fund its operations.

MUJAHADIN-E KHALQ ORGANIZATION (MEK)

aka MEK; MKO; Mujahadin-e Khalq; Muslim Iranian Students' Society; National Council of Resistance; NCR; Organization of the People's Holy Warriors of Iran; the National Liberation Army of Iran; NLA; People's Mujahadin Organization of Iran; PMOI;

National Council of Resistance of Iran; NCRI; Sazeman-e Mujahadin-e Khalq-e Iran

Description: Designated as a Foreign Terrorist Organization on October 8, 1997, the Mujahadin-E Khalq Organization (MEK) is a Marxist-Islamic Organization that seeks the overthrow of the Iranian regime through its military wing, the National Liberation Army (NLA), and its political front, the National Council of Resistance of Iran (NCRI).

The MEK was founded in 1963 by a group of college-educated Iranian Marxists who opposed the country's pro-western ruler, Shah Mohammad Reza Pahlavi. The group participated in the 1979 Islamic Revolution that replaced the Shah with a Shiite Islamist regime led by Ayatollah Khomeini. However, the MEK's ideology – a blend of Marxism, feminism, and Islamism – was at odds with the post-revolutionary government, and its original leadership was soon executed by the Khomeini regime. In 1981, the group was driven from its bases on the Iran-Iraq border and resettled in Paris, where it began supporting Iraq in its eight-year war against Khomeini's Iran. In 1986, after France recognized the Iranian regime, the MEK moved its headquarters to Iraq, which facilitated its terrorist activities in Iran. From 2003 through the end of 2011, roughly 3,400 MEK members were encamped at Ashraf in Iraq.

Activities: The group's worldwide campaign against the Iranian government uses propaganda and terrorism to achieve its objectives. During the 1970s, the MEK staged terrorist attacks inside Iran and killed several U.S. military personnel and civilians working on defense projects in Tehran. In 1972, the MEK set off bombs in Tehran at the U.S. Information Service office (part of the U.S. Embassy), the Iran-American Society, and the offices of several U.S. companies to protest the visit of President Nixon to Iran. In 1973, the MEK assassinated the deputy chief of the U.S. Military Mission in Tehran and bombed several businesses, including Shell Oil. In 1974, the MEK set off bombs in Tehran at the offices of U.S. companies to protest the visit of then U.S. Secretary of State Kissinger. In 1975, the MEK assassinated two U.S. military officers who were members of the U.S. Military Assistance Advisory Group in Tehran. In 1976, the MEK assassinated two U.S. citizens who were employees of Rockwell International in Tehran. In 1979, the group claimed responsibility for the murder of an American Texaco executive. Alhough denied by the MEK, analysis based on eyewitness accounts and MEK documents demonstrates that MEK members participated in and supported the 1979 takeover of the U.S. Embassy in Tehran and that the MEK later argued against the early release of the American hostages. The MEK also provided personnel to guard and defend the site of the U.S. Embassy in Tehran, following the takeover of the Embassy.

In 1981, MEK leadership attempted to overthrow the newly installed Islamic regime; Iranian security forces subsequently initiated a crackdown on the group. The MEK instigated a bombing campaign, including an attack against the head office of the Islamic Republic Party and the Prime Minister's office, which killed some 70 high-ranking Iranian officials, including Chief Justice Ayatollah Mohammad Beheshti, President Mohammad-Ali Rajaei, and Prime Minister Mohammad-Javad Bahonar. These attacks resulted in an expanded Iranian government crackdown that forced MEK leaders to flee to France. For five years, the MEK continued to wage its terrorist campaign from its Paris headquarters. Expelled by France in 1986, MEK leaders turned to Saddam Hussein's regime for basing, financial support, and training. Near the end of the 1980-1988 Iran-Iraq War, Baghdad armed the MEK with heavy military equipment and deployed thousands of MEK fighters in suicidal, waves of attacks against Iranian forces.

The MEK's relationship with the former Iraqi regime continued through the 1990s. In 1991, the group reportedly assisted the Iraqi Republican Guard's bloody crackdown on Iraqi Shia and Kurds who rose up against Saddam Hussein's regime. In April 1992, the MEK conducted near-simultaneous attacks on Iranian embassies and consular missions in 13 countries, including against the Iranian mission to the United Nations in New York, demonstrating the group's ability to mount large-scale operations overseas. In June 1998, the MEK was implicated in a series of bombing and mortar attacks in Iran that killed at least 15 and injured several others. The MEK also assassinated the former Iranian Minister of Prisons in 1998. In April 1999, the MEK targeted key Iranian military officers and assassinated the deputy chief of the Iranian Armed Forces General Staff, Brigadier General Ali Sayyaad Shirazi.

In April 2000, the MEK attempted to assassinate the commander of the Nasr Headquarters, Tehran's interagency board responsible for coordinating policies on Iraq. The pace of anti-Iranian operations increased during "Operation Great Bahman" in February 2000, when the group launched a dozen attacks against Iran. One attack included a mortar attack against a major Iranian leadership complex in Tehran that housed the offices of the Supreme Leader and the President. The attack killed one person and injured six other individuals. In March 2000, the MEK launched mortars into a residential district in Tehran, injuring four people and damaging property. In 2000 and 2001, the MEK was involved in regular mortar attacks and hit-and-run raids against Iranian military and law enforcement personnel, as well as government buildings near the Iran-Iraq border. Following an initial Coalition bombardment of the MEK's facilities in Iraq at the outset of Operation Iraqi Freedom, MEK leadership negotiated a cease-fire with Coalition Forces and surrendered their heavy-arms to Coalition control. From 2003 through the end of 2011, roughly 3,400 MEK members were encamped at Ashraf in Iraq.

In 2003, French authorities arrested 160 MEK members at operational bases they believed the MEK was using to coordinate financing and planning for terrorist attacks. Upon the arrest of MEK leader Maryam Rajavi, MEK members took to Paris' streets and engaged in self-immolation. French authorities eventually released Rajavi.

Strength: Estimates place MEK's worldwide membership at between 5,000 and 10,000 members, with large pockets in Paris and other major European capitals. In Iraq, roughly 3,400 MEK members were gathered at Camp Ashraf, the MEK's main compound north of Baghdad, at the end of 2011.

As a condition of the 2003 cease-fire agreement, the MEK relinquished more than 2,000 tanks, armored personnel carriers, and heavy artillery.

Location/Area of Operation: The MEK's global support structure remains in place, with associates and supporters scattered throughout Europe and North America. Operations have targeted Iranian government elements across the globe, including in Europe and Iran. The MEK's political arm, the National Council of Resistance of Iran (NCRI), has a global support network with active lobbying and propaganda efforts in major Western capitals. NCRI also has a well-developed media communications strategy.

External Aid: Before Operation Iraqi Freedom began in 2003, the MEK received all of its military assistance and most of its financial support from Saddam Hussein. The fall of Saddam Hussein's regime has led the MEK increasingly to rely on front organizations to solicit contributions from expatriate Iranian communities.

NATIONAL LIBERATION ARMY (ELN)

Description: The National Liberation Army (ELN) was designated as a Foreign Terrorist Organization on October 8, 1997. The ELN is a Colombian Marxist-Leninist group formed in 1964 by intellectuals inspired by Fidel Castro and Che Guevara. It is primarily rural-based, although it also has several urban units. The ELN remains focused on attacking economic infrastructure, in particular oil and gas pipelines and electricity pylons, and extorting foreign and local companies.

Activities: The ELN engages in kidnappings, hijackings, bombings, drug trafficking, and extortion activities. The group also uses intimidation of judges, prosecutors and witnesses and has been involved in the murder of teachers and trade unionists. Historically, the ELN has been one of the most prolific users of anti-personnel mines in Colombia. In recent years, the ELN has launched joint attacks with the Revolutionary Armed Forces of Colombia (FARC), Colombia's largest terrorist organization. Authorities believe that the ELN kidnapped at least 25 people and was involved in at least 23 attacks in 2010, some of which were carried out jointly with the FARC.

The two Colombia-based terrorist groups significantly increased their attacks in 2011 as they attempted to undermine the October 30 national elections. Attacks on Colombia's oil and gas industry also significantly increased resulting in major economic damage, and numerous deaths and kidnappings. On June 25, ELN attacked a police outpost in Colon Genova, Narino, killing eight civilians, including a child, and wounding four others. On October 30 – election day – the ELN attempted to kill the Vice President of the House of Representatives, killing his driver but missing the Vice President.

Strength: Approximately 2,000 armed combatants and an unknown number of active supporters.

Location/Area of Operation: Mostly in the rural and mountainous areas of northern, northeastern, and southwestern Colombia, as well as the border regions with Venezuela.

External Aid: The ELN draws its funding from the narcotics trade and from extortion of oil and gas companies. Additional funds are derived from kidnapping ransoms. There is no known external aid.

PALESTINE ISLAMIC JIHAD (PIJ)

Description

Originated among militant Palestinians in the Gaza Strip during the 1970s. Committed to the creation of an Islamic Palestinian state and the destruction of Israel through holy war. Because of its strong support for Israel, the United States has been identified as an enemy of the PIJ, but the group has not specifically conducted attacks against US interests in the past.

In July 2000, however, publicly threatened to attack US interests if the US Embassy is moved from Tel Aviv to Jerusalem.

Also opposes moderate Arab governments that it believes have been tainted by Western secularism.

Activities

Conducted at least three attacks against Israeli interests in late 2000, including one to commemorate the anniversary of former PIJ leader Fathi Shaqaqi's murder in Malta on 26 October 1995. Conducted suicide bombings against Israeli targets in the West Bank, Gaza Strip, and Israel.

Strength

Unknown.

Location/Area of Operation

Primarily Israel and the occupied territories and other parts of the Middle East, including Jordan and Lebanon. Headquartered in Syria.

External Aid

Receives financial assistance from Iran and limited logistic assistance from Syria.

PALESTINE LIBERATION FRONT (PLF)

Description

Broke away from the PFLP-GC in mid-1970s. Later split again into pro-PLO, pro-Syrian, and pro-Libyan factions. Pro-PLO faction led by Muhammad Abbas (Abu Abbas), who became member of PLO Executive Committee in 1984 but left it in 1991.

Activities

The Abu Abbas-led faction is known for aerial attacks against Israel. Abbas's group also was responsible for the attack in 1985 on the cruise ship Achille Lauro and the murder of US citizen Leon Klinghoffer. A warrant for Abu Abbas's arrest is outstanding in Italy.

Strength

Unknown.

Location/Area of Operation

PLO faction based in Tunisia until Achille Lauro attack. Now based in Iraq.

External Aid

Receives support mainly from Iraq. Has received support from Libya in the past.

POPULAR FRONT FOR THE LIBERATION OF PALESTINE (PFLP)

aka PFLP; Halhul Gang; Halhul Squad; Palestinian Popular Resistance Forces; PPRF; Red Eagle Gang; Red Eagle Group; Red Eagles; Martyr Abu-Ali Mustafa Battalion

Description: Designated as a Foreign Terrorist Organization on October 8, 1997, the Popular Front for the Liberation of Palestine (PFLP), a Marxist-Leninist group founded by George Habash, broke away from the Arab Nationalist Movement in 1967. The group earned a reputation for spectacular international attacks in the 1960s and 1970s, including airline hijackings that killed at least 20 U.S. citizens. A leading faction within the PLO, the PFLP has long accepted the concept of a two-state solution but has opposed specific provisions of various peace initiatives.

Activities: The PFLP stepped up its operational activity during the Second Intifada. This was highlighted by at least two suicide bombings since 2003, multiple joint operations with other Palestinian terrorist groups, and the assassination of Israeli Tourism Minister Rehavam Ze'evi in 2001, to avenge Israel's killing of the PFLP Secretary General earlier that year.

The PFLP was involved in several rocket attacks, launched primarily from Gaza, against Israel in 2008 and 2009, and claimed responsibility for numerous attacks on Israeli forces in Gaza, including a December 2009 ambush of Israeli soldiers in central Gaza. The PLFP claimed numerous mortar and rocket attacks fired from Gaza into Israel in 2010, as well as a February attack on a group of Israeli citizens. In 2011, the group continued to use rockets and mortars to target communities in Israel, including rocket attacks in August and October in Eshkolot and Ashqelon, respectively, which caused no injuries or damage. In October, the PFLP claimed responsibility for a rocket attack that killed one civilian in Ashqelon.

Strength: Unknown.

Location/Area of Operation: Syria, Lebanon, Israel, the West Bank and Gaza.

External Aid: Leadership received safe haven in Syria.

POPULAR FRONT FOR THE LIBERATION OF PALESTINE—GENERAL COMMAND (PLFP-GC)

Description: The Popular Front for the Liberation of Palestine – General Command (PFLP-GC) was designated as a Foreign Terrorist Organization on October 8, 1997. The PFLP-GC split from the PFLP in 1968, claiming it wanted to focus more on resistance and less on politics. Originally, the group was violently opposed to the Arafat-led PLO. Ahmad Jibril, a former captain in the Syrian Army, has led the PFLP-GC since its founding. The PFLP-GC is closely tied to both Syria and Iran.

Activities: The PFLP-GC carried out dozens of attacks in Europe and the Middle East during the 1970s and 1980s. The organization was known for cross-border terrorist attacks into Israel using unusual means, such as hot-air balloons and motorized hang gliders. The group's primary recent focus was supporting Hizballah's attacks against Israel, training members of other Palestinian terrorist groups, and smuggling weapons. The PFLP-GC maintained an armed presence in several Palestinian refugee camps and at its own military bases in Lebanon and along the Lebanon-Syria border. In recent years, the PFLP-GC was implicated by Lebanese security officials in several rocket attacks against Israel. In May 2008, the PFLP-GC claimed responsibility for a rocket attack on a shopping center in Ashqelon that wounded at least 10 people. In 2009, the group was responsible for wounding two civilians in an armed attack in Nahariyya, Northern District, Israel. In 2011, the PFLP-GC targeted Israeli communities in a March 20 rocket attack by its Jihad Jibril Brigades in the city of Eshkolot, Southern District, Israel. The attack caused no injuries or damage.

Strength: Several hundred.

Location/Area of Operation: Political Leadership was h eadquartered in Damascus, with bases in southern Lebanon and a presence in the Palestinian refugee camps in Lebanon and Syria. The group also maintains a small presence in Gaza.

External Aid: Received safe haven and logistical and military support, from Syria and financial support from Iran.

PEOPLE AGAINST GANGSTERISM AND DRUGS (PAGAD)

Description

PAGAD was formed in 1996 as a community anticrime group fighting drugs and violence in the Cape Flats section of Cape Town but by early 1998 had also become antigovernment and anti-Western. PAGAD and its Islamic ally Qibla view the South African Government as a threat to Islamic values and consequently promote greater political voice for South African Muslims.

The group is led by Abdus Salaam Ebrahim. PAGAD's G-Force (Gun Force) operates in small cells and is believed responsible for carrying out acts of terrorism.

PAGAD uses several front names, including Muslims Against Global Oppression (MAGO) and Muslims Against Illegitimate Leaders (MAIL), when launching anti-Western protests and campaigns.

Activities

PAGAD is suspected of conducting recurring bouts of urban terrorism—particularly bomb sprees—in Cape Town since 1998, including nine bombings in 2000. Bombing targets have included South African authorities, moderate Muslims, synagogues, gay nightclubs, tourist attractions, and Western-associated restaurants. PAGAD is believed to have masterminded the bombing on 25 August 1998 of the Cape Town Planet Hollywood.

Strength

Estimated at several hundred members. PAGAD's G-Force probably contains fewer than 50 members.

Location/Area of Operation

Operates mainly in the Cape Town area, South Africa's foremost tourist venue.

External Aid

Probably has ties to Islamic extremists in the Middle East.

Salafist Group for Preaching of Islam and Combat -Algeria

Takfir wal-Hijra -Egypt/Sudan/Algeria

Hofstad Network – Netherlands

REAL IRA (RIRA)

aka RIRA; Real Irish Republican Army; 32 County Sovereignty Committee; 32 County Sovereignty Movement; Irish Republican Prisoners Welfare Association; Real Oglaigh Na hEireann

Description: Designated as a Foreign Terrorist Organization on May 16, 2001, the Real IRA (RIRA) was formed in 1997 as the clandestine armed wing of the 32 County Sovereignty Movement, a "political pressure group" dedicated to removing British forces from Northern Ireland and unifying Ireland. The RIRA has historically sought to disrupt the Northern Ireland peace process and did not participate in the September 2005 weapons decommissioning. In September 1997, the 32 County Sovereignty Movement opposed Sinn Fein's adoption of the Mitchell principles of democracy and non-violence. Despite internal rifts and calls by some jailed members, including the group's founder Michael "Mickey" McKevitt, for a cease-fire and disbandment, the RIRA has pledged additional violence and continued to conduct attacks.

Activities: Many RIRA members are former Provisional Irish Republican Army members who left the organization after that group renewed its cease-fire in 1997. These members brought a wealth of experience in terrorist tactics and bomb making to the RIRA. Targets have included civilians (most notoriously in the Omagh bombing in August 1998), British security forces, and police in Northern Ireland. The Independent Monitoring Commission, which was established to oversee the peace process, assessed that RIRA members were likely responsible for the majority of the shootings and assaults that occurred in Northern Ireland. In October 2011, Lithuanian authorities convicted a RIRA member for attempting to arrange a shipment of weapons to Northern Ireland in 2008.

In 2011, the group was responsible for seven attacks on Northern Ireland businesses and the Police Service of Northern Ireland (PSNI) and was suspected of other incidents. In January, May, and October, the RIRA damaged office buildings, government facilities, and banks in improvised explosive device (IED) attacks, and in February authorities defused another IED before it could explode. In March, RIRA attacked PSNI officers investigating a car theft, and officials blamed RIRA for a bomb placed under a police car that killed a Catholic police officer in April. RIRA conducted two separate attacks on August 4 and August 24 that killed one civilian and wounded another, respectively.

Strength: A ccording to the Irish government, the RIRA has approximately 100 active members. The organization may receive limited support from IRA hardliners and Republican sympathizers who are dissatisfied with the IRA's continuing cease-fire and with Sinn Fein's involvement in the peace process.

Location/Area of Operation: Northern Ireland, Great Britain, and the Irish Republic.

External Aid: The RIRA is suspected of receiving funds from sympathizers in the United States and of attempting to buy weapons from U.S. gun dealers. The RIRA was also reported to have purchased sophisticated weapons from the Balkans and to have occasionally collaborated with the Continuity Irish Republican Army.

REVOLUTIONARY ARMED FORCES OF COLOMBIA (FARC)

aka FARC; Fuerzas Armadas Revolucionarias de Colombia

Description: Designated as a Foreign Terrorist Organization on October 8, 1997, the Revolutionary Armed Forces of Colombia (FARC) is Latin America's oldest, largest, most violent, and best-equipped terrorist organization. The FARC began in the early 1960s as an outgrowth of the Liberal Party-based peasant self-defense leagues, but took on Marxist ideology. Today, it only nominally fights in support of Marxist goals, and is heavily involved in narcotics production and trafficking. The FARC is responsible for large numbers of kidnappings for ransom in Colombia and in past years has held more than 700 hostages. The FARC has been degraded by a continuing Colombian military offensive targeting key FARC units and leaders that has, by most estimates, halved the FARC's numbers and succeeded in capturing or killing a number of FARC senior and mid-level commanders.

Activities: The FARC has carried out bombings, murder, mortar attacks, kidnapping, extortion, and hijacking, as well as guerrilla and conventional military action against Colombian political, military, civilian, and economic targets. The FARC has also used landmines extensively.

The group considers U.S. citizens legitimate targets, and other foreign citizens are often targets of abductions carried out to obtain ransom and political leverage.

The FARC has well-documented ties to the full range of narcotics trafficking activities, including taxation, cultivation, and distribution. In 2011, Colombian government investigators reported that the FARC controlled approximately 15 gold mines in the Bolivar Department, and was actively involved in the extortion of heavy equipment operators at the mines. According to the investigators, the FARC could be receiving approximately $850 million annually from these activities.

Over the years, the FARC has perpetrated a large number of high profile terrorist acts, including the 1999 murder of three U.S. missionaries working in Colombia, and multiple kidnappings and assassinations of Colombian government officials and civilians. In July 2008, the Colombian military made a dramatic rescue of 15 high-value FARC hostages including three U.S. Department of Defense contractors Marc Gonsalves, Keith Stansell, and Thomas Howe, who were held in captivity for more than five years along with former Colombian presidential candidate Ingrid Betancourt.

FARC attacks increased significantly during 2011 likely due to the FARC's effort to disrupt the October national elections. Among the numerous attacks was the February 11 mortar attack in San Miguel, Putumayo, killing five civilians including a child and wounding two other children. Coordinated FARC attacks in late October in Narino and Arauca killed more than 30 Colombian service members. In July, a bombing of a bus, attributed to the FARC, took place in Toribio, Cauca, resulting in two deaths and 70 injuries of members of a local indigenous community. The FARC executed four Colombian military hostages on November 25. The four had been held captive for at least 12 years and were shot at close range while in chains.

Strength: Approximately 8,000 to 9,000 combatants, with several thousand more supporters.

Location/Area of Operation: Primarily in Colombia. Activities including extortion, kidnapping, weapons sourcing, and logistical planning took place in neighboring countries.

External Aid: Cuba provided some medical care, safe haven, and political consultation. The FARC often use Colombia's border areas with Venezuela, Panama, and Ecuador for incursions into Colombia; and Venezuelan and Ecuadorian territory for safe haven, although the degree of government acquiescence is not always clear.

REVOLUTIONARY ORGANIZATION 17 NOVEMBER (17N)

aka Epanastatiki Organosi 17 Noemvri; 17 November

Description: Designated as a Foreign Terrorist Organization on October 8, 1997, the Revolutionary Organization 17 November (17N) is a radical leftist group established in 1975. Named for the student uprising in Greece in November 1973 that protested the ruling military junta, 17N is opposed to the Greek government, the United States, Turkey, and the North Atlantic Treaty Organization (NATO). It seeks the end of the U.S. military presence in Greece, the removal of Turkish military forces from Cyprus, and the severing of Greece's ties to NATO and the European Union (EU).

Activities: Initial attacks consisted of assassinations of senior U.S. officials and Greek public figures. Five U.S. Embassy employees have been murdered since 17N began its terrorist activities in 1975. The group began using bombings in the 1980s. In 1990, 17N expanded its targets to include Turkish diplomats, EU facilities, and foreign firms investing in Greece. 17N's most recent attack was a bombing attempt in June 2002 at the port of Piraeus in Athens. After the attempted attack, Greek authorities arrested 19 17N members, including a key leader of the organization. The convictions of 13 of these members have been upheld by Greek courts.

Strength: Unknown.

Location/Area of Operation: Athens, Greece.

External Aid: Unknown.

REVOLUTIONARY PEOPLE'S LIBERATION PARTY/FRONT (DHKP/C)

aka DHKP/C; Dev Sol; Dev Sol Armed Revolutionary Units; Dev Sol Silahli Devrimci Birlikleri; Dev Sol SDB; Devrimci Halk Kurtulus Partisi-Cephesi; Devrimci Sol; Revolutionary Left

Description: Designated as a Foreign Terrorist Organization on October 8, 1997, the Revolutionary People's Liberation Party/Front (DHKP/C) was originally formed in 1978 as Devrimci Sol, or Dev Sol, a splinter faction of Dev Genc (Revolutionary Youth). It was renamed in 1994 after factional infighting. "Party" refers to the group's political activities, while "Front" is a reference to the group's militant operations. The group espouses a Marxist-Leninist ideology and vehemently opposes the United States, NATO, and Turkish establishments. Its goals are the establishment of a socialist state and the abolition of harsh high-security "F-type" prisons, in Turkey. DHKP/C finances its activities chiefly through donations and extortion.

Activities: Since the late 1980s, the group has primarily targeted current and retired Turkish security and military officials. It began a new campaign against foreign interests in 1990, which included attacks against U.S. military and diplomatic personnel and facilities. Dev Sol assassinated two U.S. military contractors, wounded an Air Force officer, and bombed more than 20 U.S. and NATO military, commercial, and cultural facilities. DHKP/C added suicide bombings to its repertoire in 2001, with successful attacks against Turkish police in January and September. Since the end of 2001, DHKP/C has typically used improvised explosive devices against official Turkish targets and U.S. targets of opportunity.

Operations and arrests against the group have weakened its capabilities. In late June 2004, the group was suspected of a bus bombing at Istanbul University, which killed four civilians and wounded 21. In July 2005, in Ankara, police intercepted and killed a DHKP/C suicide bomber who attempted to attack the Ministry of Justice. In June 2006, the group killed a police officer in Istanbul;

four members of the group were arrested the next month for the attack.

The DHKP/C was dealt a major ideological blow when Dursun Karatas, leader of the group, died in August 2008 in the Netherlands. After the loss of their leader, the DHKP/C reorganized in 2009 and was reportedly competing with the Kurdistan Workers Party for influence in both Turkey and with the Turkish diaspora in Europe. In 2011, DHKP/C continued to plan terrorist attacks, and suspected members were arrested in Greece in July. In October, a suspected DHKP/C member blew himself up with a grenade in Thessaloniki, Greece. A significant cache of weapons was found in the suspect's apartment, shared with other suspected DHKP/C members.

Strength: Probably several dozen members inside Turkey, with a limited support network throughout Europe.

Location/Area of Operation: Turkey, primarily in Istanbul, Ankara, Izmir, and Adana.

External Aid: DHKP/C raises funds in Europe. The group also raises funds through extortion.

REVOLUTIONARY STRUGGLE (RS)

Description: Designated as a Foreign Terrorist Organization on May 18, 2009, Revolutionary Struggle (RS) is a radical leftist group with Marxist ideology that has conducted attacks against both Greek and U.S. targets in Greece. RS emerged in 2003 following the arrests of members of the Greek leftist groups 17 November and Revolutionary People's Struggle.

Activities: RS first gained notoriety when it claimed responsibility for the September 5, 2003 bombings at the Athens Courthouse during the trials of 17 November members. From 2004 to 2006, RS claimed responsibility for a number of improvised explosive device (IED) attacks, including a March 2004 attack outside of a Citibank office in Athens. RS claimed responsibility for the January 12, 2007 rocket propelled grenade (RPG) attack on the U.S. Embassy in Athens, which resulted in damage to the building. In 2009, RS increased the number and sophistication of its attacks on police, financial institutions, and other targets. RS successfully bombed a Citibank branch in Athens in March 2009, but failed in its vehicle-borne IED attack in February 2009 against the Citibank headquarters building in Athens. In September 2009, RS claimed responsibility for a car bomb attack on the Athens Stock Exchange, which caused widespread damage and injured a passerby.

In 2010, the Greek Government made significant strides in curtailing RS's terrorist activities. On April 10, Greek police arrested six suspected RS members, including purported leadership figure Nikos Maziotis. In addition to the arrests, the Greek raid resulted in the seizure of a RPG launcher, possibly the one used against the U.S. Embassy in Athens in January 2007. The six, plus two other suspected RS members, face charges for arms offenses, causing explosions, and multiple counts of attempted homicide. Their trial started in December 2011, and if found guilty, the suspects face up to 25 years in prison.

Strength: Unknown but numbers presumed to be small.

Location/Area of Operation: Athens, Greece.

External Aid: Unknown.

SHINING PATH (SL)

aka SL; Sendero Luminoso; Ejercito Guerrillero Popular (People's Guerrilla Army); EGP; Ejercito Popular de Liberacion (People's Liberation Army); EPL; Partido Comunista del Peru (Communist Party of Peru); PCP; Partido Comunista del Peru en el Sendero Luminoso de Jose Carlos Mariategui (Communist Party of Peru on the Shining Path of Jose Carlos Mariategui); Socorro Popular del Peru (People's Aid of Peru); SPP

Description: Shining Path (SL) was designated as a Foreign Terrorist Organization on October 8, 1997. Former university professor Abimael Guzman formed SL in Peru in the late 1960s, and his teachings created the foundation of SL's militant Maoist doctrine. SL's stated goal is to destroy existing Peruvian institutions and replace them with a communist peasant revolutionary regime. It also opposes any influence by foreign governments. In the

1980s, SL was one of the most ruthless terrorist groups in the Western Hemisphere. The Peruvian government made dramatic gains against SL during the 1990s, capturing Guzman in 1992, and killing a large number of militants. In 2011, the Upper Huallaga Valley (UHV) faction of SL was largely reduced, and in December, the faction's leader publicly acknowledged defeat. Still, he did not turn himself in or disband his organization. Separately, the much larger and stronger rival SL faction in the Apurimac and Ene River Valley (VRAE) maintained its influence.

Activities: SL activities have included intimidation of U.S.-sponsored non-governmental organizations involved in counternarcotics efforts, the ambushing of counternarcotics helicopters, and attacks against Peruvian police perpetrated in conjunction with narcotics traffickers.

SL killed an estimated 17 people in 2011, including 11 soldiers in a December attack on a military convoy and a military helicopter.

Strength: The two SL factions together are believed to have several hundred armed members.

Location/Area of Operation: Peru, with most activity in rural areas, specifically the Huallaga Valley, the Ene River, and the Apurimac Valley of central Peru.

External Aid: SL is primarily funded by the narcotics trade.

TEHRIK-E TALIBAN PAKISTAN (TTP)

Aka: Pakistani Taliban; Tehreek-e-Taliban; Tehrik-e-Taliban; Tehrik-e Taliban Pakistan; Tehrik-i-Taliban Pakistan; TTP

Description: Designated as a Foreign Terrorist Organization on September 1, 2010, Tehrik-e Taliban Pakistan (TTP) is a Pakistan-based terrorist organization formed in 2007 in opposition to Pakistani military efforts in the Federally Administered Tribal Areas. Previously disparate militant tribes agreed to cooperate and eventually coalesced into TTP under the leadership of now deceased leader Baitullah Mehsud. The group officially presented itself as a discrete entity in 2007. TTP has been led by Hakimullah Mehsud since August 2009. Other senior leaders include Wali Ur Rehman, the TTP emir in South Waziristan, Pakistan. TTP's goals include overthrowing the Government of Pakistan by waging a terrorist campaign against the civilian leader of Pakistan, its military, and NATO forces in Afghanistan. TTP uses the tribal belt along the Afghan-Pakistani border to train and deploy its operatives, and the group has a symbiotic relationship with al-Qa'ida (AQ). TTP draws ideological guidance from AQ, while AQ relies on TTP for safe haven in the Pashtun areas along the Afghan-Pakistani border. This arrangement gives TTP access to both AQ's global terrorist network and the operational experience of its members. Given the proximity of the two groups and the nature of their relationship, TTP is a force multiplier for AQ.

Activities: TTP has carried out and claimed responsibility for numerous terrorist acts against Pakistani and U.S. interests, including a December 2009 suicide attack on a U.S. military base in Khowst, Afghanistan, which killed seven U.S. citizens, and an April 2010 suicide bombing against the U.S. Consulate in Peshawar, Pakistan, which killed six Pakistani citizens. TTP is suspected of being involved in the 2007 assassination of former Pakistani Prime Minister Benazir Bhutto. TTP claimed to have supported the failed attempt by Faisal Shahzad to detonate an explosive device in New York City's Times Square on May 1, 2010. TTP's claim was validated by investigations that revealed that TTP directed and facilitated the plot.

Throughout 2011, TTP carried out attacks against the Government of Pakistan and civilian targets, as well as against U.S. targets in Pakistan. Attacks in 2011 included: a March bombing at a gas station in Faisalabad that killed 31 people; an April double suicide bombing at a Sufi shrine in Dera Ghazi Khan that left more than 50 dead; a May bombing of an American consulate convoy in Peshawar that killed one person and injured twelve; a May siege of a naval base in Karachi; the May assassination of the PNS Mehran Saudi diplomat in Karachi; and a September attack against a school bus that killed four children and the bus driver.

Strength: Several thousand.

Location: Federally Administered Tribal Areas (FATA), Pakistan

External aid: TTP is believed to raise most of its funds through kidnapping for ransom and operations that target Afghanistan-bound military transport trucks for robbery. Such operations enable TTP to steal military equipment, which they then sell in Afghan and Pakistani markets.

THE EVOLUTION OF TRANSNATIONAL EXTREMIST-MUSLIM TERRORIST GROUPS IN SOUTH-EAST ASIA

Islam in South-East Asia is predominantly moderate and tolerant. We need to understand the evolution of Muslim extremist terrorist groups in the region in that context. Islam arrived in South-East Asia peaceably, carried to the region in the thirteenth century by Muslim traders from South Asia and the Middle East. Over several centuries, as the religion spread across South-East Asia, it incorporated and adapted elements of pre-existing cultural and spiritual beliefs and traditions.

Reflecting its peaceful evolution, South-East Asian Islam has been traditionally open-minded and accepting of cultural diversity.

Every country in South-East Asia has a Muslim community-from five per cent of the population in the Philippines to around 90 per cent in Indonesia. Within these Muslim communities, Islamic identity or affiliation has grown in recent decades, in line with a global phenomenon. There is a greater observance of Islamic practices and dress codes, particularly among young Muslims. And Islamic organisations have become increasingly prominent and active on university campuses and in politics more generally.

Muslim political and social organisations play a positive role in the countries of the region. Indonesia's two largest Muslim organisations, Muhammadiyah and Nahdlatul Ulama, were central to the successful transition to democracy. They play critical roles in providing welfare and education to their fellow citizens. Both organisations are firmly opposed to terrorism. They expressed support for Indonesia's new anti-terrorism decrees in the wake of the Bali bombings.

The vast majority of South-East Asia's Muslims represent tolerant, mainstream Islam. In parliamentary elections in both Indonesia and Malaysia in 2004, Muslim political parties advocating a moderate and tolerant message outperformed those advocating a narrow conservative interpretation of Islam.

It is important to recognise that support for political Islam or a growth in Muslim piety does not translate into a greater likelihood of Muslim extremism and militancy.

An increase in identification with Islam should not be confused with the emergence of terrorist groups such as Jemaah Islamiyah, which was responsible for the Bali attack. Bali bomber Amrozi no more represents the views of the majority of Muslims in South-East Asia than Usama Bin Laden represents the majority of Muslims in the Arab world.

The vast majority of the population of South-East Asia rejects not only the callous violence of terrorist groups but also their goals and ideology.

Evolution of Militancy-Fusing Local and International Agendas

Terrorist tactics are not new in South-East Asia. Nor are they limited to a particular religious or ethnic group.

Militant separatist movements in South-East Asia since the 1940s have had a range of ethnic, political and religious motivations. And violence against civilians has been perpetrated by followers of a variety of political ideologies and religious faiths. Almost every armed nationalist and communist movement in the region has had such tactics in its repertoire. Across the region, militant sub-national groups have over past decades used terrorist attacks to advance their separatist, ethnic or religious interests.

But the emergence of systematically applied terrorism, associated with a virulent form of extremist Muslim ideology, has transformed terrorist attacks in South-East Asia. A seldom-chosen tactic has become an integral-even primary-choice for interconnected groups. Muslim militancy is not a new phenomenon in South-East Asia. In the post-colonial era, militant Muslim separatist groups formed in countries where Muslims are in the minority-Burma, the Philippines, Thailand-to fight for autonomy from national governments. In Indonesia, where Muslims make up the majority, Muslim militancy has been driven by two goals-to establish an Islamic state, governed by a rigid and doctrinaire interpretation of Islamic law, and to redress economic and political grievances. A number of South-East Asian Muslim separatist groups have been prepared to use violence or terrorism against their governments. The Moro Islamic Liberation Front (MILF) and the Abu Sayyaf Group continue to operate in the Philippines. The Pattani United Liberation Organisation (PULO) is active in Thailand, and the Rohingya Solidarity Organisation in Burma.

These groups are not primarily anti-Western. Rather, they have had long-standing disputes with national governments based on local socio-political and economic grievances. But Muslim militancy in the region has undergone a dramatic evolution over the past decade. The historical grievances of radical Muslim groups were local in nature. Now, the predominant terrorist threat in South-East Asia is transnational. It draws inspiration and support both from other South-East Asian militant groups and from outside the region.

A volatile fusion of local and international agendas has emerged. Most troubling of all, for some extremist militants, terrorist attacks have become an acceptable part of their strategy. And terrorist attacks have become more lethal, more frequent, more widespread and more focused on targeting Western interests.

Jemaah Islamiyah exemplifies the evolution of Muslim militancy in South-East Asia. It has links to Al Qaida and is strongly influenced by Usama Bin Laden's terrorist ideology and methodology. The threat posed by Jemaah Islamiyah is compounded by its development as a network that ignores national boundaries. It stretches over several regional countries. It has formed links with existing extremist Muslim groups to further its own goals.

In the southern Philippines, elements of local militant Muslim insurgency groups, the MILF and the Abu Sayyaf Group, have established links with Jemaah Islamiyah and to some extent with Al Qaida. Links with elements of the MILF are very important to Jemaah Islamiyah. They give Jemaah Islamiyah access to training camps in Mindanao and a ready-made insurgency to give new recruits combat experience.

Dangerous sub-national groups, who can or want to use terrorism to further their causes, are also present in South-East

Asia. Mujahidin KOMPAK, Laskar Jihad (supposedly disbanded) and Laskar Jundullah in Indonesia, and the Malaysian Militant Group (Kumpulan Militan Malaysia-KMM) started out with the ostensible aim of promoting the interests of political Islam. Their transition to more violent methods resulted from their greater identification with, and links to, other radical Muslim movements in the region, in South Asia and in the Middle East.

Driving the increase in terrorist activity in our region has been the exposure of South-East Asian militants to the thinking of Middle Eastern Muslim extremists. That includes the latter's message that terrorism is acceptable. Again, Afghanistan was the crucible. The most significant transmission of extremist ideology and military skills to South-East Asian militants took place in the 1980s, with their participation in the war against the Soviet Union in Afghanistan.

Origins of the Transnational Agenda: the Afghanistan Connection

South-East Asian extremism took a leap forward when militant Muslim groups-including the leaders of Jemaah Islamiyah-decided to send recruits to training camps in Afghanistan and in Pakistan from the mid-1980s. Their aim was to support their co-religionists in the fight against the Soviet Union.

The Soviet forces left Afghanistan by 1989. But the concept of militant jihad-in this case, a multinational armed struggle by Muslim believers-did not end with their departure. The Soviet-Afghanistan experience was a catalyst for radical activity in South-East Asia. There is an Afghanistan connection to many South-East Asian Muslim militant groups. Up to 1000 South-East Asian Muslims are believed to have received military training with the Afghan mujahideen in the 1980s. In some cases this included battlefield experience. Key leaders of radical Muslim groups in the region are all veterans of the Soviet-Afghan war. They include Jemaah Islamiyah key operative Hambali, Abu Sayyaf Group leaders Khaddafy and Abdurajak Janjalani (now dead), and others.

In the camps in Afghanistan, South-East Asian volunteers were infused with a sense of brotherhood and common cause with those undertaking or supporting militant jihad from other parts of the Muslim world. They were introduced to more advanced terrorist and militant ideology and techniques. They brought them back to South-East Asia and passed them on at training camps in our region.

The returnees formed a natural, transnational network in South-East Asia that is now extensive and well entrenched. This network is at the heart of the terrorist threat in South-East Asia today.

Education and Advanced Technology

Other external forces are at work to spread extremism in South-East Asia. A significant number of young South-East Asians are studying at religious schools, or madrassas, in Pakistan, Afghanistan and Yemen. They have been influenced by some of the more doctrinaire versions of Islam-particularly the closely-related Salafi and Wahhabi streams. The financial power of Saudi Arabia has also helped promote Wahhabism in South-East Asia through the funding of educational institutions.

Many South Asian and Middle Eastern madrassas teach only a rigid and doctrinaire interpretation of the Quran, with a strong emphasis on militant jihad.

South-East Asia's information technology revolution has hastened the spread of external influences, including extremist ideology. International television and information available on the Internet have led to a greater identification with Muslims in conflict around the world. They have inspired and shaped the behaviour of radicals in South-East Asia. The Internet is not merely a communications mechanism for extremists. It is also an effective vehicle for global publicity and recruitment efforts.

Some madrassas-including those run in Pakistan by the militant group Lashkar e-Tayyiba-emphasise computer literacy, even while teaching few or no other secular subjects. Within South-East Asia itself, large numbers of community-run Islamic boarding schools, or pesantren, operate outside the state control of formal Islamic education systems. Income disparity in many countries of the region has led to poorer youth taking up this option with governments unable to meet the educational needs of growing populations.

A small number of these schools have become a source of concern to regional governments as Jemaah Islamiyah has sought to use networks of pesantren across several South-East Asian countries as a vehicle to propagate extremist ideology and for recruitment purposes. Pesantren vulnerable to these approaches are few in number relative to the majority that emphasise the teaching of moral values. Al Qaida has also recruited and radicalised students with Western secular educational backgrounds. In South-East Asia some of Jemaah Islamiyah's leading operatives have had advanced technical and scientific qualifications from secular universities.

It is important to note that many leading advocates of pluralism and democracy in South-East Asia are graduates of Islamic education institutions. Former Indonesian President, Abdurrahman Wahid, and prominent Indonesian Muslim intellectuals including the Rector of the State Islamic University in Jakarta, Dr Azyumardi Azra, and the Rector of the Paramadina Mulya University, Nurcholish Madjid, are all graduates of Islamic education institutions.

Regional Vulnerabilities

Transnational terrorist groups, including Al Qaida and Lashkar e-Tayyiba, have demonstrated an interest in South-East Asia. They see it as a base for operations, a safe haven and a source of potential recruits. It is also a source of the kinds of services drawn upon by other transnational criminals. Terrorists look to exploit any vulnerabilities in the region's varied counter-terrorism capabilities. Areas of potential concern in some regional countries include limitations in institutional, governance and legislative frameworks; resource constraints; inadequate coordination arrangements, both internally and between countries in the region; and variable political will. Problem areas also include law enforcement, intelligence, transport security, defence and anti-terrorist financing. Terrorist groups can also exploit long-standing socio-political and economic grievances that persist in some countries. The lack of controlled border crossings in some South-East Asian countries is a major impediment to the monitoring and control of terrorist groups. Maritime piracy is a significant problem in the region. Porous borders, combined with massive inbound tourist and business flows, open immigration regimes, limited identity and document fraud detection, inadequately trained or corrupt officials, poor coordination between border control agencies and various security agencies, and limited immigration and customs control capacities all provide an environment in which terrorism can flourish.

All these problems can be compounded by inadequate legislation. Effective laws are important to put governments in the best possible position to investigate, detain and prosecute those involved in terrorism and its financing.

Al Qaida and other terrorist groups are known to have abused charitable organisations. They have used them for fund-raising and have diverted money donated to them towards support for extremist activities. Unregulated and unaudited Islamic charities in South-East Asia are vulnerable to misuse by extremist groups.

4

Global War against Terrorism

INTRODUCTION

The fight against terrorism is no closer to success today than it was a decade ago when, in the wake of the September 11 terror attacks, President George W. Bush declared a Global War on Terrorism. The problem is not simply that Western agencies are outfoxed by state sponsors of terror and trans-national groups, but rather that Western governments and international organizations continue to suffer self-inflicted wounds. These include a failure to reach consensus on what terrorism is; political correctness that leads Western officials to downplay or ignore the religious component to terrorism; the legitimization of terrorists' grievances; and a failure to recognize that diplomacy often does more harm than good.

Until and unless Western governments recognize that terrorist ideologies, religious or otherwise, must be delegitimized and that the military must have the primary role in defeating terrorism, then terrorists will continue to scourge Western societies. Talk cannot fill vacuums or deny terrorists control over safe-havens. While many diplomats argue that it never hurts to talk, negotiation with terrorists and legitimization of their sponsors often undercuts counterterrorism and can do far more harm than good.

Why Terrorism is like Pornography

Terrorism is a tactic of choice for state sponsors and rogue groups when its ability to achieve political aims outweighs the costs. The lack of consensus over the definition of terrorism complicates the fight against terrorism. A 1988 study found 100 different definitions of terrorism used by professionals. More than two decades later, Alex P. Schmid, editor of Perspectives on Terrorism, compiled 250 definitions. In many ways, terrorism's definition parallels U.S. Supreme Court Justice Potter Stewart's 1973 quip about pornography, "I shall not today attempt further to define [obscenity]; and perhaps I could never succeed in intelligibly doing so. But I know it when I see it...."

The UN has been no more successful at defining terrorism. In a 1994 resolution, the UN General Assembly defined terrorism in part as "Criminal acts intended or calculated to provoke a state of terror in the general public," while a bit over a decade later, UN Secretary General Kofi Annan said terrorism was any act "intended to cause death or serious bodily harm to civilians or non-combatants with the purpose of intimidating a population or compelling a Government or an international organization to do or abstain from doing any act." Neither definition, however, enjoys codified status or recognition as law. A proposed UN Comprehensive Convention on International Terrorism has gone nowhere as states seek to exempt their pet causes from the terrorism label. In effect, they argue, that if they are sympathetic to the cause, the ends justify the means. While most states condemn terrorism, they make exceptions for the groups with whom they sympathize.

The willingness of diplomats to negotiate with terrorists or engage with their sponsors bolsters terrorists' legitimacy, validates their tactics, and shields terror groups from consequence. Turkey, which Western diplomats look at as a model for Arab states in transition, provides a case in point. Its premier, Recep Tayyip Erdoan, has repeatedly embraced Hamas as a legitimate political entity. Less than a month after Hamas won the Palestinian Authority election, Erdoan invited Khalid Meshaal, the head of Hamas' most militant faction, to Ankara. The decision to receive a senior Hamas delegation prior to that group's renunciation of terrorism legitimatized both Hamas and its tactics. Yet, even as Erdoan celebrated Hamas, he denounced any suggestion of parallels between Hamas and the Kurdistan Workers Party [PKK], a group as vicious in its targeting of civilians. The PKK seized upon the precedent. "Is it not blood that is shed in the fighting between the Turkish army and the Kurdistan freedom movement, just like the Palestinian-Israeli conflict?" asked Murat Karayilan, a senior PKK commander. The Turkish Foreign Ministry's argument that elections should cleanse Hamas of its terrorist label falls flat as pro-PKK front groups repeatedly dominated elections in major cities in majority Kurdish cities like Van and Diyarbakir in southeast Turkey.

The desire of diplomats and human rights activists to take, in effect, an a la carte definition of terrorism has given solace to terrorists and made a mockery of counter-terror efforts. A decade ago, for example, histrionics were running high at the United Nations. After enduring months of Palestinian terrorism, Israel launched a military operation to root out bomb makers and their factories in the West Bank. Human rights activists and diplomats cried foul, and promoted the myth of the Jenin massacre. Professor Derrick Pounder, part of an Amnesty International investigative team, suggested civilian deaths would rival what had occurred in Bosnia and Kosovo. "I must say that the evidence before us at the moment doesn't lead us to believe that the allegations are anything other than truthful and that therefore there are large numbers of civilian dead underneath these bulldozed and bombed ruins that we see," he told the BBC. Of course, this was nonsense. Pounder was off by a factor of 5,000: 28 Israelis and 52 Palestinians dead, only a handful of who were civilians.

It was against this backdrop that on April 15, 2002, the United Nations Human Rights Commission – at the time led by former Irish President Mary Robinson – passed a resolution endorsing "the legitimacy of the struggle of peoples for independence, territorial integrity, national unity and liberation from colonial and foreign domination and foreign occupation by all available means, including armed struggle." France, Belgium, Spain, Ireland, Portugal and Sweden all supported the resolution. While diplomats may have voted for the resolution with Palestine in mind, the precedent enables terrorists to justify their actions in international humanitarian law. In effect, the UN commission engrained in humanitarian law the right to use car bombs or attack kindergarteners. Sympathy for terrorist causes and a tendency to favor David over Goliath continues to corrode the international legal response.

A la carte exceptionalism extends even to Al Qaeda. Not only did the U.S. Treasury Department label Saudi businessman al-Qadi a "specially designated global terrorist" for his support of al-Qaeda, but the United Nations Security Council also placed him on its terrorism list and demanded that all countries freeze his funds. Enter Turkey's prime minister: After Turkish newspapers reported that Erdoan confidant Cuneyd Zapsu had donated money to al-Qadi, his former business partner, Erdoan declared, "I know Mr. Qadi. I believe in him as I believe in myself," and refused to discipline Zapsu or freeze al-Qadi's funds in Turkey.

DIPLOMACY UNDERCUTS THE FIGHT AGAINST TERRORISM

The United States is not blameless in pursuing policies which undermine the fight against terrorism. The problem is not the alignment of U.S. foreign policy, but rather premature recourse to diplomacy. Between 1995 and 2000, Clinton administration diplomats—up to and including a cabinet-level official—argued that the best way to address Al Qaeda was to negotiate with the Taliban. During the course of those six years, American officials and Taliban representatives met on almost three dozen occasions. American diplomats embraced such theories that if only they could convince the Taliban to send its clerics to "moderate Islamic states such as Saudi Arabia," the problem might resolve itself. The Taliban was never sincere in its talks, however. While American officials drank tea with their Taliban hosts, Al Qaeda used Taliban territory to plot the 9/11 attacks.

Current efforts to resolve the Afghan situation diplomatically by negotiating with the Taliban simply repeat the past. Blessing a Taliban office in Qatar merely allows the militant group easier access to donors. Secretary of State Hillary Clinton acknowledged that Taliban attackers are drawn from groups to which the Americans reached out.

The American experience is not exclusive. Pakistani authorities long sought to strike a deal with the Pakistani Taliban. In February 15, 2009, they reached an agreement to effectively hand the Malakand District over to a local Taliban group. Rather than end their struggle, however, the Taliban used the territory as a springboard to expansion. With their safe-haven established, the Taliban doubled the number of forces in the Swat Valley to at least six thousand, enabling their march southward, forcing the Pakistani army into a much broader military operation than Pakistani authorities had ever expected.

Diplomacy undercuts counterterrorism in other ways. Too many senior statesmen exaggerate the efficacy of dialogue and approach terrorism as an inconvenient obstacle to diplomatic deals. On August 1, 1996, against the backdrop of evidence showing Tehran's complicity in Khobar Towers attack, former Defense Secretary Caspar Weinberger testified before a joint hearing of the Senate Select Committee on Intelligence and the Senate Judiciary Committee about how, regardless of proof of complicity, diplomatic considerations sometimes triumphed over direct action. In 1986, for example, he described how Reagan ordered retaliatory bombing against Libya for its role in the La Belle disco bombing but, two years later, neither Reagan nor George H.W. Bush retaliated militarily for the Libyan regime's role in the far deadlier Lockerbie bombing.

Diplomatic considerations regularly compromise the fight against Iranian terror sponsorship. In July 2001, an Atlantic Council team led by Lee H. Hamilton, James Schlesinger, and Brent Scowcroft largely dismissed State Department findings regarding the Iran's state sponsorship of terror and advocated lifting trade bans. They further argued for the revision of legislation linking the State Department's Terrorism List to export controls, and continued to argue that the State Department's definition of terrorism as "premeditated, politically motivated violence perpetrated against noncombatant targets by subnational groups or clandestine agents, usually intended to influence an audience," unfairly targets only "one strand of the whole spectrum of politically motivated violence," one really not much different from asymmetrical warfare. Rather than hold Iran accountable for terrorism, Scowcroft and his fellow travelers suggested ignoring its terror sponsorship. He castigated automatic sanctions imposed on state sponsors of terrorism, and lamented how the State Department's Patterns of Global Terrorism blamed the entire state apparatus, even when only some factions or groups were involved.

The Iran example is the rule rather than the exception. An as blatant case of prioritizing diplomacy over accountability involved the George W. Bush administration's desire to remove North Korea from the State Department's list of state sponsors of terrorism. With the Iraq war so unpopular in 2006, Secretary of State Condoleezza Rice decided to double down efforts to win a breakthrough on North Korea in order to cement a positive legacy for Bush. When American and North Korean diplomats met in Beijing, Christopher Hill—the Bush administration's point man on North Korea—offered to remove North Korea from the state sponsors of terrorism list. Rice scrapped the Clinton administration's demand that Pyongyang provide a written guarantee that it had ceased terrorism, would acquiescence to international agreements combating terrorism, and would address its past terrorism.

Rice's decision—motivated by a desire to facilitate a diplomatic breakthrough—in effect let North Korea off-the-hook on its terror sponsorship. North Korean terror complicity may not have been as blatant as the Rangoon and Korean Air bombings of the 1980s, but the North Korean regime refused to provide full accounting of its kidnappings of Japanese citizens in the 1970s and 1980s, a major factor in the listing. While the communist regime returned five surviving abductees in 2004 of the ten it eventually admitted seizing, the Japanese government maintains Korean agents kidnapped 80 Japanese. Rice pressured Tokyo to tone down its objections, though, and told Prime Minister Shinzo Abe that the White House was under no obligation to classify the kidnappings as terrorism. The White House and State Department proceeded to brush off evidence that North Korean kidnapping of South Korean citizens was even greater. Appeasing the enemy had trumped honoring the allies.

North Korea's delisting came despite testimony from French, Japanese, South Korean, and Israeli sources who alleged robust North Korean involvement with both Hezbollah in Lebanon and the Tamil Tigers in Sri Lanka. Ali Reza Nourizadeh, a London-based Iranian reporter close to the Iran's reformist camp, described North Korean assistance in the design of underground Hezbollah military facilities in Lebanon, assertions supported by a diverse array of reporting. Such tunnels allowed Hezbollah both to shield rockets from Israeli surveillance prior to the 2006 war. Moon Chung-in, a professor at South Korea's Yonsei University, has also reported Mossad allegations that Hezbollah missiles included North Korean components.

North Korean efforts to aid the Tamil Tigers were even more blatant. The Far Eastern Economic Review reported in 2000 that North Korea has supplied the Tamil Tigers with weaponry, citing intelligence sources in Bangkok. The State Department's Patterns of Global Terrorism made similar claims in 2001, 2002, and 2003, making subsequent claims that Pyongyang had abandoned the terrorism business curious. Three times between October 2006 and March 2007, the Sri Lankan navy intercepted cargo ships flying no flag or identifying marker found to be carrying North Korean arms. For Rice and Bush, though, diplomatic considerations trumped the reality of North Korean terror sponsorship.

Sri Lanka presents another case highlighting how counterproductive a diplomatic strategy to counter terrorism can be. In May 2009, the army of the South Asian island nation of Sri Lanka did what decades of UN diplomatic intervention and State Department pronouncements could not do. It ended its 26-year war against the Tamil Tigers. The war not only extracted a tremendous economic cost, but had a massive human cost—the UN estimated that the death toll might exceed 100,000. In the end, Sri Lankan action was both merciless and effective. The army reconquered Tamil Tiger-held territory and slaughtered the group's leadership. The final battle was messy, but with the Tigers gone, both Sri Lankan Sinhalese and Tamils can get on with their lives and, with luck and persistence, build a strong, democratic, and prosperous state. War is hell, and the Sri Lankan army was brutal during the war's climax, but this brutality was well-justified, ended the conflict, and ultimately saving lives. The Tigers seldom if ever abided by the laws of war, and so it is rich to upbraid the Sri Lankan army for showing little restraint. Rather than sully a victory over terrorism, the West should celebrate it. And rather than condemn a struggling nation and an ally, Western diplomats and UN bureaucrats should congratulate the Sri Lankan government for accomplishing what outside diplomats had long failed to do.

PLANNING AND TAKING ACTION AGAINST GLOBAL TERRORIST NETWORKS

Two unresolved debates regularly undercut international action against terrorist groups. The first is whether the West should consider terrorism a judicial rather than a military threat, and the second is whether the best long-term strategy to counter terrorism would be to resolve terrorist grievances.

Until Western states consider terrorism a military matter to be resolved primarily by force of arms, terrorists will win. The reasons are many: If terrorism is simply a criminal matter, then states cannot use military force to counter it. Exposing intelligence to conform to judicial proceedings compromises sources and threatens future defense which might rely on the same sources or codes. Differences in treatment of evidence also matters: While a military approach is proactive, judicial proceedings are necessarily reactive. In order to protect intelligence, convictions would require forensic evidence gathered in the wake of an attack. Successful counterterrorism, however, should prevent attacks, not simply punish them. Certainly, the Pentagon perceives terrorism as a military matter, even if the State Department is less sure. "This is both a battle of arms and a battle of ideas," the 2006 Quadrennial Defense Review (QDR) declared. The report continued to argue that defeat of terrorist networks depends upon augmenting human intelligence, surveillance, special operations, and willingness to conduct irregular warfare. The 2010 QDR was less explicit, but did argue that "successful COIN [counterinsurgency], stability, and CT [counterterrorism] operations are necessarily the products of strategies that orchestrate the activities of military and civilian agencies."

Little does more to undercut effective counter terrorism than the urge to address terrorist grievances. Indeed, beyond international organizations and multilateral coalitions' inability to define terrorism, little does more to undercut the fight against terrorism than embracing a grievance-centric approach to the resolution of conflicts. It has become fashionable for academics and diplomats to believe that resolving terrorist grievances. University of Chicago political scientist Robert Pape, for example, has argued that resistance to occupation motivates most suicide terrorism. Quipping "It's the occupation, stupid," he argued that "suicide terrorism such as that of 9/11 is particularly sensitive to foreign military occupation, and not Islamic fundamentalism or any ideology independent of this crucial circumstance." End occupation, he suggests, and terrorists will cease striking at Western targets.

Pape's willingness to discount ideology is a fatal flaw in his arguments, however. Occupations have spanned centuries, but suicide bombings are a relative new phenomenon, one which has grown alongside Saudi Arabia's oil wealth and the Islamic Republic's export of revolution. While adherents of the grievance school argue that resolution of the Israel-Palestine conflict is the key to stopping Islamist terrorism, the record suggests otherwise. In 1946, the Military Intelligence Division of the U.S. War Department—the predecessor of the Defense Intelligence Agency—asked its analysts to speculate on long-term threats to global security. The result was prescient. Even before the United Nations considered the partition of Palestine and two years before Israel's independence, the Division identified Islamic fundamentalism as a growing threat to U.S. interests. The problem was not grievance regarding U.S. foreign policy; U.S. involvement in the Middle East was minimal. Rather, the concern was ideological. "There have appeared in Egypt and elsewhere several societies that stress Islamic culture; these are openly anti-European and secretly anti-Christian and anti-Jewish. The best known is the Ikhwan el-Muslimin," the Muslim Brotherhood.

When it comes to Al Qaeda and most terrorism in the Middle East and South Asia, religion matters. Islamist radicals terrorizing young women in Paris housing projects, bombing nightclubs in Java, and beheading journalists in Pakistan act not in reaction to occupation, but rather on an embrace of a once radical, but increasingly common strain of Islamic interpretation.

A politically correct and whitewashed understanding of jihad further obscures the ideological motivation for terror. The Council on American-Islamic Relations (CAIR), a self-described Muslim advocacy group which often hews close to the Muslim Brotherhood's line, for example, declares, "Jihad means to strive, struggle and exert effort... There is no such thing as 'holy war' in Islam." John Esposito, a Georgetown University professor whose program is largely financed by Saudi donors, is more nuanced, but still obfuscates. "Jihad in Islam means the struggle to be a good Muslim," he told PBS, although he acknowledged. "Jihad also means the right, indeed the obligation, of a Muslim to defend himself."

Both claims mischaracterize traditional Islamic jurisprudence. During the Golden Age of Islam between the eighth and thirteenth centuries, most theologians understood jihad to be military. The ninth century Islamic scholar Muhammad bin Isma'il al-Bukhari, compiler of the most authoritative collection of reports about the Prophet Muhammad's life, dedicated one-third of a volume to jihad as holy war.

In the 1970s, against the backdrop of the oil boom and concurrent influx of luxury goods into the newly-affluent Saudi society, Saudi theologians promoted the idea that Western goods—color televisions, Cadillacs, and cosmetics—represented an assault against Islam as menacing as any military threat. They described a deliberate Western "cultural attack" seeking to undermine Muslim faith. To these paranoid preachers, David Hasselhoff posed as much a threat as an F-14 fighter over Mecca.

Into this xenophobic tinderbox came a spark in the form of a Palestinian Muslim Brotherhood adherent named Abdullah Azzam. After landing a job at Abdulaziz University in Jeddah, he took a young Osama Bin Laden under his wing. Azzam added a new dimension to the discussion of the Western cultural assault: He argued that every Muslim had a duty to defend Islamic lands against the penetration of infidels, whether in the form of armies or over the airwaves. The Muslims' obligation to fight was not optional, but rather was as mandatory as the Ramadan fast or daily prayer. Western academics may explain jihad is purely defensive in nature, but they should not assume that they and the Islamist enablers of terrorism share their view of what defense means. It is intellectually dishonest to apply a 21st century rather than 11th century notion of jihad to extremists who seek to rebuild a social order 1,000 years in the past. Likewise, it is important to remember that when jihadists and Western diplomats might discuss 'defense,' they can have very different understandings.

Diplomats may want to address grievances, but terrorists are not willing to compromise upon ideology. Sheikh Omar Abdel Rahman, mastermind of the first World Trade Center bombing, declared, "There is no truce in Jihad against the enemies of Allah." When Abu Musab al-Zarqawi, Al-Qaeda in Iraq's leader declared in January 2005, "We have declared a bitter war against democracy," there simply was no way to appease him. No government should be willing to sacrifice democracy for peace. Likewise, it would be suicidal for Israel to strike a deal with Hamas, when the Hamas charter calls for Israel's eradication and when the terrorist group underlines its unwillingness to abide by any agreement with Israel. Still, many in the West try to force other countries to make concessions, especially when the negotiating chit is not their own society. This backfires. The 2006 Quadrennial Defense Review was correct when it observed, "Victory will come when the enemy's extremist ideologies are discredited in the eyes of their host populations and tacit supporters." Few remember the Baader-Meinhof Gang simply because its ideology was so roundly discredited. If terrorists can claim victories, however, they gain adherents.

Validation bolsters terrorism. Terror sponsors and leaders calculate cost and benefits before undertaking terrorism. Every terrorist action or attack creates forensic evidence which increases the vulnerability of terrorist leaders or provides evidence to link them with their sponsors. If terror leaders can gain wider support for their cause, greater press exposure, of political concessions, they calculate that the net benefit is greater than the risk. Engaging terrorists not only legitimizes extremism, but actually encourages it. If the natural inclination of Western diplomats is to compromise with any demand, terrorists simply stake out even more extreme positions. The tendency of diplomats and journalists to condemn disproportionality in response also undercuts the fight against terror. Disproportionality is a deterrent to terrorism. Linkage between equitable distribution of casualties and legitimacy of conflict has little basis in international law. When terrorists understand that the costs of their actions will be far greater to themselves than their adversaries, they will abandon terror and either seek other strategies, or simply fade way.

IMPLICATIONS OF KEY THREATS EMANATING FROM THE MIDDLE EAST

Unfortunately, the Middle East today remains a Petri dish for terrorism. The problems emanate from two main poles: Iran and Saudi Arabia. When Ayatollah Ruhollah Khomeini launched the Islamic Revolution, he sought to export its ideology far beyond the borders of Iran. Today, Iranian leaders interpret the call to export revolution as an endorsement of violence. When, in 2008, former President Muhammad Khatami suggested that Khomeini had sought only to transform Iran into a soft-power utopia, and that Iran should therefore refrain from the more violent aspects of revolutionary export, 77 members of parliament demanded that the intelligence ministry prosecute him. Ayatollah Mahmoud Heshemi Shahroudi, at the time the head of Iran's judiciary and a close associate of the current supreme leader, quashed any further debate. Against the backdrop of the controversy, he emphasized that the export of Iran's revolution was a military strategy, telling the Islamic Revolutionary Guards Corps, "You are the hope of Islamic national and Islamic liberation movements."

The threat from Tehran will only worsen as the regime strengthens. Too many Western officials misread regime trajectory. After uprisings in 1999, 2001, and 2009, there is a common assumption that once the genie of reform is out of the bottle, it cannot be returned. Iranian officials, however, beg to differ.

Declining birthrates benefit the regime. When Khomeini seized power, he suspended Iran's family planning programs, and the birthrate skyrocketed. During the Iran-Iraq War, it was not uncommon to see posters depicting a good Islamic family with a mother, father, and six or seven children. Soon after the war concluded in 1988, however, the Iranian government realized that it could not handle such rapid population growth and authorities again authorized birth control. According to UNICEF, Iran's average annual growth rate was 3.4 percent between 1970 and 1990, but declined to 1.6 percent in the following decade, and was just 1.1 percent in the first decade of the 21st century. The result is that the post-revolutionary baby boom generation is now in their late twenties, many out of school but not yet with their own families. In five years, however, many of these protestors will settle down and begin to focus more on concerns such as salary and rent checks rather on grand notions of liberty and democracy. The regime realizes that the next generation of university students and recent graduates will be far smaller and more easily contained. It is quite probable that Supreme Leader Ali Khamenei and President Mahmoud Ahmadinejad believe that if the Revolutionary Guards can suppress protests for just a couple years, the Islamic Republic can guarantee itself decades more.

Amplifying the Iranian threat is Syria, Iran's traditional ally and the transit point for supply to Hezbollah. The Obama administration's decision to withdraw from Iraq has risked snatching defeat from the jaws of victory by enabling overland resupply from Iran into Syria. Much more than an end to atrocity in Syria is at stake. Should Bashar al-Assad survive and reassert control over his country, he will solidify a pro-Iranian block which extends from Western Afghanistan to the Mediterranean. In such a scenario, the lack of Western resolve to back up demands for Assad's ouster might lead the Syrian President both to believe that he faces no accountability for his future action and to seek revenge using terror networks he has long supported.

Assad's fall may change the nature of the terrorism threat but, thanks to five decades of Baathist rule, it will not eliminate it. The Assads, both father and son, have long played a double game that has enabled not only radical Shi'ite groups like Hezbollah, but has also empowered Sunni Islamists. The assumption that the Assad regime does not support Islamism is rooted in the regime's troubled history with radical Islam. The Muslim Brotherhood established a branch in Syria in the late 1950s. The group remained quiet for two decades but, in 1979, it began to engage in terrorism, most famously when members of the group murdered several dozen Alawi military cadets near Aleppo. Three years later, after some 200 Islamists staged an insurrection in Hama, the Syrian military razed much of the city, killing between 10,000 and 20,000 civilians. In the aftermath of Hama, many analysts note that the Syrian Muslim Brotherhood renounced violence although only the most prescient Syria hands have observed that, behind the regime's veneer of secularism, Hafiz al-Assad subsequently sought to co-opt Islamism.

While the Syrian government has, on occasion, extradited alleged Islamist terrorists to other Arab countries when diplomatic necessity dictated it do so, more often than not, it refused to hand over terrorists, suggesting that Assad lacks a principled commitment to combat Islamist terrorism. In September 2007, U.S. forces in the northern Iraqi town of Sinjar, twelve miles from the Syrian border, discovered computers and documents that traced more than 600 foreign fighters who had infiltrated into Iraq over the previous year. The files showed that contrary to Syrian protestations of opposing Islamist terror, Syrians coordinated the insertion into Iraq of almost all the fighters listed. While Saudi Arabia shares a far longer—and more porous—border with Iraq than does Syria, even Saudi terrorists preferred to infiltrate via Syria, presumably because the Saudi government was less willing to facilitate Al Qaeda after that group had struck at the Kingdom in 2003 and 2004. Even before the uprising, Syria was far less hostile to Sunni Islamist terrorists than many diplomats supposed.

Saudi authorities may not have been willing to allow Al Qaeda to base itself in the Kingdom or openly transit it, but Saudi Arabia and its Wahabi neighbor Qatar continue to support militancy. Saudi officials may assure Western officials that they have cracked down on terror finance, but Saudi-funded mosques from Turkey

to Indonesia continue to fund the most radical interpretations of Islam. Few Islamist terrorists have had no contact with Saudi-funded mosques or organizations.

Qatar is the stealth catalyst for radicalism. Because of his desire to lead from behind, President Barack Obama pushed countries like Qatar to the diplomatic forefront, a move which because of the agendas of Doha's agenda, privileges more militant and Islamist factions inside transitional Arab Spring countries. Qatar, for example, funded the most militant Libyan factions, many of which refused to subordinate themselves to the Transitional National Council in the wake of Libyan dictator Muammar Qadhafi's fall. Both Saudi Arabia and Qatar have supported not only the Muslim Brotherhood in Egypt, but also the Salafi an-Nour Party. When the Muslim Brotherhood becomes the 'moderate" faction,' it's clear something has gone wrong.

IMPLICATIONS OF THE EVOLVING NATURE OF AL QA'IDA

Al Qaeda founder Osama Bin Laden's death was a major triumph for Western counterterrorism, but Bin Laden had long ceased to be more than the symbolic leader of global terrorism. The United States and NATO's long manhunt forced him into isolation, cut him off from his network save messages passed to and from by courier. Because Bin Laden was effectively off-the-grid, jihadists had long before begun to debate how Al Qaeda should operate into the future. While some jihadist theoreticians like Abu Musab as-Suri argue for the need for a decentralized structure in order to defeat surveillance and counter-terror efforts others like Abu Bakr Naji emphasize the necessity to possess territory in order to realize their social agenda and, more importantly, to maintain a safe-haven from which they can plan and execute missions unmolested.

Al Qaeda has spawned four major subunits: Al Qaeda in the Arabian Peninsula (AQAP); Al-Qaeda in Iraq; al-Shabaab in Somalia; and Al Qaeda in the Islamic Maghreb (AQIM). In addition, various Al-Qaeda affiliates and terrorist groups operate from Pakistan: The Quetta Shura, the Haqqani network, and Tehrik-e-

Taliban Pakistan. Pakistan's Punjab province, a densely-populated plain that is home to more than half Pakistan's population, will be the counter-terror battleground of the future. In effect, each of these safe havens enable Al Qaeda to combine As-Suri and An-Naji's vision. Today, Al-Qaeda still has free reign in its Somali, Saharan, Yemeni, and Pakistani safe-havens to plan attacks against Western targets. Attacks by the underwear bomber over Detroit and the Times Square car bomb were planned in Yemen and Pakistan respectively. That they were averted had more to do with luck than counter terror skill. Western failure to deal with the existence of these safe-havens suggests the same lack of seriousness about counterterrorism that marked U.S. and European policy through the 1990s

The West may never eliminate terrorism completely, but if Western officials re-examine base assumptions, they can still triumph over many terrorist groups and convince potential sponsors that support for terrorism carries a cost too great to bear. Western leaders must recognize that just as military action and sanctions have costs, so too does diplomacy. Sometimes the cost of misapplied diplomacy can be even greater than that of limited military action. While international organizations—chief among them the United Nations—stake a claim to be the arbiters of legitimacy, the UN's inability to achieve a consensus definition of terrorism suggests that structured founded more than a half century ago may be ill-designed for a 21st century fight. Multilateralism is no panacea. Unilateralism certainly has drawbacks, but it also has strengths.

Amidst a political culture which often questions military actions and collateral damage, Western officials should remain secure in the knowledge that counterterrorism is the moral fight. Jihadists, for example, work to their own ends; they seldom have the best interests of the local population at heart. Whether in Al-Anbar or southern Afghanistan, they often run roughshod over local culture, burden local populations with taxation and property confiscation, abuse local women, commit robbery and kidnapping as a source of income, and destroy centuries-old balances between local populations and tribes.

Governments which provide safe-haven to terrorists must be made to understand that undercut their long-term survival, whether because terrorists will inevitably turn on them, or because victims of terrorist attacks will hold sponsors responsible for their proxies' actions. Supporting foreign fighters often has economic consequences as well, not only in terms of potential sanctions but also because there is seldom significant investment in areas ruled by shari'a.

As the war on terrorism enters its second decade, resolve will also become a key determinant to success. Al Qaeda succeeded until 9/11 for three reasons: First, the West failed to recognize that ideology mattered. Hesitant to enter a cycle of tit-for-tat violence, the Clinton administration opted not to respond to the 1993 World Trade Center attack or the 2000 strike on the USS Cole. Al Qaeda simply concluded that they could continue their ideological mandate with abandon. Second, the West failed to recognize that terrorists thrive in a vacuum. State failure, no matter how far away, can pose a grave threat to Western democracies. It is against this context that the looming withdrawal from Afghanistan should concern, so long as diplomats and statesmen fail to explain how they will fill the vacuum in Afghanistan should its government topple. Third, strength matters. Bin Laden famously quipped that no one supports the weak horse. Perception means more than reality. A willingness to cede territory to terrorists or retreat under fire, be it in Lebanon, Iraq, or Afghanistan promises not peace but rather greater bloodshed. A return to the status quo ante is an illusion, and a dangerous one at that.

5

Islamic Terrorism

Islamic terrorism is a form of terrorism committed by Muslims. Islamic terrorism has occurred globally, including in India, Africa,Australia, Middle East, Europe, Southeast Asia, South Asia, South America, The Caucasus, The Pacific and North America. Islamic organizations have been known to engage in tactics including suicide attacks, bombings, spree killings, hijackings, kidnappings and recruiting new members through the Internet.

HISTORY

Analysis of Relevant Quranic Verses

Beginning with the 7th-century AD Arab era of Muslim conquests, and continuing on until the 21st-century resurgence of Muslim violence on non-Muslims in the name of "Jihad", many have debated whether Islam was fundamentally a religion of peace, of violence, or perhaps of some combination of the two. Within the Quran itself, there appears to be some ambiguity regarding the infliction of injury upon non-combatants. In the Quran's *"No-Compulsion verse"* it is suggested that *"there shall be no compulsion in religion"*. However, this verse was abrogated, as later in the Quran's *"Sword verses"*, Muslims were advised to *"...Fight those who do not believe in Allah or in the last day and who do not consider unlawful what Allah and his messenger (Muhammad) have made unlawful and who do not adopt the religion of truth (Islam)."* Hence, the misinterpretation of the topic is famous among all parties. Mark Gabriel, founder and president of Hope for the Nations, alleges that certain Quranic verses such as the "Sword verses" have been instrumental in promulgating various forms of Islamic terrorism.

MOTIVATIONS AND ISLAMIC TERRORISM

The View that Western Foreign Policy is a Motivation for Terrorism

Robert Pape has argued that at least terrorists utilizing suicide attacks – a particularly effective form of terrorist attack – are driven not by Islamism but by "a clear strategic objective: to compel modern democracies to withdraw military forces from the territory that the terrorists view as their homeland." However, Martin Kramer, who debated Pape on origins of suicide bombing, stated that the motivation for suicide attacks is not just strategic logic but also an interpretation of Islam to provide a moral logic. For example,Hezbollah initiated suicide bombings after a complex reworking of the concept of martyrdom. Kramer explains that the Israeli occupation of Lebanon raised the temperature necessary for this reinterpretation of Islam, but occupation alone would not have been sufficient for suicide terrorism. "The only way to apply a brake to suicide terrorism," Kramer argues, "is to undermine its moral logic, by encouraging Muslims to see its incompatibility with their own values."

Former CIA analyst Michael Scheuer argues that terrorist attacks (specifically al-Qaeda attacks on America) are *not* motivated by a religiously inspired hatred of American cultureor religion, but by the belief that U.S. foreign policy has oppressed, killed, or otherwise harmed Muslims in the Middle East, condensed in the phrase "They hate us for what we do, not who we are." U.S. foreign policy actions Scheuer believes are fueling Islamic terror include: the U.S.-led intervention in Afghanistan and invasion of Iraq; Israel–United States relations, namely, financial, military, and political support for Israel.; U.S. support for "apostate" police states in Muslim nations such as Saudi Arabia, Egypt,Pakistan, Algeria, Morocco, and Kuwait; U.S. support for the creation of an independent East Timor from territory previously held by Muslim Indonesia; perceived U.S. approval or support of actions against Muslim insurgents in India, the Philippines, Chechnya, and

Palestine; U.S. troops on Muslim 'holy ground' in Saudi Arabia; the Western world's religious discrimination against Muslim immigrants'; historical justification, such as the Crusades.

Maajid Nawaz, in a debate with Mehdi Hasan, countered Scheuer's contention: "a tiny minority, from within the non-Iraqi British Muslim communities, reacted with violence on 7 July 2005. To interpret this simply as a "nationalist struggle" to remove occupation ignores the blatantly obvious fact that, first, the terrorists were not Iraqis, they were British-Pakistanis (though British Iraqis have lived here for a long time); second, the vast majority of the Stop the War protesters were non-Muslims, yet only a handful from among a minority of Muslims reacted to the war with terrorism.

Even though occupation may have caused agitation among the 7 July bombers, these northern-born lads with thick Yorkshire accents confessed in their suicide tapes to considering themselves soldiers with a mission to kill our people (Britons) on behalf of their people (Iraqis). The prerequisite to such a disavowal of one's country of birth is a recalibration of identity; this is the undeniable role of ideological narratives."

The View that Islamic Terrorism Predates U.S. Action and is justified by Quranic Teachings

According to others, Islamic terrorism is linked to the practice of divinely sanctioned warfare against apostates. Many Muslim groups including the Council on American-Islamic Relations argue that references to violence in Muslim sources have been taken out of context. They argue that these Koranic ayahs are only for self-defense when non-believers endanger Muslim life. It should be noted that a number of well documented religiously motivated massacres by Muslims of largely Christian ethnic groups in the Near East occurred long before the United States became a presence on the world stage, such as the massacres conducted by Tamurlane in the 14th century, theMassacres of Bader Khan in the 1840s, the Hamidian massacres of the 1890s, the Armenian Genocide, Assyrian Genocide and Greek Genocide between 1915 and 1921, and the Simele massacre of 1933.

Societal Motivations

Scholar Scott Atran, research director and involved in a NATO group studying suicide terrorism, asserts that there is no single root cause of terrorism. The greatest predictors of suicide bombings, Atran concludes, is not religion but group dynamics: "small-group dynamics involving friends and family that form the diaspora cell of brotherhood andcamaraderie on which the rising tide of martyrdom actions is based".

Economical Motivations

The Muslim world has been afflicted with economic stagnation for many centuries. In 2011, U.S. President Barack Obama stated that apart from crude oil, the exports of the entire Greater Middle East with its 400 million population roughly equals that of Switzerland. It has also been estimated that the exports of Finland, a European country of only five million, exceeded those of the entire 260 million-strong Arab world, excluding oil revenue. This economic stagnation is argued by historian David Fromkin in his work A Peace to End All Peace to have commenced with the demise of the Ottoman Caliphate in 1924, with trade networks being disrupted and societies torn apart with the creation of new nation states; prior to this, the Middle East had a diverse and growing economy and more general prosperity.

Another cause of embarrassment and resentment is that for several decades, Muslim immigrants have been forced to emigrate to western countries in large numbers because fellow Muslim countries that are well-off economically and socially do not accept them. Out of the 57 Muslim majority countries, only two nations (Turkey and Malaysia) offer a formal path to becoming a naturalized citizen regardless of your religious beliefs, marital status or ethnic origin. Even the oil-rich Gulf states do not grant citizenship to Muslim immigrants, regardless of how long they have resided in those countries.

Profiles

Forensic psychiatrist and former foreign service officer Marc Sageman made an "intensive study of biographical data on 172 participants in the jihad," in his book *Understanding Terror Networks*. He concluded social networks, the "tight bonds of family and friendship", rather than emotional and behavioral disorders of "poverty, trauma, madness, [or] ignorance", inspired alienated young Muslims to join the jihad and kill.

Lawrence Wright described the characteristic of "displacement" of members of the most famous Islamic terrorist group, al-Qaeda: What the recruits tended to have in common – besides their urbanity, their cosmopolitan backgrounds, their education, their facility with languages, and their computer skills – was displacement.

Most who joined the jihad did so in a country other than the one in which they were reared. They were Algerians living inexpatriate enclaves in France, Moroccans in Spain, or Yemenis in Saudi Arabia. Despite their accomplishments, they had little standing in the host societies where they lived."

Scholar Olivier Roy describes the background of the hundreds of *global* (as opposed to local) terrorists who were incarcerated or killed and for whom authorities have records, as being surprising for their Westernized background; for the lack of Palestinians, Iraqis, Afghans "coming to avenge what is going on in their country"; their lack of religiosity before being "born again" in a foreign country; the high percentage of converts to Islam among them; their "de-territorialized backgrounds" – "For instance, they may be born in a country, then educated in another country, then go to fight in a third country and take refuge in a fourth country"; their nontraditional belief that jihad is permanent, global, and "not linked with a specific territory."

This profile differs from that found among recent local Islamist suicide bombers in Afghanistan, according to a 2007 study of 110 suicide bombers by Afghan pathologist Dr. Yusef Yadgari. Yadgari found that 80% of the attackers studied had some kind of physical or mental disability. The bombers were also "not celebrated like their counterparts in other Arab nations. Afghan bombers are not featured on posters or in videos as martyrs." Daniel Byman, a Middle East expert at the Brookings Institute, and Christine Fair, an assistant professor in peace and security studies at Georgetown

University say that many of the Islamic terrorists are foolish and untrained, perhaps even untrainable.

Ideology

One ideology that plays a role in Islamic terrorism is the principle of Jihad, which broadly means strive. Militants generally use jihad to mean defensive or retaliatory warfare against actors that have allegedly harmed Muslims.

Transnational Islamist ideology, specifically of the militant Islamists, assert that Western policies and society are actively anti-Islamic, or as it is sometimes described, waging a "war against Islam". Islamists often identify what they see as a historical struggle between Christianity and Islam, dating back as far as the Crusades, among other historical conflicts between practitioners of the two respective religions. Osama bin Laden, for example, almost invariably described his enemy as aggressive and his call for action against them as defensive. Defensive jihad differs from offensive jihad in being "fard al-ayn," or a personal obligation of all Muslims, rather than "fard al-kifaya", a communal obligation, that is, some Muslims may perform it but it is not required from others. Hence, framing a fight as defensive has the advantage of both appearing to be a victim rather than an aggressor, and of giving the struggle the very highest religious priority for all good Muslims.

Many of the violent terrorist groups use the name of jihad to fight against certain Western nations and Israel. An example is bin Laden's al-Qaeda, which is also known as "International Islamic Front for Jihad Against the Jews and Crusaders". Most militant Islamists oppose Israel's policies, and often its existence.

According to U.S. Army Colonel Dale C. Eikmeier, "ideology", rather than any individual or group, is the "center of gravity" of al-Qaeda and related groups, and that ideology is a "collection of violent Islamic thought called Qutbism." He summarizes the tenets of Qutbism as being:

- A belief that Muslims have deviated from true Islam and must return to "pure Islam" as originally practiced during the time of theProphet.

- The path to "pure Islam" is only through a literal and strict interpretation of the Qur'an and Hadith, along with implementation of the Prophet's commands.
- Muslims should interpret the original sources individually without being bound to follow the interpretations of Islamic scholars.
- That any interpretation of the Quran from a historical, contextual perspective is a corruption, and that the majority of Islamic history and the classical jurisprudential tradition is mere sophistry.

The historic rivalry between Hindus and Muslims in the Indian subcontinent has also often been the primary motive behind some of the most deadly terrorist attacks in India. According to a U.S. State Department report, India topped the list of countries most affected by Islamic terrorism.

In addition, Islamist militants, scholars, and leaders opposed Western society for what they see as immoral secularism. Islamists have claimed that such unrestricted free speech has led to the proliferation of pornography, immorality, secularism, homosexuality,feminism, and many other ideas that Islamists often oppose. Although bin Laden almost always emphasized the alleged oppression of Muslims by America and Jews when talking about them in his messages, in his "Letter to America" he answered the question, "What are we calling you to, and what do we want from you?," with We call you to be a people of manners, principles, honour, and purity; to reject the immoral acts of fornication, homosexuality, intoxicants, gambling's, and trading with interest (...) You separate religion from your policies, (...) You are the nation that permits Usury, which has been forbidden by all the religions (...) You are a nation that permits the production, trading and usage of intoxicants (...) You are a nation that permits acts of immorality (...) You are a nation that permits gambling in its all forms. (...) You use women to serve passengers, visitors, and strangers to increase your profit margins. You then rant that you support the liberation of women.

Given their perceived piety, *The Times* noted the irony when a major investigation by their reporters uncovered a link between

Islamic Jihadis and child pornography; a discovery that, according to the London paper, "is expected to improve understanding of the mindsets of both types of criminals and has been hailed as a potentially vital intelligence tool to undermine future terrorist plots.". Similarly, Reuters reported that pornography was found among the materials seized from Osama bin Laden's Abbottabad compound that was raided by U.S. Navy SEALs.

In 2006 Britain's then head of MI5 Eliza Manningham-Buller said of Al-Qaeda that it "has developed an ideology which claims that Islam is under attack, and needs to be defended". "This" she said "is a powerful narrative that weaves together conflicts from across the globe, presenting the West's response to varied and complex issues, from long-standing disputes such as Israel/Palestine and Kashmir to more recent events as evidence of an across-the-board determination to undermine and humiliate Islam worldwide." She said that the video wills of British suicide bombers made it clear that they were motivated by perceived worldwide and long-standing injustices against Muslims; an extreme and minority interpretation of Islam promoted by some preachers and people of influence; their interpretation as anti-Muslim of UK foreign policy, in particular the UK's involvement in Iraq and Afghanistan." She also cautioned how difficult it was to gain a proper perspective, saying that although there are more important dangers we face daily without feeling so threatened by them such as climate change and road deaths and though terrorist deaths were few the intelligence services had prevented some potentially large threats and that vigilance was needed.

Interpretations of the Qur'an and Hadith

The role played by the Qur'an, Islam's sacred text, in opposing or in encouraging attacks on civilians is disputed.

The Princeton University Middle Eastern scholar Bernard Lewis, states that Islamic jurisprudence does not allow terrorism. In 2001, Professor Lewis noted:

At no time did the (Muslim) jurist approve of terrorism. Nor indeed is there any evidence of the use of terrorism (in Islamic tradition). Muslims are commanded not to kill women, children, or the aged, not to torture or otherwise ill-treat prisoners, The rules and regulations concerning prisoners of war in Islam to give fair warning of the opening of hostilities, and to honor agreements. Similarly, the laws of Jihad categorically preclude wanton and indiscriminate slaughter. The warriors in the holy war are urged not to harm non-combatants, women and children, "unless they attack you first." A point on which they insist is the need for a clear declaration of war before beginning hostilities, and for proper warning before resuming hostilities after a truce. What the classical jurists of Islam never remotely considered is the kind of unprovoked, unannounced mass slaughter of uninvolved civil populations that we saw in New York two weeks ago. For this there is no precedent and no authority in Islam.

But Bernard Lewis says Jihad is an unlimited offensive to bring the whole world under Islamic law; Christian crusades a defensive, limited response to, and imitation of, jihad.

Even the Christian crusade, often compared with the Muslim jihad, was itself a delayed and limited response to the jihad and in part also an imitation. But unlike the jihad it was concerned primarily with the defense or reconquest of threatened or lost Christian territory...The Muslim jihad, in contrast, was perceived [by Muslims] as unlimited, as a religious obligation that would continue until all the world had either adopted the Muslim faith or submitted to Muslim rule.... The object of jihad is to bring the whole world under Islamic law.

Bernard Lewis says Islam imposes, without limit of time or space, the duty to subjugate non-Muslims.

"...it is the duty of those who have accepted them [Allah's word and message] to strive unceasingly to convert or at least to subjugate those who have not. This obligation is without limit of time or space. It must continue until the whole world has either accepted the Islamic faith or submitted to the power of the Islamic state."

Michael Sells and Jane I. Smith (a Professor of Islamic Studies) write that barring some extremists like al-Qaeda, most Muslims do not interpret Qura'nic verses as promoting warfare; and that the phenomenon of radical interpretation of scripture by extremist groups is not unique to Islam. According to Sells, "[Most Muslims] no more expect to apply [the verses at issue] to their contemporary non-Muslim friends and neighbors than most Christians and Jews consider themselves commanded by God, like the BiblicalJoshua, to exterminate the infidels."

According to Robert Spencer, Muhammad said in one Hadith:

"Allah's Apostle said, "I have been sent with the shortest expressions bearing the widest meanings, and I have been made victorious with terror (cast in the hearts of the enemy), and while I was sleeping, the keys of the treasures of the world were brought to me and put in my hand." Abu Huraira added: Allah's Apostle has left the world and now you, people, are bringing out those treasures (i.e. the Prophet did not benefit by them). Narrated in Abu Huraira. — Sahih al-Bukhari, 4:52:220, see also Sahih Muslim, 4:1062,Sahih Muslim, 4:1063,Sahih Muslim, 4:1066,Sahih Muslim, 4:1067 and Sahih al-Bukhari, 5:59:512

Furthermore Muhammad said in another Hadith:

The Prophet said, "Who is ready to kill Ka'b ibn al-Ashraf who has really hurt Allah and His Apostle?" Muhammad bin Maslama said, "O Allah's Apostle! Do you like me to kill him?" He replied in the affirmative. So, Muhammad bin Maslama went to him (i.e. Ka'b) and said, "This person (i.e. the Prophet) has put us to task and asked us for charity." Ka'b replied, "By Allah, you will get tired of him." Muhammad said to him, "We have followed him, so we dislike to leave him till we see the end of his affair." Muhammad bin Maslama went on talking to him in this way till he got the chance to kill him. Narrated Jabir bin 'Abdullah — Sahih al-Bukhari, 4:52:270, see also Sahih al-Bukhari, 5:59:369,Sahih Muslim, 19:4436

And another Hadith:

The Prophet passed by me at a place called Al-Abwa or Waddan, and was asked whether it was permissible to attack the pagan warriors at night with the probability of exposing their women and children to danger. The Prophet replied, "They (i.e. women and children) are from them (i.e. pagans)." I also heard the Prophet saying, "The institution of Hima is invalid except for

Allah and His Apostle. Narrated As-Sab bin Jaththama — Sahih al-Bukhari, 4:52:256, see also Sahih Muslim, 19:4321 Sunan Abu Dawood, 38:4390

Militant Islamic fundamentalist organisations portray their struggle in simply uncompromising terms. According to Antar Zouabri, a leader of a 1990s movement to establish an Islamic republic in Algeria, there can never be either dialogue or truce in his organisation's struggle against the illegitimate, secular government. The word of God, he argued, is immutable: God does not negotiate or engage in discussion.

CRITICISM OF ISLAMIC TERRORIST IDEOLOGY

Although "Islamic" terrorism is commonly associated with the Salafis (or "Wahhabis"), the scholars of the group have constantly attributed this association to ignorance, misunderstanding and sometimes insincere research and deliberate misleading by rival groups. Following the September 11 attacks, Abdul-Azeez ibn Abdullaah Aal ash-Shaikh, the Grand Mufti of the Kingdom of Saudi Arabia, made an official statement that "the Islamic Sharee'ah (legislation) does not sanction" such actions. A Salafi Committee of Major Scholars"in Saudi Arabia has declared that "Islamic" terrorism, such as the May 2003 bombing in Riyadh, are in violation of Sharia law and aiding the enemies of Islam.

Criticism of Islamic terrorism on Islamic grounds has also been made by Abdal-Hakim Murad (Timothy Winter):

Certainly, neither bin Laden nor his principal associate, Ayman al-Zawahiri, are graduates of Islamic universities. And so their proclamations ignore 14 centuries of Muslim scholarship, and instead take the form of lists of anti-American grievances and of Koranic quotations referring to early Muslim wars against Arab idolaters. These are followed by the conclusion that all Americans, civilian and military, are to be wiped off the face of the Earth. All this amounts to an odd and extreme violation of the normal methods of Islamic scholarship. Had the authors of such fatwâs followed the norms of their religion, they would have had to acknowledge that no school of mainstream Islam allows the targeting of civilians. An insurrectionist who kills

> *non-combatants is guilty of baghy, "armed aggression," a capital offense in Islamic law.*

Colonel Eikmeier points out the "questionable religious credentials" of many Islamist theorists, or "Qutbists," which can be a "means to discredit them and their message":

> *With the exception of Abul Ala Maududi and Abdullah Yusuf Azzam, none of Qutbism's main theoreticians trained at Islam's recognized centers of learning. Although a devout Muslim, Hassan al-Banna was a teacher and community activist. Sayyid Qutb was a literary critic. Muhammad Abd al-Salam Faraj was an electrician. Ayman al-Zawahiri is a physician. Osama bin Laden trained to be a businessman.*

Fethullah Gülen, a prominent Turkish Islamic scholar, has claimed that "a real Muslim," who understood Islam in every aspect, could not be a terrorist. There are many other people with similar points of view such as Karen Armstrong, Prof. Ahmet Akgunduz, Harun Yahya and Muhammad Tahir-ul-Qadri. Huston Smith, an author on comparative religion, noted that extremists have hijacked Islam, just as has occurred periodically in Christianity, Hinduism and other religions throughout history. He added that the real problem is that extremists do not know their own faith.

Ali Gomaa, former Grand Mufti of Egypt, stated not only for the Islam but in general: "Terrorism cannot be born of religion. Terrorism is the product of corrupt minds, hardened hearts, and arrogant egos, and corruption, destruction, and arrogance are unknown to the heart attached to the divine."

Identity-based Frameworks for Analyzing Islamist-based Terrorism

Islamist-based fundamentalist terrorism against Western nations and the U.S. in particular, has numerous motivations and takes place the larger context of a complex and tense relationship between the 'West' and the Arab and Muslim 'world,' which is highlighted in the previous section on motivations and Islamic terrorism. Identity-based theoretical frameworks including theories of social identity, social categorization theory, and psychodynamics are used to explain the reasons terrorism occurs.

Social identity is explained by Karina Korostelina as a "feeling of belonging to a social group, as a strong connection with social category, and as an important part of our mind that affects our social perceptions and behavior" This definition can be applied to the case of Osama bin Laden, who, according to this theory, had a highly salient perception of his social identity as a Muslim, a strong connection to the social category of the Muslim Ummah or 'community,' which affect his social perceptions and behaviors. Bin Laden's ideology and interpretation of Islam led to the creation of al-Qaeda in response to perceived threats against the Muslim community by the Soviet Union, the U.S. in particular due to its troop presence in Saudi Arabia, and American support for Israel. The Islamist terrorist group al-Qaeda has a group identity, which includes "shared experiences, attitudes, beliefs, and interests of ingroup members," and is "described through the achievement of a collective aim for which this group has been created," which in this case is to achieve "a complete break from the foreign influences in Muslim countries, and the creation of a new Islamic caliphate."

Social categorization theory has been discussed as a three-stage process of identification, where "individuals define themselves as members of a social group, learn the stereotypes and norms of the group, and group categories influence the perception and understanding of all situations in a particular context" This definition can be applied to the U.S.-led war on terror, in which conflict features such as the phenomenon of Anti-Americanism and the phenomenon of non-Arab countries like Iran and Afghanistanlending support to Islamist-based terrorism by funding or harboring terrorist groups such as Hezbollah and al-Qaeda against Western nations, particularly Israel and theUnited States are, according to social categorization theory, influenced by a three-stage process of identification. In this three-stage process of identification, the Arab and Muslim world(s) are the social group(s), in which their members learn stereotypes and norms which categorize their social group vis-à-vis the West. This social categorization process creates feelings of high-level in-group support and allegiance among Arabs and Muslims and the particular context within which members of the Arab and Muslim world(s) social group(s) understand all situations that involve the

West. Social categorization theory as a framework for analysis indicates causal relationships between group identification processes and features of conflict situations.

MUSLIM ATTITUDES TOWARD TERRORISM

Muslim popular opinion on the subject of attacks on civilians by Islamist groups varies. Fred Halliday, a British academic specialist on the Middle East, argues that most Muslims consider these acts to be egregious violations of Islam's laws. Muslims living in the West denounce the September 11th attacks against United States, while Hezbollah contends that their rocket attacks against Israeli civilian targets are defensive Jihad by a legitimate resistance movement rather than terrorism. Subsequently, however, on Osama Bin Laden's death, many Muslims in the UK came out on streets in support of Osama, announcing him as an Islamic hero and condemned the role of US and west in killing him. The protest against Bin Laden's death was organised by controversial preacher Anjem Choudary – who praised both 7/7 and the September 11 attacks. Statistics compiled by the United States government's Counterterrorism Center present a complicated picture: of known and specified terrorist incidents from the beginning of 2004 through the first quarter of 2005, slightly more than half of the fatalities were attributed to Islamic extremists but a majority of over-all incidents were considered of either "unknown/unspecified" or a secular political nature. The vast majority of the "unknown/ unspecified" terrorism fatalities did however happen in Islamic regions such as Iraq andAfghanistan, or in regions where Islam is otherwise involved in conflicts such as the West Bank, the Gaza Strip, southern Thailand and Kashmir.

View of Islamic law

Although the murder of Muslims is always forbidden in Islam, the murder of non-Muslims is also prohibited in certain circumstances. Many Muslim scholars have presented subjective evidence against the religious justification of terrorism against certain non-Muslims, a notable example being that of Muhammad ibn al Uthaymeen who states regarding killing a non-Muslim who is living in an Islamic state or with whom Muslims have a peace treaty: "As for a non-Muslim living under Muslim rule and a Mu'âhid (a Non-Muslim ally with whom Muslims have a treaty, trust, peace, or agreement), the prophet said: "Whoever kills a Mu'âhid will not even smell the fragrance of paradise and its fragrance can be smelled from the distance of forty years away." and he also said: "Certainly, one of the most difficult situations for which there is no turning back for whomever casts himself into it - shedding sacred blood without right." However this does not address the killing of non-Muslims living outside the Islamic world who do not have a specific treaty with Muslims.

Another example is that of late scholar Abd al-Aziz Ibn Baz who stated: "It is well-known to anyone with the slightest amount of common sense that hijacking planes and kidnapping embassy officials and similar acts are some of the greatest universal crimes that result in nothing but widespread corruption and destruction. They place such extreme hardships and injuries upon innocent people, the extent of which only Allâh knows."

Numerous fatwâs (rulings) condemning terrorism and suicide bombing as *haram* have been published by Islamic scholars worldwide, one of the most extensive being the 600-page ruling by Sheikh Tahir-ul-Qadri, whose fatwa condemned them as *kufr*. On 2 March 2010, Qadri's fatwa was an "absolute" condemnation of terrorism without "any excuses or pretexts." He said that "Terrorism is terrorism, violence is violence and it has no place in Islamic teaching and no justification can be provided for it, or any kind of excuses or ifs or buts." Qadri said his fatwa, which declares terrorists and suicide bombers to be unbelievers, goes further than any previous denunciation. Iranian Ayatollah Ozma Seyyed Yousef Sanei issued a fatwa (ruling) that suicide attacks against civilians are legitimate only in the context of war. The ruling did not say whether other types of attacks against civilians are justified outside of the context of war, nor whether jihad is included in Sanei's definition of war.

An influential group of Pakistani scholars and religious leaders declared suicide attacks and beheadings as un-Islamic. 'Ulema' (clerics) and 'mushaikh' (spiritual leaders) of the Jamaat Ahl-e-Sunnah, who gathered for a convention, declared suicide attacks and beheadings as un-Islamic in a unanimous resolution. Chairman of the Pakistani Ruet-e-Hilal Committee, Mufti Muneeb-ur-Rehman, said in his address that those who were fighting in the name of implementing Shariah or Islamic law must first abide by these same laws and killing minors is contrary to the teachings of Islam.

Some contemporary scholars who have followed a textual based approach to the study of the Qur'an with an emphasis over the coherence in the Book and the context of situation offered a radical interpretation on the verses and prophetic narratives that are usually quoted by the militants to promote militancy. According to Javed Ahmad Ghamidi(his booklet on Jihad is considered one of his most important contribution towards understanding the religion according to the principles of interpreting the Qur'an introduced byFarahi and Islahi) the Qur'an does not allow waging war except for against oppression under a sovereign state. He holds that jihad without a state is nothing but creating nuisance in the land when hijacked by the individuals and groups independent of the state authority defeats the purpose. The principle behind this study of the issue in the basic sources is the principle that there are divine injunctions in the Qur'an which are specific to the age of the Messenger. He says that nobody can be punished for apostasy or being non-Muslim after the Prophet who acted as the divine agent when he punished the disbelievers by sword who had rejected the message of God and his messenger even after the truth was made manifest to them. Ghamidi and his associates have written extensively on the topics related to these issues. In his book Meezan Ghamidi has concluded that:

1. Jihad can only waged against persecution Islamic jihad has only two purposes : putting an end to persecution even that of the non-Muslims and making the religion of Islam reign supreme in the Arabian peninsula. The latter type was specific for the messenger of God and is no more operative .
2. Under a sovereign state.
3. There are strict ethical limits for jihad which do not again allow fighting for example non-combatants.

4. Seen in this perspective acts of terrorism including suicide bombing becomes prohibited.

Opinion Surveys

- Gallup conducted tens of thousands of hour-long, face-to-face interviews with residents of more than 35 predominantly Muslim countries between 2001 and 2007. It found that more than 90% of respondents condemned the killing of non-combatants on religious and humanitarian grounds.
- A 2004, a year after the invasion of Iraq, Pew Research Center survey found that suicide bombings against Americans and other Westerners in Iraq were seen as "justifiable" by many Jordanians (70%), Pakistanis (46%), and Turks (31%). At the same time, the survey found that support for the U.S.-led War on Terror had increased.
- A 2005 Pew Research study that involved 17,000 people in 17 countries showed support for terrorism was declining in the Muslim world along with a growing belief that Islamic extremism represents a threat to those countries. A *Daily Telegraph* survey showed that 88% of Muslims said the July 2005 bombings in the London Underground were unjustified, while 6% disagreed. However it also found that 24% of British Muslims showed some sympathy with the people who carried out the attacks.
- Polls taken by Saudi owned Al Arabiya and Gallup suggest moderate support for the September 11 terrorist attacks within the Islamic world, with 36% of Arabs polled by Al Arabiya saying the 9/11 attacks were morally justified, 38% disagreeing and 26% of those polled being unsure. A 2008 study, produced by Gallup, found similar results with 38.6% of Muslims questioned believing the 9/11 attacks were justified. Another poll conducted, in 2005 by the Fafo Foundation in the Palestinian Authority, found that 65% of respondents supported the September 11 attacks.
- In Pakistan, despite the recent rise in the Taliban's influence, a poll conducted by Terror Free Tomorrow in Pakistan in January 2008 tested support for al-Qaeda, the Taliban,

other militant Islamist groups and Osama bin Laden himself, and found a recent drop by half. In August 2007, 33% of Pakistanis expressed support for al-Qaeda; 38% supported the Taliban. By January 2008, al-Qaeda's support had dropped to 18%, the Taliban's to 19%. When asked if they would vote for al-Qaeda, just 1% of Pakistanis polled answered in the affirmative. The Taliban had the support of 3% of those polled.

- Pew Research surveys in 2008 show that in a range of countries – Jordan, Pakistan, Indonesia, Lebanon, and Bangladesh – there have been substantial declines in the percentages saying suicide-bombings and other forms of violence against civilian targets can be justified to defend Islam against its enemies. Wide majorities say such attacks are, at most, rarely acceptable. The shift of attitudes against terror has been especially dramatic in Jordan, where 29% of Jordanians were recorded as viewing suicide-attacks as often or sometimes justified (down from 57% in May 2005). In the largest majority-Muslim nation, Indonesia, 74% of respondents agree that terrorist attacks are "never justified" (a substantial increase from the 41% level to which support had risen in March 2004); in Pakistan, that figure is 86%; in Bangladesh, 81%; and in Iran, 80%.
- A poll conducted in Osama bin Laden's home country of Saudi Arabia in December 2008 shows that his compatriots have dramatically turned against him, his organisation, Saudi volunteers in Iraq, and terrorism in general. Indeed, confidence in bin Laden has fallen in most Muslim countries in recent years.

EXAMPLES OF ORGANIZATIONS AND ACTS

Some prominent Islamic terror groups and incidents include the following:

South America

Argentina

The 1992 attack on Israeli embassy in Buenos Aires was a

suicide bombing attack on the building of the Israeli embassy of Argentina, located in Buenos Aires, which was carried out on 17 March 1992. Twenty-nine civilians were killed in the attack and 242 additional civilians were injured. A group called Islamic Jihad Organization, which has been linked to Iran and possibly Hezbollah, claimed responsibility.

Central Asia

Afghanistan

According to Human Rights Watch, Taliban and Hezb-e-Islami Gulbuddin forces have "sharply escalated bombing and other attacks" against civilians since 2006. In 2006, "at least 669 Afghan civilians were killed in at least 350 armed attacks, most of which appear to have been intentionally launched at civilians or civilian objects."

Tajikistan

The government blamed the IMU (Islamic Movement of Uzbekistan) for training those responsible for carrying out a suicide car bombing of a police station in Khujand on September 3, 2010. Two policemen were killed and 25 injured.

Uzbekistan

On February 16, 1999, six car bombs exploded in Tashkent, killing 16 and injuring more than 100, in what may have been an attempt to assassinate President Islam Karimov. The IMU was blamed.

The IMU launched a series of attacks in Tashkent and Bukhara in March and April 2004. Gunmen and female suicide bombers took part in the attacks, which mainly targeted police. The violence killed 33 militants, 10 policemen, and four civilians. The government blamed Hizb ut-Tahrir, though the Islamic Jihad Union (IJU) claimed responsibility.

Furkat Kasimovich Yusupov was arrested in the first half of 2004, and charged as the leader of a group that had carried out the March 28 bombing on behalf of Hizb ut-Tahrir.

On July 30, 2004, suicide bombers struck the entrances of the US and Israeli embassies in Tashkent. Two Uzbek security guards were killed in both bombings. The IJU again claimed responsibility.

Foreign commentators on Uzbek affairs speculated that the 2004 violence could have been the work of the IMU, Al-Qaeda, Hizb ut-Tahrir, or some other radical Islamic organization.

Eurasia

Russia

Politically and religiously motivated attacks on civilians in Russia have been traced to separatist sentiment among the largely Muslim population of its North Caucasus region, particularly in Chechnya, where the central government of the Russian Federation has waged two bloody wars against the local secular separatist government since 1994. In theMoscow theater hostage crisis in October 2002, three Chechen separatist groups took an estimated 850 people hostage in the Russian capital; at least 129 hostages died during the storming by Russian special forces, all but one killed by the chemicals used to subdue the attackers (whether this attack would more properly be called a nationalist rather than an Islamist attack is in question). In the September 2004 Beslan school hostage crisis more than 1,000 people were taken hostage after a school in the Russian republic ofNorth Ossetia–Alania was seized by a pro-Chechen multiethnic group aligned to Riyad-us Saliheen Brigade of Martyrs; hundreds of people died during the storming by Russian forces.

Since 2000, Russia has also experienced a string of suicide bombings that killed hundreds of people in the Caucasian republics of Chechnya, Dagestan and Ingushetia, as well as in Russia proper including Moscow. Responsibility for most of these attacks were claimed by either Shamil Basayev's Islamic-nationalist rebel faction or, later, by Dokka Umarov's pan-Islamist movement Caucasus Emirate which is aiming to unite most of Russia's North Caucasus as an emirate since its creation in 2007. Since the creation of the Caucasus Emirate, the group has abandoned its secular nationalist goals and fully adopted the ideology of Salafist-takfiri Jihadism which seeks to advance the cause of Allah on the earth by waging war against the Russian government and non-Muslims in the North Caucasus, such as the local Sufi Muslim population, whom they view asmushrikeen (hypocrites) who do not adhere to true Islamic teachings. In 2011, the U.S. Department of State included the Caucasus Emirate on its list of terrorist organisations.

Turkey

Hezbollah in Turkey (unrelated to the Shia Hezbollah in Lebanon) is a Kurdish Sunni terrorist group accused of a series of attacks, including the November 2003 bombings of two synagogues, the British consulate in Istanbul and HSBC bank headquarters that killed 58. Hizbullah's leader, Hüseyin Velioðlu, was killed in action by Turkish police in Beykoz on 17 January 2000. Besides Hizbullah, other Islamic groups listed as a terrorist organization by Turkish police counter-terrorism include Great Eastern Islamic Raiders' Front, al-Qaeda in Turkey, Tevhid-Selam (also known as *al-Quds Army*) and Caliphate State. Islamic Party of Kurdistan and Hereketa Ýslamiya Kurdistan are also Kurdish Islamist groups active against Turkey, however unlike Kurdish Hizbullah they're yet to be listed as active terrorist organizations in Turkey by Turkish police counter-terrorism.

Europe

Major lethal attacks on civilians in Europe credited to Islamist terrorism include the 1985 El Descanso bombing in Madrid, the 1995 Paris Metro bombings, 11 March 2004 bombings of commuter trains in Madrid, where 191 people were killed, and the 7 July 2005 London bombings, also of public transport, which killed 52 commuters. According to EU Terrorism Report, however, there were almost 500 acts of terrorism across the European Union in 2006, but only one, the foiled suitcase bomb plot in Germany, was related to Islamist terror. In 2009, a Europol report also showed that more than 99% of terrorist attacks in Europe over the last three years were, in fact, carried out by non-Muslims. In terms of arrests, out of a total of 1,009 arrested terror suspects in 2008, 187 of them were arrested in relation to Islamist terrorism. The report also showed that the majority of Islamist terror suspects were not first generation immigrants, but were rather children of immigrants who no longer identified with the culture of their parents and at the same time felt excluded from Western society, "which still perceives them as foreigners," thus they became "more attracted to the idea of becoming 'citizens' of the virtual worldwide Islamic community, removed from territory and national culture."

MIDDLE EAST / SOUTHWEST ASIA

Iraq

The area that has seen some of the worst terror attacks in modern history has been Iraq as part of the Iraq War. In 2005, there were 400 incidents of one type of attack (suicide bombing), killing more than 2,000 people – many if not most of them civilians. In 2006, almost half of all reported terrorist attacks in the world (6,600), and more than half of all terrorist fatalities (13,000), occurred in Iraq, according to the National Counterterrorism Center of the United States. Along with nationalist groups and criminal, non-political attacks, the Iraqi insurgency includes Islamist insurgent groups, such as Al-Qaeda in Iraq, who favor suicide attacks far more than non-Islamist groups. At least some of the terrorism has a transnational character in that some foreign Islamic jihadists have joined the insurgency.

Israel and the Palestinian territories

Hamas ("zeal" in Arabic and an acronym for Harakat al-Muqawama al-Islamiyya) began support for attacks on military and civilian targets in Israel at the beginning of the First Intifada in 1987. The 1988 charter of Hamas calls for the destruction of Israel, and remains in effect today. Its "military wing" has claimed responsibility fornumerous attacks in Israel, principally suicide bombings and rocket attacks. Hamas has also been accused of sabotaging the Israeli-Palestine peace process by launching attacks on civilians during Israeli elections to anger Israeli voters and facilitate the election of harder-line Israeli candidates. Hamas has been designated as a terrorist group by theEuropean Union, Canada, the United States, the United Kingdom, Israel, Australia, Japan, the United Nations Commission on Human Rights and

Human Rights Watch. It is banned in Jordan. Russia does not consider Hamas a terrorist group as it was "democratically elected". During the second intifada (September 2000 through August 2005) 39.9 percent of the suicide attacks were carried out by Hamas. The first Hamas suicide attack was the Mehola Junction bombing in 1993. Although Hamas justifies these attacks as necessary in fighting the Israeli occupation of Palestinian territory, the attacks continue despite the 2005 Israeli withdrawal from Hamas controlled territory and Hamas still states its goal to be the elimination of Israel. The wider Hamas movement also serves as a charity organization and provides services to Palestinians.

Islamic Jihad Movement in Palestine is a Palestinian Islamist group based in the Syrian capital, Damascus, and dedicated to waging jihad to eliminate the state of Israel. It was formed by Palestinian Fathi Shaqaqi in the Gaza Strip following the Iranian Revolution which inspired its members. From 1983 onward, it engaged in "a succession of violent, high-profile attacks" on Israeli targets. The intifada which "it eventually sparked" was quickly taken over by the much larger Palestine Liberation Organization and Hamas. Beginning in September 2000, it started a campaign of suicide bombing attacks against Israeli civilians. The PIJ's armed wing, the Al-Quds brigades, has claimed responsibility for numerous militant attacks in Israel, including suicide bombings. The group has been designated as a terrorist organization by several Western countries.

Lebanon

Hezbollah first emerged in 1982 as a militia during the Israeli invasion of Lebanon, also known as Operation Peace for Galilee. Its leaders were inspired by the ayatollah Khomeini, and its forces were trained and organized by a contingent of Iranian Revolutionary Guards. Hezbollah's 1985 manifesto listed its three main goals as "putting an end to any colonialist entity" in Lebanon, bringing the Phalangists to justice for "the crimes they [had] perpetrated," and the establishment of an Islamic regime in Lebanon. Hezbollah leaders have also made numerous statements calling for the destruction of Israel, which they refer to as a "Zionist entity... built on lands wrested from their owners."

Hezbollah, which started with only a small militia, has grown to an organization with seats in the Lebanese government, a radio and a satellite television-station, and programs forsocial development. They maintain strong support among Lebanon's Shi'a population, and gained a surge of support from Lebanon's broader population (Sunni, Christian,Druze) immediately following the 2006 Lebanon War, and are able to mobilize demonstrations of hundreds of thousands. Hezbollah alongside with some other groups began the 2006–2008 Lebanese political protests in opposition to the government of Prime Minister Fouad Siniora. A later dispute over Hezbollah preservation of its telecoms network led to clashes and Hezbollah-led opposition fighters seized control of several West Beirut neighborhoods from Future Movement militiamen loyal to Fouad Siniora. These areas were then handed over to the Lebanese Army.

A national unity government was formed in 2008, in Lebanon, giving Hezbollah and its opposition allies control of 11 of 30 cabinets seats; effectively veto power. Hezbollah receives its financial support from the governments of Iran and Syria, as well as donations from Lebanese people and foreign Shi'as. It has also gained significantly in military strength in the 2000s. Despite a June 2008 certification by the United Nations that Israel had withdrawn from all Lebanese territory, in August, Lebanon's new Cabinet unanimously approved a draft policy statement which secures Hezbollah's existence as an armed organization and guarantees its right to "liberate or recover occupied lands." Since 1992, the organization has been headed by Hassan Nasrallah, its Secretary-General. The United States, Canada, Israel, Bahrain, France, Gulf Cooperation Council, and the Netherlands regard Hezbollah as a terrorist organization, while the United Kingdom, the European Union and Australia consider only Hezbollah's military wing or its external security organization to be a terrorist organization. Many consider it, or a part of it, to be a terrorist group responsible for blowing up the American embassy and later its annex, as well as the barracks of American and French peacekeeping troops and a dozens of kidnappings of foreigners in Beirut. It is also accused of being the recipient of massive aid from Iran, and of serving "Iranian foreign policy calculations and interests," or serving as a "subcontractor of Iranian initiatives" Hezbollah denies any involvement or dependence on Iran. In the Arab and Muslim worlds, on the other hand, Hezbollah is regarded as a legitimate and successful resistance movement that drove both Western powers and Israel out of Lebanon. In 2005, the Lebanese Prime Minister said of Hezbollah, it "is not a militia. It's a resistance."

Fatah al-Islam is an Islamist group operating out of the Nahr al-Bared refugee camp in northern Lebanon. It was formed in November 2006 by fighters who broke off from the pro-Syrian Fatah al-Intifada, itself a splinter group of the Palestinian Fatah movement, and is led by a Palestinian fugitive militant named Shaker al-Abssi. The group's members have been described as militant jihadists, and the group itself has been described as a terrorist movement that draws inspiration from al-Qaeda. Its stated goal is to reform the Palestinian refugee camps under Islamic sharia law, and its primary targets are the Lebanese authorities, Israel and the United States.

NORTH AFRICA

Algeria

The Armed Islamic Group, active in Algeria between 1992 and 1998, was one of the most violent Islamic terrorist groups, and is thought to have takfired the Muslim population of Algeria. Its campaign to overthrow the Algerian government included civilian massacres, sometimes wiping out entire villages in its area of operation. It also targeted foreigners living in Algeria, killing more than 100 expatriates in the country. In recent years it has been eclipsed by a splinter group, the Salafist Group for Preaching and Combat (GSPC), now called Al-Qaeda Organization in the Islamic Maghreb.

NORTH AMERICA

Canada

According to recent government statements Islamic terrorism is the biggest threat to Canada. The Canadian Security Intelligence

Service (CSIS) reported that terrorist radicalization at home is now the chief preoccupation of Canada's spy agency. The most notorious arrest in Canada's fight on terrorism, was the 2006 Ontario terrorism plotin which 18 Al-Qaeda cell members were arrested for planning a mass bombing, shooting, and hostage taking terror plot throughout Southern Ontario. There have also been other arrests mostly in Ontario involving terror plots.

United States

Between 1993 and 2001, the major attacks or attempts against US interests stemmed from militant Islamic jihad except for the 1995 Oklahoma City bombing. In 2001 nearly 3,000 people were killed in the massive September 11 attacks organised by al-Qaeda and largely perpetrated by Saudi nationals, sparking the War on Terror. Former CIA Director Michael Hayden considers homegrown terrorism to be the most dangerous threat and concern faced by American citizens today. On April 15, 2013 two Muslim suspected terrorists detonated two pressure cooker bombs in the City of Boston during the Boston Marathon, killing 3 people and injuring an estimated 264 others. As of July 2011, there have been 52 homegrown jihadist plots or attacks in the United States since the September 11 attacks.

SOUTH ASIA

Bangladesh

In Bangladesh the group Jamaat-ul-Mujahideen Bangladesh was formed sometime in 1998 and gained prominence in 2001. The organization was officially banned in February 2005 after attacks on NGOs, but struck back in August when 300 bombs were detonated almost simultaneously throughout Bangladesh, targeting Shahjalal International Airport, government buildings and major hotels.

India

Lashkar-e-Taiba and Jaish-e-Mohammed are militant groups seeking accession of Kashmir to Pakistan from India or Bharat. The Lashkar leadership describes Indian andIsrael regimes as the main enemies of Islam and Pakistan that is an extremist thought but is not real. Lashkar-e-Toiba, along with Jaish-e-Mohammed, another militant group active in Kashmir are on the United States' foreign terrorist organizations list, and are also designated as terrorist groups by the United Kingdom, India, Australia and Pakistan. Jaish-e-Mohammed was formed in 1994 and has carried out a series of attacks all over India. The group was formed after the supporters of Maulana Masood Azhar split from another Islamic militant organization, Harkat-ul-Mujahideen. Jaish-e-Mohammed is viewed by some as the "deadliest" and "the principal terrorist organization in Jammu and Kashmir". The group was also implicated in the kidnapping and murder of American journalist Daniel Pearl.

Several major blasts and attacks in India were perpetrated by Islamic extremists from Pakistan like 26/11(or Mumbai attack),attack on parliament(Sansad Bhawan)of India in 2001 .The terrorist accused of Sansad Bhawan attack was sentenced to death by Supreme Court of India. Attacks by Islamic militants in India continue even now.

SOUTHEAST ASIA

The Philippines

The Abu Sayyaf Group, also known as al-Harakat al-Islamiyya, is one of several militant Islamic-separatist groups based in and around the southern islands of the Philippines, inBangsamoro (Jolo, Basilan, and Mindanao) where for almost 30 years various Muslim groups have been engaged in an insurgency for a state, independent of the predominantlyChristian Philippines. The name of the group is derived from the Arabic ÇÈæ, *abu* ("father of") and *sayyaf* ("Swordsmith"). Since its inception in the early 1990s, the group has carried out bombings, assassinations, kidnappings and extortion in their fight for an independent Islamic state in western Mindanao and the Sulu Archipelago with the stated goal of creating a pan-Islamic superstate across southeast Asia, spanning from east to west; the island of Mindanao, the Sulu Archipelago, the island of Borneo (Malaysia, Indonesia), the South China Sea, and the Malay Peninsula (Peninsular Malaysia, Thailand and Myanmar).

The U.S. Department of State has branded the group a terrorist entity by adding it to the list of Foreign Terrorist Organizations.

Transnational

Al-Qaeda's stated aim is the use of jihad to defend and protect Islam against Zionism, Christianity, Hinduism, the secular West, and Muslim governments such as Saudi Arabia, which it sees as insufficiently Islamic and too closely tied to the United States. Formed by Osama bin Laden and Muhammad Atef in the aftermath of the Soviet war in Afghanistan in the late 1980s, al-Qaeda called for the use of violence against civilians and military of the United States and any countries that are allied with it.

TACTICS

Suicide attacks

An increasingly popular tactic used by terrorists is suicide bombing. This tactic is used against civilians, soldiers, and government officials of the regimes the terrorists oppose. A recent clerical ruling declares terrorism and suicide bombing as forbidden by Islam. However, groups who support its use often refer to such attacks as "martyrdom operations" and the suicide-bombers who commit them as "martyrs" (Arabic: shuhada, plural of "shahid"). The bombers, and their sympathizers often believe that suicide bombers, as martyrs (shaheed) to the cause of jihad against the enemy, will receive the rewards of paradise for their actions.

Hijackings

Islamic terrorism sometimes employs the hijacking of passenger vehicles. The most famous were the "9/11" attacks that killed nearly 3,000 people on a single day in 2001, effectively ending the era of aircraft hijacking.

Kidnappings and Executions

Along with bombings and hijackings, Islamic terrorists have made extensive use of highly publicised kidnappings and executions, often circulating videos of the acts for use as propaganda. A frequent form of execution by these groups is decapitation, another is shooting. In the 1980s, a series of abductions of American citizens by Hezbollah during theLebanese Civil War resulted in the 1986 Iran–Contra affair. During the chaos of the Iraq War, more than 200 kidnappings foreign hostages (for various reasons and by various groups, including purely criminal) gained great international notoriety, even as the great majority (thousands) of victims were Iraqis. In 2007, the kidnapping of Alan Johnston byArmy of Islam resulted in the British government meeting a Hamas member for the first time.

Internet Recruiting

In the beginning of the 21st century emerged a worldwide network of hundreds of web sites that inspire, train, educate and recruit young Muslims to engage in jihad against America and the West, taking less prominent roles in mosques and community centers that are under scrutiny. According to *The Washington Post,* "Online recruiting has exponentially increased, with Facebook, YouTube and the increasing sophistication of people online".

6

Homegrown Violent Jihadists

This report focuses on geography and citizenship in its characterization of homegrown terrorism by defining the phenomenon as jihadist terrorist activity or plots perpetrated within the United States or abroad by American citizens, legal permanent residents, or visitors radicalized largely within the United States. These homegrown groups or individuals can focus their plots on foreign targets. They can have operational ties to foreign terrorist groups, but most of the plots after April 2009 have not. Homegrown violent jihadists potentially either come from Muslim immigrant communities or are converts to Islam. A review of the numerous arrests of homegrown violent jihadists on terrorism-related charges since 9/11 suggests a wide array of incidents. There have been those who have plotted or attempted terrorist attacks. Others have provided material support to terrorist groups. Some have recruited individuals to travel abroad—or have gone themselves—to acquire terrorist training, conduct terrorism, or join in other forms of jihadist conflict, such as the fighting in Somalia or Afghanistan.

SHORTCOMINGS AND STRENGTHS

Homegrown violent jihadists may exhibit a number of conventional shortcomings when compared to international terrorist networks such as Al Qaeda. Because some homegrown terrorists are not tied to international groups, some say they possibly lack deep, hands-on understanding of specialized tradecraft such as bomb making and may not have the financing, training camps, support networks, and broad expertise housed in international organizations with extensive rosters and greater resources. Also, homegrown groups tend to be much less formally structured than international organizations. A former Central Intelligence Agency (CIA) case officer has commented that the threat posed by self-radicalized "lone" bombers lacking support networks, "even those who have been in contact with either Al Qaeda or the Taliban, will be hit or miss at best."

These apparent shortcomings may keep some homegrown violent jihadists from independently planning, coordinating, and implementing large-scale suicide strikes such as 9/11 or the Mumbai attacks of November 2008. Because of this, they may turn to violence involving less planning and preparation, such as assaults using firearms.

Al Qaeda appears to have embraced such homegrown lone wolf terrorist plots. In March 2010, As Sahab, Al Qaeda's media wing, released an English language video titled "A Call to Arms" featuring American-born spokesperson Adam Gadahn. In the video directed toward jihadists in the United States, Israel, and the United Kingdom, Gadahn extols alleged Fort Hood shooter Nidal Hasan as a "trailblazer" who did not attract law enforcement attention by training abroad or relying on conspirators. Gadahn encourages would-be terrorists to select realistically hittable targets that are familiar to them and have some broadly symbolic—especially economic— resonance. In an early June 2011 English language video message titled "Do Not Rely on Others, Take the Task upon Yourself," Gadahn even more clearly emphasized lone wolf operations. In the video he suggests possible weapons,

Let's take America as an example. America is absolutely awash with easily obtainable firearms. You can go down to a gun show at the local convention center and come away with a fully automatic assault rifle, without a background check, and most likely without having to show an identification card. So what are you waiting for?

Gadahn stresses "targeting major institutions—after a clip showing the logos of such firms as Exxon, Merrill Lynch and Bank of America—and 'influential public figures.'" At about the same time as this video was released, users of jihadist websites apparently began posting potential targets and developing hit lists.

In the same vein as Gadahn's video, Al Qaeda in the Arabian Peninsula (an Al Qaeda affiliate) has issued an English language propaganda magazine titled Inspire. The magazine has encouraged homegrown violent jihadist activity in the West, focusing on smaller scale strategies such as using a vehicle to run over victims. It has featured articles attributed to three prominent violent jihadist propagandists with strong American ties: Gadahn, radical U.S.-born imam Anwar al-Awlaki, and Saudi-born American citizen Samir Khan. In September 2011, the latter two died in a widely reported U.S. air strike in Yemen.

This does not mean that homegrown terrorists are incapable of sophisticated, coordinated action or linking up with international groups. For example, in 2008 foiled New York City subway bomber Najibullah Zazi received explosives instruction from Al Qaeda in Pakistan. He and co-conspirators then tried to implement this training in the United States. U.S. authorities assert that senior Al Qaeda official Adnan el-Shukrijumah possibly recruited Zazi and his fellow plotters. Shukrijumah—a Saudi-born, naturalized American citizen who spent part of his youth in Brooklyn—and others involved in Al Qaeda's "external operations" program allegedly planned the attack. The relative sophistication of Zazi's plot may have actually exposed it to greater law enforcement scrutiny. Authorities likely learned of the plot while monitoring a known Al Qaeda e-mail account.

The conventionally perceived shortcomings of homegrown terrorists may actually pose some challenges for law enforcement, intelligence, and security officials charged with detecting, preventing, or disrupting terrorist plots. According to terrorism analyst Steve Emerson, "The smaller cells tend to be less powerful than a central terrorist organization like Al Qaeda, but they are harder to detect.... When the group of conspirators are [sic] small it's much more difficult for the FBI.... The larger the group, the greater the chances the FBI can infiltrate." Former Director of National Intelligence Dennis C. Blair noted that many of the terrorist schemes disrupted in 2009—including homegrown activity—relied on short-term planning. These quickly generated schemes are harder to identify and disrupt than more traditional and more highly organized international terrorist conspiracies, which can gestate for years.

According to at least one study, homegrown terrorists can be nimble adversaries, because as U.S. citizens or legal permanent residents, they can travel easily between the United States and foreign countries. While abroad, they could receive training from foreign terrorist organizations, conduct surveillance operations against foreign targets, and plan attacks. In the case of recent immigrants to the United States, they are particularly comfortable moving between American and foreign cultural contexts. English language skills, the ability to navigate Western culture, society, and context are likely key ingredients for successful strikes. Three cases involving homegrown terrorists illustrate how these factors possibly facilitate terrorist plotting:

- In February 2011, Colleen LaRose (aka "Jihad Jane") pled guilty "to all counts of a superseding indictment charging her with conspiracy to provide material support to terrorists, conspiracy to kill in a foreign country, making false statements, and attempted identity theft." She allegedly discussed with her co-conspirators how her mainstream American physical appearance would allow her to "blend in with many people."
- On March 18, 2010, David Headley, born Daood Sayed Gilani to an American mother and Pakistani father, pled guilty to helping plan the 2008 terrorist attacks in Mumbai, India, and for plotting to attack the offices of a newspaper in Copenhagen, Denmark. Headley was able to use his American citizenship and Pakistani heritage to move between the United States and abroad for seven years during which time he received terrorist training in Pakistan and scouted locations in India and Denmark for terrorist attacks.
- For 10 years prior to his involvement in a September 2009 plot to trigger explosive devices in New York City's subways, Najibullah Zazi, an Afghan immigrant legally

present in the United States, lived in the New York City borough of Queens and had family in Pakistan.

In 2010, the Department of Homeland Security's (DHS's) Office of Intelligence and Analysis warned, "probable terrorist perception of success in challenging the U.S. even through failed attacks, suggest[s] Al Qaeda and associated groups will try to conduct operations in the United States with increased frequency." It appears that for the foreseeable future, American citizens and legal permanent residents of the United States radicalized within the nation's borders will continue to pose a violent jihadist threat.

RADICALIZATION AND VIOLENT EXTREMISM

Radicalization and violent extremism are terms that are sometimes used interchangeably but do not mean the same thing. Radicalization has been described as the exposure of individuals to ideological messages and the movement of those individuals from mainstream beliefs to extremist viewpoints. Others say radicalization consists of changes in belief and behavior to justify intergroup violence and personal or group sacrifice to forward specific, closely held ideas. Still others use the term to more closely link extremist beliefs to violent action, as in this definition by the DHS, which states that radicalization "entails the process of adopting an extremist belief system, including the willingness to use, support, or facilitate violence, as a method to effect societal change." But there is an important distinction between the terms "radicalization" and "violent extremism" as it relates to the threshold of U.S. law enforcement interest and action. This is because Americans have the right under the First Amendment to adopt, express, or disseminate ideas, even hateful and extremist ones. But when radicalized individuals mobilize their views (i.e., they move from a radicalized viewpoint to membership in a terrorist group, or to planning, materially supporting, or executing terrorist activity) then the nation's public safety and security interests are activated. Thus, the terms may be differentiated as follows:

- "Radicalization" describes the process of acquiring and holding radical, extremist, or jihadist beliefs.

- "Violent extremism," for this report, describes violent action taken on the basis of radical or extremist beliefs. For many, this term is synonymous with "violent jihadist" and "jihadist terrorist."

From Radicalization to Violent Extremism

Combating homegrown violent jihadists requires an understanding of how radicalization works and formulating ways to prevent the radicalization from morphing into violent extremism. In 2007, the New York City Police Department's (NYPD's) Intelligence Division released a study of domestic jihadist radicalization that has been widely circulated within the law enforcement community.

The study describes a general four-step process of radicalization leading to violent extremism. First, individuals exist in a pre-radicalization phase in which they lead lives unaware of or uninterested in either violent jihad or fundamentalist Salafi Islam. Next, they go through self-identification in which some sort of crisis or trigger (job loss, social alienation, death of a family member, international conflict) urges them to explore Salafism. Third, individuals undergo indoctrination or adoption of jihadist ideals combined with Salafi views. The study indicates that, typically, a "spiritual sanctioner" or charismatic figure plays a central role in the indoctrination process. Finally, radicalizing individuals go through "jihadization," where they identify themselves as violent jihadists, and are drawn into the planning of a terrorist attack. At this point, according to the NYPD, they can be considered violent extremists. The FBI's own four-stage model of radicalization closely follows that of the NYPD.

This model and the process it describes—though useful—should, however, be read with caution, according to some observers. The radicalization process is best depicted in broad brush strokes. Brian Michael Jenkins has suggested that

There is no easily identifiable terrorist-prone personality, no single path to radicalization and terrorism. Many people may share the same views, and only a handful of the radicals will go further to become terrorists. The transition from radical to terrorist is often a matter of happenstance. It depends on whom one meets and probably on when that meeting occurs in the arc of one's life.

Some experts have warned against viewing the radicalization process as a "conveyer belt," somehow starting with grievances and inevitably ending in violence. The NYPD report itself acknowledges that individuals who begin this process do not necessarily pass through all the stages nor do they necessarily follow all the steps in order, and not all individuals or groups who begin this progression become terrorists. Studies by the DHS Office of Intelligence and Analysis indicate that the radicalization dynamic varies across ideological and ethno-religious spectrums, different geographic regions, and socio-economic conditions. Moreover, there are many diverse "pathways" to radicalization and individuals and groups can radicalize or "de-radicalize" because of a variety of factors.

Forces and Factors in the Forging of Terrorists

What drives radicalization and spurs the creation of terrorists remains open to debate. Poverty, alienation, brainwashing, or personal humiliation—commonly seen as factors driving radicalization and terrorism—may not play particularly significant roles. Likewise, failed multiculturalism or failed integration into the larger society does not predict radicalization or terrorist activity. The radicalization process and jihadist violence may offer participants powerful but intangible spiritual incentives such as salvation and paradise in the afterlife.

Other forces are key in radicalization and the evolution of jihadist terrorists. Family ties and socialization are critical. Moral outrage or perceptions that the West is harming the global community of Muslims (the Ummah), or even waging war against it may also spur radicalization and violence. And travel to regions featuring terrorist activity can foster radicalization. Religious conversion plays a key role in the radicalization of some individuals. CRS analysis of the 63 plots since 9/11 suggests that 26 of them included converts to Islam.

As all of this may suggest, in fact, "pre-radicalization" indicators are subtle and may not be detectable and the forces driving jihadists can be described in only the most general of terms. Certainly, radicalizing individuals and terrorists connect larger grievances about the world to their own direct experiences. A study of 2,032 foreign fighters who joined Al Qaeda and its affiliated organizations broadly suggests that these individuals can be categorized as revenge seekers, status seekers, identity seekers, or thrill seekers who possessed "an unfulfilled need to define themselves." Even more broadly and fundamentally, one author has suggested that psychologically, individual terrorists "see the world in Manichean, black-and-white terms; they identify with others; and they desire revenge."

Overall, many scholars and counterterrorism analysts who have studied post-9/11 jihadist terrorist attacks have noted the prominence of a number of forces impacting radicalization and extremism. These include intermediaries (the "spiritual sanctioners" identified by the NYPD report on radicalization), social networks, the Internet, and prisons.

Intermediaries

Intermediaries are critical in the development of terrorist plots and radicalization. They quicken the formulation of individual or group beliefs regarding violent jihad. Terrorist recruiters from Al Qaeda or extremist clerics tied to such organizations can play this role in the radicalization process. They can interact with individuals interested in terrorism either directly (face-to-face discussion groups) or in online forums. Some post 9/11 terrorist plots have included an intermediary. In some cases a key intermediary may be a government informant or undercover agent. Four charismatic U.S. citizens have played especially prominent roles in international jihadist propaganda, but determining the impact—if any—of these and other intermediaries can be difficult.

Anwar al-Awlaki was a radical imam and key international charismatic figure in jihadist circles prior to being killed in a U.S. air strike in Yemen in September 2011. Awlaki allegedly served as a leader in the terrorist group known as Al Qaeda in the Arabian Peninsula (AQAP). He was a U.S. citizen born in New Mexico in 1971 and had been linked to a number of domestic jihadist plots.

U.S. officials have said that he directed foreign terrorist Umar Farouk Abdulmutallab's failed Christmas Day 2009 bombing attempt. However, according to publicly available sources, his exact connections to homegrown violent jihadists are largely unclear. Before his alleged November 5, 2009, gun rampage at Fort Hood, Texas, U.S. Army Major Nidal Hasan purportedly exchanged e-mails with Awlaki. It remains publicly unknown how the contact influenced Hasan. After the Fort Hood shootings, Awlaki issued a statement dubbing Hasan a hero.

The imam also likely influenced people involved in other homegrown violent jihadist plots. Jose Pimentel was allegedly building explosive devices when he was arrested after two years of surveillance by the NYPD. He purportedly sympathized with Al Qaeda and drew inspiration from Awlaki. The alleged would-be bomber is reputed to have tried but failed to correspond with Awlaki via e-mail, and the cleric's death may have sped up his plotting. In December 2010, federal officials charged Antonio Martinez, a Muslim convert, in a plot to bomb an Armed Forces recruiting station. A sting operation by the FBI ensnared Martinez. He allegedly planned to attack an Armed Forces recruiting station in Maryland, using a sport utility vehicle loaded with what he believed was a bomb. During the course of his plot, he also allegedly praised Awlaki. Naturalized U.S. citizen Farooque Ahmed was arrested in October 2010 for attempting to assist people he believed to be terrorists in planning the bombing of Washington, DC Metrorail stations. Ahmed allegedly possessed a biography of Awlaki and listened to his online sermons. Also apprehended in October 2010, U.S. citizen Abdel Hameed Shehadeh, who allegedly tried to join overseas extremist groups such as the Taliban, modeled one of the jihadist websites he managed after Awlaki's teachings. The website offered hyperlinks to Awlaki's online lectures. According to DOJ, Shehadeh also discussed Awlaki's ideas with an individual he tried (and failed) to recruit for violent jihad. Zachary Chesser, who allegedly tried to join the Somali terrorist group al-Shabaab as late as July 2010 and propagandized online, e-mailed Awlaki. The cleric responded twice, according to court documents. In July 2010, Paul Rockwood Jr. pled guilty to making false statements in a domestic terrorism investigation. He closely followed Awlaki's online pronouncements and developed an "execution" hit list that included 15 people Rockwood believed had desecrated Islam. According to court documents, Shaker Masri encouraged an FBI cooperating source to "review speeches" by Awlaki. Arrested in June 2010 while allegedly trying to join al-Shabaab, Mohamed Alessa and Carlos Almonte, watched videos of and listened to sermons by Awlaki.

According to media sources, Faisal Shahzad, a Pakistani immigrant who admitted that he attempted to detonate an explosives-filled vehicle in New York City's Times Square on May 1, 2010, cited Awlaki and another cleric, Abdullah Faisal from Jamaica, as key influences on him. Also, a surveillance recording from 2007 captured one of six individuals eventually convicted of plotting to attack Fort Dix in New Jersey talking about an Awlaki lecture.

U.S. officials believe Awlaki also had contact with Umar Farouk Abdulmutallab, the young Nigerian who concealed an explosive device in his underwear and attempted to detonate it on a Northwest Airlines flight from Amsterdam to Detroit on Christmas Day 2009. In October 2011, when he pled guilty to his involvement in the plot, Abdulmutallab stated, "I was greatly inspired to participate in jihad by the lectures of the great and rightly guided mujahedeen who is alive, Sheikh Anwar al-Awlaki, may Allah preserve him and his family and give them victory, Amin, and Allah knows best." A U.S. official, who spoke on the condition of anonymity because of the topic's sensitivity, told The Washington Post that Awlaki was the first U.S. citizen added to a list of suspected terrorists the CIA is authorized to kill.

Samir Khan—before he was killed in the same alleged airstrike as Awlaki—served as the editor of Inspire magazine, launched in 2010 by AQAP. Inspire has been described as "a slick magazine for jihadists ... that featured political and how-to articles written in a comfortable American vernacular." The magazine is intended to attract would-be jihadists in the West.

The Saudi-born Khan lived in Queens, New York, and Charlotte, North Carolina. He radicalized after the Al Qaeda attacks on September 11, 2001, and moved with his parents to Charlotte in 2004. He left Charlotte in 2009 and joined AQAP in Yemen. Prior to leaving the United States, Khan had gained some notoriety as a jihadist blogger and as creator of the online magazine, Jihad Recollections—Inspire's forerunner.

Reportedly, Khan and his online publications may have influenced homegrown jihadists.

- In November 2012, Miguel Alejandro Santana Vidriales was arrested for allegedly plotting with three others to join either Al Qaeda or the Taliban in Afghanistan. According to DOJ, he had read articles from Inspire about bomb making and weapons training.
- In July 2011, U.S. Army private Naser Abdo was arrested near Fort Hood in Texas for allegedly plotting a shooting spree and bombing in the area. Abdo intended to kill soldiers near the same place where Army Major Nidal Hasan reportedly killed 13 individuals in 2009. Federal officials noted that Abdo also possessed an article on how to construct an explosive device, among other items. The article was from Inspire.
- In November 2010, Mohamed Osman Mohamud, a Somali-born naturalized U.S. citizen, was arrested as part of an FBI sting operation, moments after he tried to detonate a van he believed was packed with explosives in Portland's Pioneer Courthouse Square. According to DOJ, Mohamud wrote articles for Khan's first magazine, Jihad Recollections.

Aside from editing Inspire Khan also contributed to it. Additionally, the magazine included commentary from Awlaki and another American Al Qaeda propagandist, Adam Gadahn.

Adam Gadahn has served as a translator and English-language propagandist for Al Qaeda and has been charged with treason by the United States. He has appeared in a number of the organization's videos widely circulated on the Web. Born in 1978 and raised in California, Gadahn converted to Islam as a teenager and moved to Pakistan by 1999. As a young convert in California, Gadahn was influenced by two jihadists involved with a discussion group he attended. One of these men also likely introduced him into Al

Qaeda circles in Pakistan and Afghanistan. In 2004, he first appeared in a widely released video threatening attacks on the United States, and in another dispatch he urged Americans to convert to Islam. In a video posted on June 20, 2010, Gadahn rails against President Barack Obama, describing him as "treacherous, bloodthirsty, and narrow-minded."

Omar Hammami, also known as "Abu Mansour al-Amriki," is originally from Daphne, Alabama. In 2007, he emerged as a key international intermediary for the Somali terrorist group al-Shabaab but has since broken with the group. The son of a Syrian-born father and an American mother, he has been featured in propagandist videos distributed by the group. In one he instructs recruits in urban warfare. Zachary Chesser saw Hammami as a role model. He even imitated Hammami's adoption of "al-Amriki" (the American) as part of his own jihadist name— "Abu Talhah Al-Amrikee." Somali officials tie Hammami to al-Shabaab recruitment and financial management. He may also have led battlefield skirmishes. On August 5, 2010, DOJ unsealed a 2009 superseding indictment against him. In October 2011, Hammami released a video calling Western Muslims to violent jihad.

As a child, Hammami lived between the Christian world of his mother and the Muslim beliefs of his father. He converted to Islam in high school, and while a student at the University of South Alabama, he led the Muslim Student Association and began adhering to Salafi doctrine. His Salafism allegedly sprang in part from a desire to rebel against his father. In 2002, he dropped out of school, and by 2004 he had found his way to Toronto, Canada, where American combat in Iraq and Afghanistan encouraged him to reconsider his nonviolent Salafi views. One of his friends alleges that Hammami began surfing the Web for information on jihad at this time. While in Canada, he married a Somali woman. In 2005 they moved to Cairo, and by late 2006 he was in Somalia pursuing violent jihad.

Social Networks

Social networks appear to be central to the radicalization process and to terrorist plots as well. Networks can be actual groups—encompassing intimate kinship ties, bonds of friendship, links forged in student associations, or cliques tied to radical mosques. They may also be virtual and fostered by the Internet. Group loyalties can form around jihadist messages entailing moral outrage over the perceived suffering of fellow Muslims and a sense that the West is at war with Islam. Networks help place these messages into the context of an individual's personal experiences.

Beyond the radicalization experience, the development and strengthening of affective ties with like-minded individuals may play a prominent role in the formation of terrorist groups. According to The New York Times, Faisal Shahzad befriended Shahid Hussain, a fellow Pakistani, while the two were enrolled at the University of Bridgeport in Connecticut in the early 2000s. Shahzad appears to have started to radicalize in the United States by 2004. During trips to Pakistan prior to his attempted Times Square bombing, Shahzad reestablished ties with Hussain. The latter had also returned to Pakistan. Together, the two grew more militant, especially when in 2007 Pakistani forces stormed Lal Masjid, the "Red Mosque," a center of Islamic fundamentalism. The two friends socialized with a third individual, Muhammad Shouaib Mughal. The three were keenly interested in global jihad. Mughal eventually trained with the Pakistani Taliban, the Tehrik-e-Taliban Pakistan. He brought Shahzad and Hussain into the group's camps for training in 2009.

Intermediaries within Networks

Social networks often feature their own internal intermediaries or charismatic leaders. In 2009 and 2010, Daniel Boyd and several others were indicted on terrorism charges. From November 2006 to 2009, Boyd, a charismatic leader, led a conspiracy involving a network of associates that included his sons Dylan and Zakariya to radicalize, recruit, and assist young men interested in terrorism. The conspiracy also purportedly included fundraising for and provision of material support to terrorist groups. Using stories of his past violent jihadist exploits in Pakistan and Afghanistan, Boyd recruited and trained individuals for violent terrorist activity, according to FBI courtroom testimony. From 1989-1992, Boyd supposedly trained at terrorist camps in Afghanistan and Pakistan and may have been a fighter in Afghanistan. In 2011, the Boyds pled guilty to charges related to the case.

Jihadi Cool

Recent plots suggest that intermediaries and social networks can emphasize persuasive messages featuring elements outside of jihadist religious rhetoric. Adventurism and romanticized notions of revolution seem to have some prominence in the radicalization process. A desire to protect the Ummah against what he perceived as Western incursion may have been more important to Faisal Shahzad than more overtly religious rhetoric. Terrorist recruiters are also promoting "jihadi cool" by producing rap videos advocating terrorism and releasing them on the Web. In 2007, Cabdulaahi Ahmed Faarax, a charismatic recruiter for al-Shabaab, enticed young Somali men in Minnesota with a jihadi cool message replete with war stories. According to federal court documents, he emphasized jihad but also stressed the sense of brotherhood he had experienced while fighting. He detailed his own experiences in guerilla combat and reassured his listeners that it was fun and not to be afraid. He further underscored that recruits would get the chance to use firearms.

"Jihadi cool" may have also played a role in pushing five young Northern Virginia Muslim men to travel in 2009 to Pakistan, where they were arrested for allegedly attempting to join jihadist organizations in the region. On June 24, 2010, the five were convicted on terrorism charges and sentenced to 10 years in prison in Pakistan. Muslim leaders from Alexandria, Virginia, indicated that they had no inkling of radicalization among the five. Abroad, as early as 2006, Dutch officials noted an "intensification of radicalization tendencies" among young Muslims in the Netherlands and a perception that jihad was "cool."

The Internet

The Web may also play a role in the experiences of many would-be and actual terrorists, just as it does in the lives of so many people. The interactivity of chat rooms, blogs, social networking sites, message boards, video hosting sites, and e-mail blurs the lines between readership and authorship that previous generations of terrorists and sympathizers encountered with pamphlets, newspapers, and newsletters. This blurring possibly encourages people who interact in such forums to more easily see themselves as part of broader jihadist movements and not just casual readers or online spectators. They may eventually engage in more substantive activity—actual propagandizing, financial support, or joining a terrorist network.

The Web's impact on individual would-be jihadists likely varies. In some cases accessing and engaging in online jihadist rhetoric possibly prods an individual toward violence. A study of 18,130 entries in 2,112 online discussions from more than 15 Arabic-language jihadist forums revealed that "[o]ne fifth of all discussions included an explicit call for more terrorist attacks.... Overall, two thirds of all discussions contain[ed] some form of call for or encouragement of terrorist attacks." One author asserts that Internet activity has been central in the development of a "self-starter" phenomenon and offers would-be violent jihadists what has been described as a "de-formalized" radicalization experience. "Self-starters" are groups that lack ties to major international terrorist networks and do not receive orders from such organizations. However, instances of solely virtual radicalization without face-to-face interaction seem to be rare. Most radicalization apparently requires experience with real-world social networks.

In other instances, terrorist "wannabes" may see online activity as a suitable substitute for direct violence and face-to-face contact with hardcore terrorists. Simply, individuals interested in violent jihad no longer have to physically travel to formal terrorist camps for indoctrination and rudimentary training. One author has also indicated that activity in the virtual realm may even play a much more profound, "cathartic" role, "allow[ing] aspiring jihadists to be part of the broader global jihad but crucially without engaging in direct violence." In essence, online activity may channel individuals away from the violent expression of their radical beliefs by allowing them to air their grievances. While such activity may be seen in terrorist circles as an increasingly legitimate option—instead of violent jihad—it does not come without repercussions for online supporters of terrorism. Individuals absorbed in such activities may run afoul of law enforcement for materially aiding terrorist organizations.

Regardless of whether jihadist online activity drives individuals to violence, the Internet arguably serves to spur radicalization in three ways. First, it allows jihadists to augment their messages with suggestive audio and video. Second, it makes it easier for would-be jihadists to find and interact with like-minded people around the world. Finally, the Internet "normal[izes] behaviors considered unacceptable or inappropriate in real-world environments." Terrorists publish rhetoric online that displaces culpability for their violent actions, which they commonly describe as inevitable responses when faced with overpowering enemies such as the West.

Radicalizing material is readily accessible online, as are virtual communities in which one can discuss violent jihad. Since 2005, video sharing websites have broadened the availability of jihadi video material. All sorts of other texts and graphic images supporting violent jihad exist on the Web, as does a great volume of tradecraft, such as bomb-making guides.

Social networking, now inherently part of the Internet, is likely a tool that is used in the development of contacts among radicalized individuals and recruitment into violent jihadist groups. Before he died, Anwar al-Awlaki circulated jihadist lectures online and managed his own popular Facebook page and blog. The five Virginia men convicted on June 24, 2010, in Pakistan on terrorism charges allegedly contacted an Al Qaeda operative via social networking websites, according to press coverage of their trial in the city of Sarghoda.

Another case that highlights Internet-related issues involves Tarek Mehanna. Mehanna, a pharmacist living with his parents in Sudbury, a wealthy Boston suburb, was arrested on terrorism charges in October 2009. Among other alleged activities, Mehanna and co-conspirators translated from Arabic to English documents advocating terrorism and posted them on jihadist websites. They viewed themselves as the "media wing" for Al Qaeda in Iraq. In the eyes of some terrorism experts, the Mehanna case highlights the shift away from core members of Al Qaeda toward Internet-inspired, homegrown radicalization and self-starting terrorists. The Mehanna case emphasizes how recruiters from foreign terrorist organizations no longer seem necessary to shepherd radicalized individuals into terrorist training abroad. (Mehanna, himself, allegedly tried but failed to get into such camps.) Sam Rascoff, a former New York Police Department terrorism specialist, notes that "there is a sense that these guys are radicalizing on their own." Frank J. Cilluffo notes that the Web has supplanted mosques as a recruitment venue, especially as terrorists try to draw Westerners into their organizations. In December 2011, Mehanna was convicted of "conspiracy to provide material support to al-Qaeda; providing material support to terrorists (and conspiracy to do so); conspiracy to commit murder in a foreign country; conspiracy to make false statements to the FBI, and two counts of making false statements."

Aside from its possible impact on the radicalization process, the Internet potentially offers terrorists operational capabilities. Its decentralized form mirrors the flattened, cellular structures of most terrorist organizations. Among other things, it could help them to collect intelligence about their targets, communicate with one another, propagandize, recruit foot soldiers, provide training, raise funds, and communicate operational direction.

JAILHOUSE JIHADISM

In the last several years, terrorism experts and some Members of Congress have shown interest in jihadist prison radicalization. But the research is decidedly unclear regarding the threat posed by radicalization behind bars. A scholar of the prison phenomenon in the United Kingdom notes that jail time potentially accelerates the radicalization process for many individuals. Prison brings together disaffected people who may be receptive to anti-social messages offering "clear, albeit intolerant, solutions to complex problems of identity and belonging." Experts have sounded warnings about the unknown level of threat posed by radicalization and terrorist recruitment in U.S. jails.

Others are quick to point out, however, that while conversion to Islam and radicalization occur among incarcerated populations, the jump to terrorist plotting in the United States is rare. This is at least partly due to prison officials' efforts to counter jailhouse jihadism, according to a study involving interviews with 210 prison officials and 270 inmates mostly from state correctional systems. The Federal Bureau of Prisons acknowledges the possibility of inmate radicalization but "do[es] not believe that there is widespread terrorist-inspired radicalization or recruiting in federal prisons," where between 5% and 6% of prisoners identify as Muslims. Based on CRS analysis of the 63 violent jihadist plots since 9/11, only one clearly involved radicalization in prison. A study of 117 homegrown jihadist terrorists from the United States and United Kingdom found seven cases in which prison had a significant impact on an individual's radicalization process.

The lack of conclusive prison-based radicalization among the jihadist terrorism plots and foiled attacks since 9/11 suggests that the threat emanating from prisons does not seem as substantial as some experts may fear. One case, commonly known as the Newburgh Four plot, included at least two individuals who converted to Islam while in state prison, but it remains unclear whether they radicalized behind bars.

The most prominent post-9/11 example of domestic violent jihadist activity inspired in prison implicated the group, Jamiyyat Ul-Islam Is-Saheeh (JIS or the "Authentic Assembly of God"). Kevin James, Levar Washington, Gregory Patterson, and Hammad Samana were arrested and charged in August 2005 for their participation in a plot to attack Jewish institutions and other targets in the Los Angeles area, including synagogues, the Israeli Consulate, Los Angeles International Airport (LAX), U.S. military recruiting offices, and military bases.

According to DOJ, the incarcerated James founded JIS in 1997 based on his interpretation of Islam. His views are apparent in several of his prison writings, including a 104-page document titled the "JIS Protocol." In this document, James supports the establishment of an Islamic Caliphate in the United States and describes "Jihad [as] the only true 'anti-terrorist action[,]' a defensive battle against the aggression of theological imposters led by Zionism." The document also advocated the killing of "lawful targets," including non-Muslims. Reportedly, James met Washington in prison in 2004 and introduced him to JIS and its beliefs. After his release, Washington, who converted to Islam while he was in prison, recruited Patterson, an employee at LAX, and Samana at the Jamaat-E-Masijudal mosque in Inglewood, California, where they all worshipped. Both Patterson and Samana swore allegiance to Washington and pledged to serve as "mujahideen," according to court documents. One study has pointed out that James' radicalization manifested itself in prison but may not have been heavily influenced by his experiences behind bars. Two points suggest that factors outside of prison may have at least partly driven his radicalization: his "JIS Protocol" does not focus on jailhouse conditions, and his father had been a member of the Black Panther Party.

OSAMA BIN LADEN: JIHAD AGAINST 'JEWS AND CRUSADERS'

Osama bin Laden was the last of a trio of charismatic Arab leaders who emerged in the second half of the 20th century to challenge the dominion of Western values and influence in the Arab world. If Gamal Abdul Nasser in Egypt, Saddam Hussein in Iraq and Osama bin Laden in Saudi Arabia and Afghanistan all enjoyed a measure of success, they ultimately brought catastrophe on their supporters. All three sought, with varying degrees of sincerity, to assuage the sense of injury that can be traced back, in the first instance, to the Allies' betrayal of Arab hopes at the collapse of the Ottoman Empire at the end of the First World War. Bin Laden sought to extend his constituency to the entire Muslim world and found adherents as far east as the Philippines and as far west as the continental United States.

All three overestimated their own strength and underestimated that of their foes. All ended up at odds with the greatest power on earth, the United States, and, through their recklessness, brought Western armies back into the Middle East. The popular uprisings this year in Tunisia, Egypt and Syria suggest that younger Arabs may have turned their backs on all three men and concluded that the path to Arab independence and dignity runs not through the suicide belt but the ballot box.

Six feet three inches in height, Osama bin Laden was a handsome man. Visitors remarked on his beautiful manners and quiet speech, his accurate Arabic free of seminary affectation, his Hatim-like generosity with his inherited fortune, his hypochondria and good humour. Kalashnikov semi-automatic weapon at the ready, a master of international commerce and satellite communication, Bin Laden seemed to embody a new and romantic model of Arab masculinity. Unlike many Muslim revolutionaries, he did not waste his breath on Western social customs or in hectoring respectable women. While Bin Laden sought to imitate the Prophet of Islam in his personal conduct, his unconscious models were the anti-colonial revolutionaries of the 1960s. His love of mountains, "clean air you can breathe without humiliation", was European, even touristic. In retrospect, he was a synthetic creation of two cultures at the point of collision, a sort of Arabian Crazy Horse.

Bin Laden's message combined the pious xenophobia of Saudi Arabia with the brutality of the Islamic movements of Egypt and Algeria. Though his purpose was to seize power in the Arab capitals, such as Cairo and Riyadh, his principal target was not the Arab kings or dynastic presidents but their ally, the United States. The US was for him an idol to be smashed, like the colossal Buddhas in the Bamiyan Valley destroyed by his Afghan allies, the Pashtun movement known as the Taliban, or the twin towers of the World Trade Centre in New York.

Muslim rulers, including those of his native Saudi Arabia, were to him merely apostates deserving of death. The Islamic government he financed for the Taliban, which reduced 1,400 years of Islamic civilisation to a gruesome moral police known as amr bil-maaroof wa hayy an al-munkar [Encouraging the Proper and Discouraging the Improper] was never likely to appeal to the Arabic- or Persian-speaking mainstreams. The brutality of his self-styled successors, such as Abu Musab al-Zarqawi in Iraq and Jordan, threatened a sectarian bloodbath that revolted Arab opinion.

In reality, Bin Laden's world was a Manichean waste in which a self-professed vanguard of Muslims battled "Jews and Crusaders" to annihilation.

Bin Laden's preferred weapon, which he did not originate but deployed to catastrophic effect, was the suicide attack. In the course of the 1990s, Bin Laden and his Egyptian allies built up a network of cells in the Middle East and Africa of men willing to give their lives to kill those whom they perceived to be enemies of Islam. The older of these were so-called Arab Afghans: foreign veterans of the war in Afghanistan who had been stranded at the Soviet withdrawal in 1989 with a taste for soldiering but no cause.

The suicide bomber had both tactical and propaganda merits. A cause for which a young man will murder women and children and also die must, self-evidently, be a very important one. Meanwhile, at each action the perpetrating cell destroyed itself, leaving investigators baffled at the chain of responsibility. The devastating potential of the suicide attack was revealed on 11 September 2001.

Tactical patience was not matched by strategic caution. Bin Laden, his Egyptian allies and the Taliban were unprepared for US retaliation. While many Arabs drew a sort of bleak satisfaction at the carnage on 11 September, they saw what its outcome would be and, once the war turned against Bin Laden, occupied themselves with other matters.

Once the American assault on Afghanistan began on 7 October 2001, both the Taliban and their Arab allies melted away, though Bin Laden managed to make his escape from the Tora Bora mountains of south-eastern Afghanistan some time in December. The US invasion of Iraq in 2003 offered al-Qa'ida an opportunity to regroup in a new territory, but the opportunity was squandered in an orgy of sectarian murder.

Osama bin Mohammed bin Awad bin Laden was born in Riyadh, the desert capital of Saudi Arabia, in 1957. His family, which hailed from the village of Rubat in Wadi Hadhramawt in Yemen, had come to the newly created Kingdom in 1930. His father, Mohammed bin Laden, founded a contracting company which prospered under the patronage of the Saudi royal family, building palaces, highways and works to accommodate the pilgrims at the two holy cities of Mecca and Medina. Osama, who was no doubt named after the Prophet's general Osama bin Zeid, was brought up first in Medina and then in Jeddah.

His father was the very model of a pious Arabian businessman. A pioneer of aviation in the country, he once claimed that his aircraft permitted him to pray in all three of Islam's holiest mosques in a single day. He died in an air accident in 1967. According to a historian of the Arabian merchants Michael Field, King Faisal banned the young Bin Ladens from flying their own aircraft: something of an omen, in retrospect. Osama's elder brother Salem, who built up the multi-billion-dollar business now known as the Saudi Binladin Group, himself died at the controls of a small aircraft in Texas in 1988.

Unlike Salem, who was educated in England, married an Englishwoman and charmed the expatriate society of Jeddah, Osama once said he gravitated towards Islamic opposition from as early as 1973. Ever since the 1960s, the Saudi universities had given refuge to Muslim Brothers fleeing persecution in the secular Arab republics, notably Egypt. At King Abdul Aziz University in Jeddah, where he studied for a degree in economics and public administration, Osama may have come into contact with Abdullah Azzam, the Palestinian Islamist, and Mohammed Qutb, brother of the radical philosopher Sayyid Qutb and a leading influence on the Egyptian Islamic underground that was about to break into the open with the assassination of President Anwar Sadat in 1981. Osama was to join forces with Azzam in Peshawar in recruiting Arab Afghans and later amalgamate with the Egyptian group responsible for Sadat's murder, Islamic Jihad.

At the close of 1979 (or rather the opening of the Muslim year 1400), Saudi Arabia was convulsed first by the capture of the Grand Mosque in Mecca by millenarian insurgents and, in the next month, by the Soviet invasion of Afghanistan. By his own account, Bin Laden was in Afghanistan within a few weeks of the invasion, and the next decade was to see him shuttling back and forth, marshalling his family's international contacts, its expertise in explosives and military construction, and its money in the support of the Afghan resistance. In 1984, he set up with Abdullah Azzam in Peshawar the so-called Services Office, or Maktab al-Khidamat, to recruit and ship Arab volunteers into Afghanistan. He struck people at that time as sincere and vigorous, but no leader of fighting men.

In 1986, he founded a camp in Paktia province in Afghanistan, al-Ansar (the name for the Prophet's companions in Medina) which was attacked by the Soviets the following spring. Bin Laden's conduct at that battle, and again in fighting for Jalalabad in 1989, gave him a reputation as something more than a builder and financier.

Despite ill-health, which caused him to walk with the help of a stick, Bin Laden at that period gave an air of omnipotence. He later told Peter Arnett of CNN: "The glory and myth of the superpower was destroyed not only in my mind, but also in the minds of all Muslims." In Peshawar, he came into contact with the Egyptian revolutionaries of Islamic Jihad, including Ayman al-Zawahiri, who had come to Peshawar to work as a physician among the Afghan refugees. In 1988 or 1989, as the Soviets prepared to withdraw from Afghanistan and Azzam was assassinated, Bin Laden and al-Zawahiri founded al-Qa'ida (The Base). While its original purpose is not clear, al-Qa'ida developed into an organisation to deploy the Arab Afghans – those latter-day Wild Geese – on his enemies outside Afghanistan.

Back in Saudi Arabia, at the age of 32, Bin Laden came into conflict with the House of Saud. With Saddam's invasion of Kuwait in the summer of 1990, Bin Laden volunteered the services of the Afghan veterans to expel the Iraqis, as they had the Russians from Afghanistan. The Saudi royal family instead invoked the help of the US, which began despatching troops to the kingdom on 7 August 1990. For Prince Turki al-Faisal, the son of the old King who was director of Saudi general intelligence and had co-ordinated Saudi support for the Afghan resistance, this was the turning point: "I saw radical changes in his personality," he told the Arab News of Jeddah in November 2001, "as he changed from a calm, peaceful and gentle man interested in helping Muslims into a person who believed that he would be able to amass and command an army to liberate Kuwait. It revealed his arrogance and his haughtiness."

Osama bitterly opposed the presence of Christian forces in Arabia, and his opposition was echoed by several popular preachers. Frustrated, in 1991, he moved to Sudan, where he found a welcome from Hassan al-Turabi, the founder and leader of the National Islamic Front.

While in Sudan, Bin Laden set up commercial enterprises, none of which appears to have prospered, while preparing his first action against American interests, with the bombing of two hotels housing US servicemen in Aden in December 1992. He was also to claim credit for training the Somali insurgents that brought down two US Sikorsky Black Hawk helicopters in Mogadishu the following October, killing 18 Americans. The sudden US withdrawal from Somalia caused him to jeer at the "weakness, frailty and cowardice of US troops". The first bombing of the World Trade Centre by the Baluchi explosives expert Ramzi Yousef in 1993, and the attacks on US servicemen in Riyadh in 1995 and Dhahran in 1996, may or may not have had his direct involvement.

In 1994, Osama was stripped of his Saudi citizenship and disowned by his family. Two years later, the Sudanese were seeking to be rid of him, and in May 1996 he returned with his three wives and some of his children to Jalalabad, which fell to the Taliban that August. In November, Abdul Bari Atwan, editor of the London newspaper Al-Quds Al-Arabi, visited Bin Laden in his cave hide-out, surrounded by grenades and books of devotion and theology. Early the next year, Bin Laden moved to Kandahar, where he became friendly with Mullah Omar, the leader of the Taliban, and gained a mysterious command over the newly acclaimed Prince of the Faithful.

On 23 February 1998, he announced the creation of a World Islamic Front for Jihad against Jews and Crusaders. In rhyming Arabic prose which has been admired by some connoisseurs, Bin Laden, Ayman al-Zawahiri and other radicals accused the US of occupying and despoiling the "sacred lands of Islam" and issued this fatwa, or legal ruling: "It is an individual obligation for every

Muslim who is able to do so in any country to kill and fight Americans and their allies, whether civilians or military..." On 7 August, at 10.30am, a lorry containing hundreds of pounds of TNT and aluminium nitrate blew up in the car park of the US embassy in central Nairobi, killing 201 Kenyans and 12 Americans. Nine minutes later, a second suicide bomb exploded at the embassy in Dar es Salaam in Tanzania, killing 11 Tanzanians, almost all of them Muslim.

Five years of planning went into the suicide attacks, code-named Holy Kaaba (Kenya) and al-Aqsa (Tanzania). Their complexity, scope, precision and indiscriminate savagery set an ominous precedent that the Clinton administration did not take to heart. Instead, the US fired dozens of cruise missiles at al-Qa'ida camps in the Khost district of eastern Afghanistan, and a Khartoum factory. The Afghan missiles had no effect except to infuriate Mullah Omar and embarrass Prince Turki's negotiations in Kandahar to have Bin Laden extradited to Saudi Arabia. By the middle of 1999, Bin Laden was exulting in the Nairobi bombing: "God's grace to Muslims that the blow was successful and great."

An attack on the American mainland to coincide with the new Christian millennium was frustrated. But on 12 October of the next year, two suicide bombers brought a dinghy alongside the destroyer USS Cole in Aden harbour, and detonated it, killing 17 sailors. By the beginning of 2001, reports began to surface in London and elsewhere that al-Qa'ida would soon launch another long-prepared attack. But nothing had prepared the world for the airliners that drove into the towers of the World Trade Centre, killing almost 3,000 people. It is possible that Bin Laden expected, even invited, a US assault on Afghanistan. On 9 September, two days before the suicide attacks on the World Trade Centre and Pentagon, two Moroccan Arabs posing as journalists blew up Ahmad Shah Massoud, the United Front commander most feared by the Taliban.

Of his escape from Afghanistan and life in hiding, we know little. His communications with the outside world by means of audio- and video-tape slowed to a trickle, and by 2007, dried up. Even before then, he seemed to be commenting on events rather than initiating them. In any case, the cause of violent jihad had long passed to new recruits, many of them European Muslims of the second generation, to whom Osama was an inspiration rather than a guide.

In his violent career, his fatwas and his interviews, Osama bin Laden attempted to portray Islam as a civilisation that had no choice but to murder, or kill itself. Whether his death has broken the spell of this nihilism, or inaugurates a new cycle of violence, is a question that may be asked but not yet answered. While the West seems determined, through its military actions in Iraq, Afghanistan and Libya, to give the Arabs and Muslims new cause for grievance, the "Arab Spring" may tell us that history has moved on.

AL-QAEDA IN PAKISTAN AND AFGHANISTAN

The importance of Afghanistan and Pakistan for al-Qaeda is clear from Bin Laden's letters that were seized in his hideout after he was killed, and from the location of the organization's headquarters in Waziristan in Pakistan. The organization fought in Pakistan at the side of the Pakistani Taliban and members of the Haqqani network in cooperation with local and foreign terrorist organizations engaged in the struggle against the Pakistani army in the tribal area in Waziristan province. Al-Qaeda's contribution to the fghting was in separate brigade frameworks operating as part of the Taliban forces under the designation of Lashkar al-Zil name and as part of Brigade 313, which is considered the military wing of al-Qaeda in Pakistan and was under the command of Ilyas Kashmiri until he (allegedly) was killed on June 3, 2011.

At the same time, over the past two years al-Qaeda has been engaged in fghting with the Taliban against US and NATO forces operating in Afghanistan in large numbers on a major scale, especially following the surge ordered by President Obama in 2010. A large percentage of the important senior commanders in this area were killed by American UAVs; the most prominent of them were Mustafa Abu al-Yazid, considered one of al-Qaeda's three most important commanders and spokesmen, who previously commanded the organization's activity in Afghanistan and was responsible for its fnances; Atiya Abd al-Rahman, one of Bin Laden's associates in the leadership, who served as his most senior liaison while Bin Laden remained in hiding in Abbottabad and was responsible for transmitting Bin Laden's instructions to the organization's operatives and ensuring their implementation; and Abu Yahya al-Libi, formerly a senior commander in the Libyan Islamic Fighting Group, who was arrested in Afghanistan by American forces in 2003, escaped from Bagram Prison in 2005, and became one of al-Qaeda's leading propagandists There was a $1 million reward offered for his capture. After Bin Laden was killed, he was appointed second in command to al-Zawahiri and chief of staff.

Despite the ongoing offensive against it, however, al-Qaeda has continued to aid the Taliban and the Haqqani network in their struggle against the coalition forces, drawing on its vast experience in planning and executing suicide bombings and high level attacks. The organization also continues to promote its militant agenda by training foreign operatives to take part in jihad and prepare them for participation in the violent campaign against the Western forces in the region. In effect, the organization wants them to accumulate experience and operational know how that they will be able to use upon their return to their countries of origin to carry out terrorist attacks on behalf of al-Qaeda or some of the independent terrorist networks operating in the name of global jihad. At the same time, the organization's efforts to launch terrorist attacks abroad continue, even though for a long time these attempts have not been successful, due to thorough preventive activity by security services around the world. Nevertheless, Shukrijumah, the current commander of the organization's overseas terrorist apparatus and an experienced and well-known operative who was responsible for a series of unsuccessful attacks in the UK and Scandinavia, is still alive. With other experienced surviving terrorists and reinforcements of new battle hardened members flling the ranks, al-Zawahiri is thus able to make further attempts at showcase attacks in accordance with al-Qaeda's modus operandi.

AL-QAEDA HEJAZ

The most senior and active partner of global al-Qaeda is al-Qaeda Hejaz. Founded in 2009 as a merger of the Saudi Arabian branch with its Yemeni counterpart, the organization is headed by Nasir al-Wuhayshi, who was Bin Laden's personal secretary for many years. Since the merger, al-Qaeda has carried out deadly terrorist attacks in Yemen and Saudi Arabia. By conducting an uncompromising anti-terrorist campaign, Saudi Arabia succeeded in killing most of the organization's members, while those who survived escaped to Yemen, a much more favorable environment for them.

Yemen's unstable government, dispersed tribal structure, and topography have enabled al-Qaeda to establish itself in the Hejaz and operate around the country relatively freely, particularly in the south, where control exercised by the central government, located in Sana'a, is weak.

When the upheaval in the Arab world reached Yemen, President Ali Abdullah Saleh, who ruled the country for 33 years, was forced out of offce and fed the country. In February 2012 he was succeeded by Vice President Abd Rabbuh Mansur Hadi. The new President encountered many diffculties in establishing his rule in Yemen, as a result of internal disputes between him and followers of the ousted leader. Adding to his leadership challenges were the bitterness among the Shiite Houthis in the north and activity by al-Qaeda and Ansar al-Sharia, an organization founded in 2012 as al-Qaeda's political front in order to create a more moderate image for joint activity. The goal of this activity was to take over Yemen or part of it in order to establish a state ruled by Islamic religious law.

Information seized with the death of Bin Laden reveals that Bin Laden warned the organization's commander in Yemen against attacks against the army and friction with tribesmen, and urged him to concentrate on attacks on American targets in order to win public sympathy and support. Yet despite this directive, over the past year the organization has focused its activity against the government and the army. Al-Qaeda conducted several attacks on Yemeni army bases, killing many soldiers, and carried out a dozen suicide attacks - one of the calling cards of al-Qaeda and its affliates – against administration and security forces personnel. In one of these suicide attacks, a lone suicide attacker succeeded in killing approximately one hundred soldiers and wounding dozens more. In its operations, the organization exposed the central government's weakness and inability to control the country effectively, while forcing President Hadi to reorganize the armed forces in order to liberate and regain control in cities conquered by al-Qaeda in the southern part of the country. With the help of American aid in money, training, instruction, and direct operational assistance in the form of armed UAVs, the Yemeni army managed to deal the organization and its senior operational personnel a severe blow. Anwar al-Awlaki, one of the organization's leading propagandists, who was accused of direct involvement in terrorism, was killed in an air attack in September 2011, together with Samir Khan, editor of the organization's online mouthpiece, *Inspire*. Fahd al-Quso, who escaped from prison in Yemen after taking part in the 2000 attack on the destroyer *Cole* in Aden Port, was killed in March 2012. Al-Quso headed a squad that planned to send a suicide terrorist in April 2012 to detonate a sophisticated bomb on an American plane while in American airspace, a continuation of previous terrorist attempts by the organization to blow up airplanes en route to the US.

Full scale fghting in Yemen between the authorities and al-Qaeda and Ansar al-Sharia is ongoing. It appears that despite the success achieved by the Yemeni army and security forces in recent months in pushing al-Qaeda out of the cities they had taken, attacking their bases, and killing their personnel, the organization still enjoys much strength and can be expected to continue its activity in and outside of Yemen with the active support of al-Zawahiri. Furthermore, given the support from al-Zawahiri and al-Qaeda and the recruitment of foreign volunteers, which the organization trains to fght alongside its forces and in other jihad theaters, the organization remains a signifcant threat to the stability of the Yemeni government and poses a dangerous security risk for the US and its allies overseas.

AL-QAEDA MAGHREB AND GLOBAL JIHAD FACTIONS IN NORTH AND WEST AFRICA

The al-Qaeda Maghreb organization, which merged with the central al-Qaeda in 2007, has also adopted the strategies and operating methods of the parent organization. The organization focuses its attacks on senior government offcials, the military, and targets identifed with the West. It has carried out a series of suicide missions and also developed expertise in kidnapping Western civilians, which reaped large sums that helped fnance operations. During most of its existence, al-Qaeda has operated principally in Algeria, but it has also sent operatives to other countries, and maintains close connections with the Salaf jihád organizations in Morocco, Libya, Mauritania, and now Mali as well. Indeed, in recent years, as a result of Algeria's tough and effective policy against terrorism in active cooperation with other Maghreb countries, the organization's activity has declined in Algeria itself, forcing it to divert its efforts to other felds of operation, mainly in northern Mali, which has recently become its most important center of activity. In addition, following the coup staged by the military junta in Mali last March, global jihad forces streamed into the region. Besides al-Qaeda Maghreb personnel who escaped from Algeria, these included fghters who escaped from Niger, Mauritania, Libya, and members of the Boko Haram organization in Nigeria seeking to take an active part in the fghting.

In Mali, al-Qaeda Maghreb cooperates with a number of terrorist organizations, including MOJWA and Ansar al-Din, which work together to establish a base for global jihad activity. For example, Ansar al-Din, backed by al-Qaeda Maghreb forces and other global jihad operatives, took control of a number of key cities in northern Mali, with their main goal being the founding of an Islamic state based on *sharia*. As part of this takeover, a meeting took place in April 2012 in Timbuktu, one of the largest cities in northern Mali, which fell to the jihadists. Al-Qaeda Maghreb leaders met with their counterparts from Ansar al-Din, supported by local religious fgures, and the Ansar al-Din commander announced the appointment of al-Qaeda Maghreb commander Yahya Abou Al-Hammam as emir of Timbuktu. The region has since become the permanent residence of the leaders of this "coalition," which controls two thirds of northern Mali. A systematic terror campaign against the civilian population is currently underway, which has damaged the ancient holy shrines there. Security has declined precipitously, due in part to a fow of armaments of various types from Qaddaf's arsenal that fell into al-Qaeda hands. In spite of this cooperation, internal power struggles have prevented the terrorist coalition from reaching agreement and acting jointly to achieve their goals through coordinated activity. At times sharp differences of opinion, originating in national and or ethnic differences, such as between the Algerian "elite," which includes "Afghan alumni," and the Islamists in Mali and Nigeria, constitute an obstacle to coordinated joint activity aimed at achieving their Islamic vision in Africa.

Following the fall of the Qaddaf regime in Libya, Libyan global jihad operatives, who formerly operated in the framework of the Libyan Islamic Fighting Group, stepped up their activity. Since the uprising they have adopted the name Ansar al-Sharia in order to camoufage their links to al-Qaeda. The most notorious operation by global jihad elements operating in Libya since Qaddaf was deposed was the assassination of the US ambassador and three US consulate employees in Benghazi on September 11, 2012. According to the accumulated evidence, elements close to al-Qaeda in Ansar al-Sharia and former members of the Libyan Islamic Fighting Group carried out the attack. This strike was apparently planned under the guidance of al-Zawahiri, and according to those who assumed responsibility for it, was designed to avenge the killing of Abu Yahya al-Libi in the UAV attack in Waziristan.

The rising threat to regional stability posed by al-Qaeda Maghreb and the coalition of local terrorist organizations led to a major investment of resources and political, intelligence, and military cooperation between countries in the region to combat the growing danger of terrorism in the Sahel and Mali, and prevent its spread to other countries in the region. In December 2011, Algerian forces crossed the northern border with Mali in order to assist the local army in dealing with elements identifed with al-Qaeda. In June 2012, the Organization of African Unity considered the possibility of military intervention in Mali. In August 2012, at the security conference on the Sahel that took place in Niger, representatives from Algeria, Mali, Mauritania, and Niger expressed concern about the terrorist threat from Islamist parties in northern Mali to the neighboring countries, and called for active intervention by the international community in northern Mali. In early October 2012, the UN Security Council decided that in order to eliminate the threat of terrorism, a comprehensive military operation by the member countries of the Economic Community of West African States (ECOWAS) was needed. American security agencies, which reassessed the situation with regard to the danger of terrorism to Western targets in these countries and the region as a whole, stated that the US was likely to offer military assistance and even act independently to expel al-Qaeda operatives who found refuge in northern Mali.

AL-QAEDA AND GLOBAL JIHAD ELEMENTS IN THE ARAB LEVANT AND THE MIDDLE EAST

The importance of the Arab Levant in Muslim history has given it a special status in the aspirations of al-Qaeda and its affliates to establish the Islamic caliphate in one of the countries in the region. Hence the supreme importance that al-Qaeda attaches to the fghting that developed in Iraq following the American occupation. The organization invested much effort and extensive resources to take advantage of the upheaval to reinvigorate global jihad. Bin Laden, and especially al-Zawahiri, who was already the organization's chief spokesman when Bin Laden was alive, encouraged the operatives in Iraq to continue the struggle to infict severe damage on the US and its allies, and supported the establishment of the Islamic country in Iraq declared by al-Qaeda Iraq in 2006.

A concrete expression of the importance attributed to Iraq by the organization appeared in a letter from al-Zawahiri to al-Zarqawi, who was the organization's frst "emir" in this country, and who was known for his murderous actions against his opponents, including Muslims, especially Shiites. The letter emphasizes the importance of preserving the gains already scored by al-Qaeda in Iraq, and requested that al-Zarqawi refrain from alienating the local population in order to avoid losing their support. Over the years al-Qaeda leaders have continued to support the struggle in Iraq, and they appointed fgures they trusted to replace Zarqawi when he was killed in an American attack. Since he assumed his chief role, al-Zawahiri has also made statements in support of the local organization's activity and stressed its great importance. In a speech celebrating the eleventh anniversary of the terrorist attacks in the US, he claimed that the US had been defeated and in effect "was running away for its life, leaving behind a government of puppets to rule in Iraq, a government that was now feeling the might of the mujahidin...Allah gave them the honor of leading the local struggle and defeating the American ambition of controlling the Middle East."

Iraq is no longer the main theater of jihad for al-Qaeda and its affliates that it was when foreign forces, headed by the US, occupied the country in 2003. Even after the last American soldier left Iraq on December 18, 2011, however, and despite President Obama's statement that the purpose for which the US had entered Iraq had been achieved – the overthrow of Saddam Hussein and the establishment of a stable democracy in Iraq– terrorism was not eliminated from the country. In practice, al-Qaeda Iraq (operating under the title Islamic State of Iraq - ISI) and its affliates continue their activity. They focus their attacks primarily on targets identifed with the current regime in Iraq, which is clearly under Shiite rule. Particularly in the second half of 2012, the organization carried out hundreds of attacks, principally in the cities of Baghdad, Nasiriyah, and Basra, where dozens of suicide bombings demonstrated the organization's ability to strike and disrupt the current regime's efforts to stabilize the country and control the level of inter-ethnic violence. The organization's attacks became even more frequent and daring in the fnal months of 2012. During several days of intense activity, simultaneous attacks were staged against army and police targets, combining multi-casualty suicide attacks with attacks aimed at freeing prisoners. For example, an armed squad broke into a prison in Tikrit on September 27, 2012 in a combined attack that included suicide terrorists and freed dozens of prisoners, some from al-Qaeda Iraq who had been sentenced to death. Furthermore, many of the organization's attacks were aimed directly at the Shiite civilian population – on Shiite holidays and against local Shiite leaders and institutions –

heightening anxiety about a renewal of the sectarian civil war in Iraq.

In tandem with its local activity, al-Qaeda Iraq has devoted resources and manpower to supporting the opposition forces in Syria. This new policy was adopted as an answer to a public appeal by al-Zawahiri, who declared that Syria was a key theater of jihad and urged Muslims from around the world to go to Syria and help the local mujahidin in their fght to oust the "murderer of all murderers," who will continue to slaughter Muslims until his regime is deposed. Al-Zawahiri called for the establishment of a regime that would free the Golan Heights and continue the jihad until the fag of victory fies over the hills of conquered Jerusalem. Following al-Zawahiri's call, al-Qaeda Iraq operatives, under the name Jabhat al-Nusra – a name designed to prevent the group from accepting support from Western and leading Arab countries acting to overthrow the Assad regime – arrived in Syria. These operatives are conducting organized activity, based on their military ability and experience acquired during their years of fghting in Iraq. It appears that they were responsible for most of the especially daring and deadly attacks in Syria in recent months, particularly suicide attacks. Sporadic and less organized activity by global jihad elements from Yemen, Saudi Arabia, Libya, Jordan, and Gaza, who came to Syria without belonging to any group and joined the Free Syrian Army, is also underway.

Estimates of the number of fghters identifed with global jihad vary from several hundred to several thousand.

The third key front emphasized in particular by al-Zawahiri, refecting his new policy of exploiting the upheaval in the Arab world to escalate the struggle of global jihad parties in general and in the Levant in particular, is Egypt, particularly in Sinai. Al-Zawahiri hailed the fall of Mubarak's regime and its replacement by a religious Islamic regime as a supreme strategic target and a personal ideal for him and his Egyptian cohorts in the al-Qaeda leadership, who were part of the Egyptian jihadist organization that formally merged with al-Qaeda in 2001. Following Mubarak's fall from power and the subsequent governmental vacuum in Egypt, global jihad elements took advantage of the situation to promote their goals. The escape and release of their operatives from prison, where they were serving lengthy sentences for past activity, enabled these organizations to bolster their ranks with loyal foot soldiers with operational experience. Many of them found their way to Sinai and joined the local terrorist organizations, while taking advantage of the Egyptian government's lack of control in the area to solidify their religious Islamic autonomy there.

A number of groups identifed with al-Qaeda and global jihad appeared in Sinai over the past year, the most prominent being Ansar Bayt al-Maqdis, al-Tawhid wal-Jihad, and Ansar al-Jihad. These organizations, and Ansar Bayt al-Maqdis in particular, operate in some measure against Egyptian targets but mostly against Israel. The terrorist attacks for which they took responsibility refect al-Qaeda's ideology and operating strategy. For example, following the rocket attacks on Eilat and the strikes against the pipeline for transporting natural gas from Egypt to Israel, Ansar Bayt al-Maqdis published a short flm taking responsibility and listing the attacks designed to prevent the looting of the natural resources granted to Muslims by Allah through sale at a fnancial loss to the enemies of Islam, headed by Israel. This subject was frequently mentioned in the propaganda that described past activity by the central al-Qaeda organization that caused serious economic damage to the attacked countries. The organization also took care to include speeches by al-Zawahiri in which he praised the repeated strikes against the gas pipeline, and added a call to the new Egyptian government to cancel the peace agreement with Israel and institute Islamic religious law in Egypt.

Ansar Bayt al-Maqdis, considered the most active and dangerous of the Egyptian global jihad organizations in Sinai, was responsible for several of the deadliest attacks on the border between Egypt and Israel: the August 2011 attack on Highway 40 to Eilat, in which eight Israelis were murdered; the August 5, 2012 attack at the Egyptian-Israeli border, in which 16 Egyptian border guards were murdered; and the attack at Har Harif, on September 12, 2012, in which an IDF soldier was killed. In these attacks, the organization proved that it does not hesitate to kill Muslims serving regimes that oppose its views, and does not recognize borders between countries, as these were not determined by Allah. For its part, Ansar al-Jihad (which is probably identical to the Salaf Sinai Front), founded in December 2011, declared "that it would follow Bin Laden's example," and swore loyalty to Sheikh Ayman al-Zawahiri, the new al-Qaeda leader. Its members also swore to Allah "to do all they could to fght the corrupt government of the Jews, the Americans, and their allies," to fulfll Bin Laden's promise that "America, and those living in America, will never be secure as long as Palestine does not exist, and until the armies of the unbelievers leave the land of Muhammed," and swore to work for the vision they shared with al-Qaeda – the founding of an Islamic caliphate in Egypt.

In addition to the Egyptian organizations in Sinai, Salaf jihadist organizations from Gaza are also exploiting Sinai as a key region for terrorist activity against Israel, along with activity against Israel in Gaza. The use of Sinai as a theater for activity is a result of pressure exerted on them by Hamas to restrict their activity against Israel from Gaza, owing to the fear of a harsh Israeli military strike against Hamas in Gaza in a way that would escalate to an all-out war. The most prominent of the Gaza organizations active in Sinai over the past year is the Mujahidin Shura Council in Greater Jerusalem, which serves as an umbrella organization for a number of Salaf Palestinian organizations, the most active and prominent of which is the Palestinian al-Tawhid wal-Jihad. The Mujahidin Shura Council in Greater Jerusalem claimed responsibility for the attack in the Be'er Milka area on June 18 that killed Said Fashfasha, an Israeli Arab who worked on the security fence on the border with Egypt. In a flm about the attack, the organization noted that it had been prepared "as a gift to our brothers in al-Qaeda and Sheikh al-Zawahiri," and in response to the assassination of Bin Laden. In the flm, the terrorists who took part in the operation, who were of Egyptian and Saudi Arabian origin, expressed their commitment to al-Zawahiri that the organization would uphold its commitment to "the way of jihad," and asserted that it "did not recognize the international border, but only the 'border of Allah.'"

Alongside this prominent organization, older Salaf organizations in Gaza operate directly against Israel, while using

Sinai for their activity in order to evade restrictions enforced by Israel and to avoid inviting Israeli retaliation against Hamas in Gaza. Among these organizations, Jaish al-Islam (Army of Islam) is particularly noteworthy. Founded in 2006 by Mumtaz Dughmush, after he split off from the Popular Resistance Committees, the organization was very active in launching rockets and in attacks against Israel, and was involved in the Gilad Shalit kidnapping. Its activity extended beyond Sinai; it sent operatives to fght in Syria, a fact that became publicly known when one of its members was killed in battle. Another organization is the Popular Resistance Committees (PRC), which is active on both sides of the border, and enjoys close ties with global jihad groups in Sinai. The organization was linked directly to a number of attacks on the Egyptian border that were also attributed to Ansar Bayt al-Maqdis, which may indicate close cooperation between the Gaza organizations and their Egyptian counterparts. There are currently over ten groups belonging to the jihadist Salaf movement in Gaza, which presents a challenge to Hamas hegemony in Gaza. Their growing ability to conduct attacks from Gaza and from Sinai is liable to earn them support from al-Zawahiri, win his offcial recognition, and give them the title of al-Qaeda Gaza or part of a unifed al-Qaeda Gaza force in Sinai.

As a result of the international campaign waged against it for over a decade, which brought about the arrest and elimination of many of the older leaders of the central al-Qaeda organization as well as its mythological commander, al-Qaeda has confronted complex challenges to its survival, its ability to undertake showcase terrorist attacks like the one in the US, and progress toward its goals. Furthermore, the organization's dire straits and the assessment voiced by administration sources and leading intelligence fgures around the world that al-Qaeda stood on the brink of destruction has forced al-Zawahiri to decide how his organization will continue and what operational strategy it will employ. This choice, whose signifcance is also clear to al-Zawahiri, will to a great extent determine whether al-Qaeda can survive and continue leading its supporters and affliates on the road to the global jihad it has proclaimed as its supreme goal. In order to achieve its goals, al-Zawahiri is also careful to maintain his links to powerful elements in Pakistan and Afghanistan, which enable him to solidify his status as an effective partner in their armed struggle, retain his ability to manage his organization from a base that is relatively secure from the long arm of the US and its allies, and at the same time continue to train al-Qaeda fghters.

Given the challenge posed by the upheaval in the Arab world, which erupted in the name of values and operational modes opposed to those of al-Qaeda, it appears that al-Zawahiri has chosen to carve his leadership and design al-Qaeda's path by grasping the opportunity presented to him and supporting the insurrectionists and their activity in the belief that they will serve al-Qaeda's long term goals. Indeed, the weakening of the regimes in a number of Arab countries and the governmental instability in others have generated opportunities for jihadist Salaf organizations to establish themselves in border regions where government is ineffective. These organizations have used these areas to set up infrastructures for training, weapons smuggling, and the transport of personnel to join a regional or global jihad, and some of them have even instituted *sharia* law. Al-Zawahiri, who is aware of the limitations and weaknesses of his organization, chose to do his best to turn the "Arab Spring" into an "Islamic Spring" by focusing on the role of guide and supporter, at least at this stage. This choice differs from the role outlined by Bin Laden for the organization – to serve as an operational vanguard inspiring its supporters by its actions, and not confning itself to declarations of support and provision of indirect aid. At the same time, this does not mean that al-Zawahiri has decided to completely abandon his efforts to carry out showcase attacks. Despite the damage suffered by the organization's forces responsible for its international terrorism and the effective thwarting of its attempted attacks in Europe and the US in recent years, it still exists, and Shukrijumah, its chief of staff, is still its commander. Furthermore, based on the organization's tradition, past record, and dozens of Muslim volunteers from Western countries it has trained, al-Qaeda will presumably not dissolve in the face of these obstacles, particularly when it remains committed to its path and terrorist attacks, including revenge operations for the death of the movement's leader.

The results of the anti-terrorist campaigns against the global al-Qaeda organization and its local affliates in Pakistan and Afghanistan, and against al-Qaeda's afliates in the Hejaz, the Maghreb and North Africa, and the Levant will have an effect on the future of regional and international terrorism. If the countries bordering Israel become bases of operations for jihadist Salaf groups, Israel, which up until now has not been the target of focused and intensive by al-Qaeda and global jihad elements, is liable to fnd itself in a different security situation. The frst signs of this were visible over the past year on Israel's southern border, following the attacks conducted there by Egyptian and Palestinian jihadist Salaf groups identifed with al-Qaeda operating in Sinai. Global jihad operatives arriving from outside the region were also among those taking part in those attacks. There is likewise a risk that the chaotic situation in Syria could lead to such activity against Israel from Syrian territory. Whether Assad's regime survives or falls, an effect on activity against Israeli territory by similar groups from Lebanon, and in the future perhaps also from Jordan, is quite possible.

On a number of occasions al-Zawahiri has expressed his determination to take action against the existence of Israel, which he regards as a foreign imperialistic import into the region. He encourages terrorist activity in Sinai, and stresses in his statements the critical importance of fghting in Syria on the way to liberating the Golan Heights and Jerusalem, i.e., of destroying Israel. The development of events in the countries bordering Israel and the results of activity by al-Qaeda and its affliates in more distant theaters will certainly infuence al-Zawahiri's future decisions whether to focus on terrorist action against Israel, and perhaps even to declare it a preferred theater of jihad on the road to global jihad, or whether to encourage this activity from a distance, while focusing his efforts on other areas of armed combat.

OVERVIEW OF POST-9/11 HOMEGROWN JIHADIST TERRORISM PLOTS AND ATTACKS

Scholars and law enforcement officials have noted that no workable general profile of domestic violent jihadists exists.

According to the NYPD's Intelligence Division, there is no effective profile to predict exactly who will radicalize. Another study found only broad trends among domestic jihadist terrorists, specifically that they are overwhelmingly male and about two-thirds of them are younger than 30 years old.

Indeed, there does not appear to be a common thread connecting the U.S. Army psychiatrist Major Nidal Hasan with the Caucasian convert, Daniel Patrick Boyd; the Afghan immigrant Najibullah Zazi with Carlos Bledsoe, an African American of a happy childhood who converted to Islam and renamed himself Abdulhakim Muhammad; David Headley, who was born Daood Gilani to a successful Pakistani immigrant father and American mother, with Talib Islam, who was born Michael Finton and raised in multiple foster homes; or the educated pharmacist Tarek Mehanna, with the Somali American from Minneapolis Shirwa Ahmed, who traveled to the land of his birth and became the first U.S. citizen suicide bomber. The plots and attacks drew in first- and second-generation Muslim American immigrants and native-born Americans who converted to the faith. Some included individuals acting alone, while others had multiple co-conspirators. Some plots were aspirational. Many believe others appear to have been pushed along by government informants or undercover agents, and still others were serious and calculating until uncovered by intelligence and/or law enforcement officials.

Overarching Themes

Homegrown violent jihadist activity since 9/11 defies easy categorization. For example, conventional notions of "homegrown" may suggest plots that are hatched and executed solely within the United States. But in a globalized environment, many domestic jihadist terrorist plots have some sort of international dimension. For example, some plotters train abroad. Some receive cues from terrorist Internet propagandists operating in foreign lands. And as suggested above, homegrown terrorists can focus their violent plans on domestic or international entities. Since 9/11, 38 homegrown plots featured domestic targets, 22 focused on foreign ones, and three conspiracies had both domestic and foreign targeting elements. From another perspective, 35 involved intent to or actual travel abroad for training or to plan for terrorist attacks. The 63 homegrown jihadist attacks and plots since 9/11 do exhibit four broad themes: a variety of endgames, little stomach for suicide or martyrdom among plotters, successful attacks by lone wolves, and varied capabilities among the plots.

A Variety of Endgames

Homegrown violent jihadists pursue a number of endgames. Some seek involvement in foreign conflicts or insurgencies. Others plan and attempt to execute either bombings or assaults with firearms. Finally, some jihadists apparently intended from the start only to fund or materially support the activities of their brethren.

Foreign Fighters

Twenty-two of the post-9/11 homegrown plots have featured individuals exclusively seeking to become foreign fighters with terrorist groups entangled in insurgency-type conflicts. Al-Shabaab-related cases concerning young men leaving the United States to fight in Somalia are the paramount example. Other cases include the following:

- Five men from Northern Virginia (Northern Virginia Five) were arrested in Sarghoda, Pakistan, in December 2009. They purportedly traveled there hoping to join jihadist groups and battle U.S. troops in Afghanistan. On June 24, 2010, they were convicted of terrorism charges in a special Pakistani anti-terror court. Prosecutors say the five men also began planning attacks against a Pakistani nuclear plant and an air base and other targets in Afghanistan and "territories of the United States."
- In February 2006, three residents of Toledo, Ohio—Mohammad Zaki Amawi, a dual U.S. and Jordanian citizen; Marwan Othman El-Hindi, a naturalized U.S. citizen from Jordan; and Wassim Mazloum, a legal permanent resident from Lebanon (Toledo, Ohio Plotters)—were charged with conspiracy to kill or maim persons in locations outside the United States, to include U.S. Armed Forces personnel

serving in Iraq. On June 13, 2008, a federal jury convicted all three of conspiring to commit terrorist acts against Americans overseas and material support to terrorists.

Explosives and Firearms

Eighteen of the 63 homegrown jihadist plots targeting the United States since 9/11 exclusively involved explosives or incendiary devices. Suspects at least discussed the use of bombs, hand grenades, or missiles in these cases. From a broader perspective, 33 cases in whole or in part included schemes revolving around explosives or incendiary devices. Historically, most terrorist incidents in the United States have involved bombs or fires. According to research drawn from the National Consortium for the Study of Terrorism and Responses to Terrorism's Global Terrorism Database, about 83% of all terrorist incidents on U.S. soil between 1970 and 2007— including violent jihadists as well as non-jihadists—have included explosives or incendiary devices. Roughly 9% involved firearms.

The Zazi case (as mentioned elsewhere) and the attempt by Faisal Shahzad to detonate an explosives-filled 1993 Nissan Pathfinder in New York City's Times Square stand out as examples of plots incorporating explosive or incendiary devices. On May 1, 2010, investigators discovered fireworks, clocks, wiring, filled propane tanks, gasoline canisters, and fertilizer that Shahzad had rigged for explosion in his vehicle. The Tehrik-e-Taliban Pakistan helped facilitate the failed attack by training Shahzad and sending him $12,000 in funding. Three plots intended to use firearms exclusively, while 19 plots involved in whole or in part the use of firearms. The three plots that focused on firearms include two of the successful post-9/11 attacks.

- The deadlier of the two attacks was the shooting at Fort Hood, Texas, on November 5, 2009. U.S. Army Major Nidal Hasan was charged in the attack which killed 13 and injured 43 others.
- Abdulhakim Muhammad was arrested on June 1, 2009, in connection with a shooting at the U.S. Army-Navy Career Center in Little Rock, Arkansas, that killed one soldier and

wounded another. He was charged with capital murder, attempted capital murder, and 10 counts of unlawful discharge of a firearm. In Arkansas state court, in July 2011, Muhammad pled guilty to these charges.

The third case that centered on firearms involved six men. They were arrested in May 2007 in a plot against Fort Dix, a U.S. Army base in New Jersey. The plan focused on firearms and included attacking and killing soldiers. In December 2008, a jury found five of the six guilty of conspiring to kill military personnel but cleared them of attempted murder.

Multiple, Unclear, or Unique Tactics

In total, 22 attacks and plots incorporated multiple or unique tactics or the tactics were not clear from the public record. One attack involving multiple tactics occurred abroad but targeted members of the U.S. Armed Forces at a base. In that attack, which occurred on March 23, 2003,

U.S. Army Sergeant Hasan Akbar used hand grenades (explosives) and his military-issued M-4 rifle to kill two fellow U.S. servicemen and wound 14 others at Camp Pennsylvania in Kuwait. Other examples of multiple, unique, or unspecified tactics include the following:

- Members of the plot involving Daniel Boyd allegedly attempted to travel abroad to engage in jihad as foreign fighters and also likely prepared to attack a domestic site—the U.S. Marine Corps Base in Quantico, Virginia, using firearms.
- Bryant Vinas, who plotted to blow up (explosives) the Long Island railroad in New York, admitted to U.S. officials that he met with Al Qaeda leaders in Pakistan and, between March and July 2008, attended three Al Qaeda training courses. In September 2008, as a foreign fighter he took part in a rocket attack targeting a U.S. military base in Afghanistan.
- Even though the plotters discussed using explosives, the four individuals tied to JIS and arrested in 2005 used firearms in robberies to generate funding for their scheme.

- In a case involving unspecified tactics, Ehsanul Islam Sadequee, a U.S. citizen born in Virginia, and Syed Haris Ahmed, a naturalized U.S. citizen from Pakistan, scouted targets in Washington, DC, in 2005.
- In an attack that did not feature guns or bombs, on March 3, 2006, Mohammed Reza Taheri-Azar, a naturalized U.S. citizen, crashed his SUV into a crowd near the University of North Carolina, Chapel Hill. No one was seriously injured in the attack, and he pled guilty to two counts of attempted murder. The assailant allegedly hoped to avenge the deaths of Muslims abroad that he believed were caused by the United States.

Material Support

Although this report largely focuses on radicalization and violent jihadist plotting, there is at least one other illegal method for individuals to assist terrorists. Radicalization may lead people to help terrorist organizations by illegally providing them material support unrelated to specific violent jihadist plots. How frequently this has occurred since 9/11 is difficult to discern, because material support charges are often part of the illegal activity in violent plots. DOJ has publicly released information on unsealed terrorism convictions between September 11, 2001, and March 18, 2010. CRS analysis of this information indicates that homegrown jihadists unconnected to any specific violent plots were prosecuted for materially supporting terrorists in at least six schemes. The six schemes supported violent jihadist or jihadist-linked groups such as Al-Qaeda, Jemaah Islamiyah, Abu Sayyaf, and Lashkar-e-Tayyiba (LeT). They included the following:

- Rahmat Abdhir: A U.S. citizen living in San Jose, California, Abdhir was indicted in 2007 for providing material support to his brother, Zulkifli Abdhir, a member of Jemaah Islamiyah based in the Philippines. The U.S. government accused Rahmat of sending to his brother more than $10,000 in supplies, including chocolates, underwear, knives, guns, and radios.
- Ahmed Abdellatif Sherif Mohamed: According to DOJ, during a routine traffic stop in Goose Creek, South Carolina

on August 4, 2007, law enforcement officials found explosive materials (PVC pipe containing potassium nitrate and kitty litter as well as about 20 feet of fuse) during a consensual search of the trunk of the Toyota Camry Mohamed was driving. A laptop retrieved from the car yielded a video produced by Mohamed depicting how components from a remote controlled toy car could be used to fashion a detonator for an explosive device. Mohamed had uploaded the recording to YouTube. Although no specific terrorist group was linked to Mohamed, he did admit that he intended the recording as instruction to "suiciders" on how to spare themselves in attacks. An Egyptian resident of Tampa, Florida, Mohamed entered the United States on an F-1 student visa.

- Tarik Shah, Rafiq Abdus Sabir, Mahmud Faruq Brent: In an investigation stretching back at least to December 2001, the FBI infiltrated a group of acquaintances interested in supporting international jihadist terrorist organizations. Shah and Brent pled guilty to material support in 2007 and Sabir was convicted of the charge the same year. In 2005, Shah, a Bronx, New York City, jazz musician and martial arts instructor, had sworn allegiance to Al Qaeda in the presence of an FBI agent who posed as a recruiter for the group. He had also allegedly offered to train Al Qaeda fighters in hand-to-hand combat. Shah purported to have been interested in traveling to Afghanistan in 1998 to attend terrorist training camps. Sabir, a doctor from Florida, swore allegiance to Al Qaeda in the same ceremony as his friend, Shah. Sabir also offered his medical skills to treat injured Al Qaeda fighters. Brent, a Washington, DC, cab driver, traveled to Pakistan in 2002 to attend a LeT training camp. A fourth individual was arrested in the investigation but did not get convicted of material support.
- Ronald Grecula: In an FBI sting operation, Grecula negotiated to build and sell an explosive device with individuals he believed were tied to Al Qaeda.
- Ilyas Ali: In a drugs-for-arms case, Ali, a naturalized U.S. citizen born in India, admitted to conspiring in 2002 with

two Pakistanis to supply Al Qaeda with anti-aircraft missiles bought using proceeds from the sale of heroin and hashish.

- Cedric Carpenter and Lamont Ranson: In February 2005, the duo from New Orleans pled guilty to conspiring to sell false Mississippi Driver's licenses, Social Security cards, and birth certificates to undercover informants they believed were members of the Abu Sayyaf terrorist organization.

Aside from the convictions derived from the DOJ's list covering the period between 9/11 and March 18, 2010, several other material support cases have come to light. It is unclear what accounts for this recent flurry of arrests. It may be a parallel to the uptick in violent jihadist plotting. Some of the cases include the following:

- In May 2011, FBI agents arrested Hafiz Khan (a naturalized U.S. citizen and resident of Miami) and two of his sons Izhar Khan and Irfan Khan (both naturalized U.S. citizens). They were allegedly involved in efforts to provide financing and other material support to the Pakistani Taliban. The trio was purportedly assisted by three other indicted individuals at large in Pakistan. This second group included Amina Khan—Izhar Khan's daughter—and her son, Alam Zeb, as well as an individual named Ali Rehman. Hafiz and Izhar Khan are imams in South Florida mosques. The federal government dropped its charges against Irfan Khan in June 2012 and Izhar Khan in January 2013.
- Nima Ali Yusuf: A permanent resident of the United States living in San Diego, Yusuf was arrested on November 12, 2010, on charges of conspiracy to provide material support to al-Shabaab and for making false statements to a government agency regarding an international terrorism matter. In December 2011, Yusuf pled guilty to conspiring to provide material support to al-Shabaab.
- Mohamud Abdi Yusuf, Abdi Mahdi Hussein, and Duwayne Mohamed Diriye participated in a scheme to provide material support to al-Shabaab, according to an indictment unsealed November 3, 2010. Yusuf, a resident of St. Louis, Missouri, is accused of sending funds to people tied to the

terrorist organization in Somalia, including Diriye. Yusuf purportedly worked with Hussein to structure financial transactions while the latter was an employee of a licensed money-remitting business. In November 2011, Yusuf "pled guilty to providing material support to a foreign terrorist organization."

- According to an indictment unsealed on November 2, 2010, San Diego residents, Basaaly Saeed Moalin, Mohamed Mohamed Mohamud, and Issa Doreh conspired to provide material support to al-Shabaab. The indictment states that Moalin received a request for financial support from one of al-Shabaab's military leaders in December 2007 and subsequently worked with Mohamud and Doreh to fill the request. In a separate indictment unsealed on December 3, 2010, Anaheim resident Ahmed Nasir Taalil Mohamud was tied to the scheme.
- Barry Bujol: According to DOJ, Bujol, a U.S. citizen living in Texas, allegedly attempted to provide money, pre-paid telephone calling cards, and global positioning system receivers (among other items), to Al Qaeda in the Arabian Peninsula after he had communicated with radical cleric Anwar al-Awlaki. He was arrested on May 30, 2010. In November 2011, he was convicted of attempting to provide material support or resources to a designated foreign terrorist organization as well as aggravated identity theft.
- Khalid Quazzani: On May 19, 2010, Quazzani, a naturalized U.S. citizen originally from Morocco and living in Kansas City, Missouri, pled guilty to participating in a material support scheme that provided more than $23,000 to Al Qaeda.
- Syed Hashmi: A Pakistan-born U.S. citizen, Hashmi pled guilty to material support charges on April 27, 2010. He admitted that while he was a graduate student in London, he allowed a roommate to store in his apartment ponchos, sleeping bags, and waterproof socks destined for Al Qaeda. Hashmi also loaned the individual $300 to travel to Waziristan, Pakistan, to deliver the goods.

- Raja Lahrasib Khan: On March 25, 2010, Khan, a naturalized U.S. citizen born in Pakistan, was charged with providing material support (in the form of money) to Al Qaeda. The criminal complaint alleges that Khan accepted $1,000 from an undercover agent and assured him that the money would be used to purchase weapons and possibly other supplies. In February 2012, he pled guilty to material support charges.
- Between November 2007 and March 2010, U.S. citizens Wesam El-Hanafi and Sabirhan Hasanoff allegedly engaged in a scheme to, among other things, provide computer expertise to and purchase seven Casio digital watches for Al Qaeda. In June 2012, El-Hanafi and Hasanoff pled guilty to providing material support Al Qaeda associates in Yemen and elsewhere and to conspiring to provide material support to al Qaeda.

LITTLE STOMACH FOR SUICIDE OR MARTYRDOM

Relatively few of the terrorist conspiracies examined in this report clearly contained suicidal or martyrdom overtones. Two terrorist plots clearly had suicide missions as core elements. Najibullah Zazi and his associates planned their attack on New York's subways as suicide missions.

Additionally, some Americans from Minneapolis, Minnesota, who were recruited into al-Shabaab reportedly committed suicide attacks. On October 29, 2008, al-Shabaab recruit Shirwa Ahmed became the first known American suicide bomber when he drove an explosives-laden truck into a government building in Somalia, one of five simultaneous assaults that killed 22 U.N. aid workers and others. The FBI also identified Farah Mohamed Beledi as a suicide bomber who died as he tried to detonate his suicide vest in a May 2011 attack in Mogadishu, Somalia.

According to media reports, al-Shabaab has claimed that Abdisalan Hussein Ali purportedly blew himself up while attacking African Union troops in Mogadishu in October 2011.

Individuals in 10 other plots clearly expressed a willingness to engage in suicide missions. For example, Daniel Maldonado told authorities that he would be willing to become a suicide bomber if he were wounded and could not otherwise fight. Al Qaeda member and U.S. citizen Bryant Neal Vinas wanted to become a suicide bomber but was rebuffed by the group. In e-mails intercepted by law enforcement authorities, Colleen LaRose ("Jihad Jane") wrote that she was prepared to be a martyr. And, in recordings of his conversations with an informant, Shaker Masri stated that he would be willing to walk up to a group of U.S. Army soldiers and blow himself up as a martyr.

The Success of Lone Wolves

Lone wolves (Nidal Hasan, Abdulhakim Muhammad, Hasan Akbar, and Mohammed Taheri-Azar) have conducted the four successful homegrown attacks since 9/11. Three other plotters acted alone. The remaining disrupted or failed plots have involved two or more participants in a group or network of one type or another. Three of the four lone wolf attacks involved firearms and they targeted U.S. military personnel.

It is difficult to generalize from such a small pool of cases. However, the success of four solo actors may highlight two contrasting points. First, law enforcement may face significant challenges in identifying and stopping lone wolf terrorists involved in technically uncomplicated plots unconnected to terrorist groups. Second, U.S. Law enforcement has been successful in disrupting and dismantling homegrown terrorist groups or networks since 9/11. Bolstering this point, undercover agents or cooperating witnesses infiltrated and monitored groups involved in 33 of the plots.

Varied Capabilities

Among the 63 homegrown plots since 9/11, the operational capabilities of participants diverge greatly. Some evinced terrorist tradecraft such as bomb making skills. Others appeared to be far less experienced. For instance, long before Derrick Shareef was apprehended in 2006, he likely intended to commit terrorist acts. However, he appears not to have possessed the capability to do so on his own until he was approached by an undercover FBI informant.

Shareef, a Muslim convert and 22 years old at the time of his arrest, plotted to set off hand grenades at a shopping mall in Rockford, Illinois. FBI informant William "Jamaal" Chrisman played a central part in the plot. At the behest of authorities, Chrisman befriended Shareef in September 2006 while the latter was working in a video store and had nowhere to live. Chrisman invited the young man to move in with him and began reporting to his law enforcement handlers regarding Shareef's jihadist tendencies. Shareef was unaware that Chrisman secretly recorded their conversations. The duo talked about violent jihad against civilians, public buildings, and a judge in DeKalb, IL. They concocted a plan to attack a local shopping mall. Chrisman told the young jihadist of a friend who could procure weapons for them. Unknown to Shareef, the "friend" was an undercover FBI agent. On December 6, 2006, the duo met the undercover FBI agent in the mall's parking lot where Shareef attempted to trade stereo speakers for hand grenades and was arrested. Shareef, who pled guilty to one count of attempting to use a weapon of mass destruction, was sentenced in September 30, 2008, to 35 years in prison.

Conversely, two of the homegrown jihadist terrorist plots appear to stand out for the capability their plotters. Both came to public attention in 2009. Both involved homegrown jihadists who had strong ties to foreign terrorist organizations. Attorney General Eric Holder characterized one of those plots—Najibullah Zazi's plan to blow up explosives on the New York City subway—as one of the most serious terrorist threats to our nation since September 11, 2001, and were it not for the combined efforts of the law enforcement and intelligence communities, it could have been devastating. This attempted attack on our homeland was real, it was in motion, and it would have been deadly. We were able to thwart this plot because of careful analysis by our intelligence agents and prompt actions by law enforcement.

While a complete picture of Zazi's radicalization process is not publicly available, some details regarding his plot have emerged. In his youth, he may have listened to the radical messages of Saifur Rahman Halimi, an imam who advocated jihad, attended the same mosque as Zazi's family, and lived in the same Queens building. Regardless, Zazi pled guilty on February 22, 2010, to a number of terrorism charges. The young man admitted to receiving Al Qaeda training in the Waziristan region of Pakistan in 2008. There, he learned about explosives and discussed specific targets with Al Qaeda members. He returned to the United States in January 2009 and moved to Denver. He also traveled to New York to discuss the timing for the attacks with a network of conspirators. In July and early September in Denver, he gathered materials for detonator components and assembled them based on the detailed training he had received in Afghanistan. Zazi admitted to bringing the explosive Triacetone Triperoxide (TATP) into New York on Thursday September 10, 2009. He intended to finish bomb construction over the weekend and planned to target New York's subway lines early the next week.

On March 18, 2010, David Headley pled guilty to terrorism charges. He admitted that he helped plan two plots for the Pakistani terrorist group, LeT—the November 2008 Mumbai attack and an un-executed conspiracy targeting a Danish newspaper. He received training from LeT and claimed membership in the organization. Headley attended the group's training camps five times between 2002 and 2005. These stints in Pakistan provided him with weapons training, indoctrination in jihad as well as instruction in close combat, survival skills, and counter-surveillance, among other things.

Between 2005 and 2008, he received extensive direction from LeT members and engaged in reconnaissance for the group in preparation for its Mumbai attack. To provide cover for his surveillance activity, Headley encouraged a co-conspirator in Chicago, who owned an immigration services business, to open a satellite office in Mumbai. Headley conducted video surveillance of potential Mumbai targets for LeT, and using a global positioning system device, he pinpointed landing sites for a waterborne assault. At the behest of LeT, Headley also conducted reconnaissance of the offices of the Danish newspaper Morgenavisen Jyllands-Posten. Representatives of both LeT and Al Qaeda schemed with him to strike the newspaper after it had published unflattering cartoons of the Prophet Muhammad.

COMBATING HOMEGROWN TERRORISM: ENFORCEMENT ACTIVITIES

The Obama Administration has recognized the significance of the homegrown jihadist threat in its June 2011 National Strategy for Counterterrorism. The strategy focuses on Al Qaeda, its affiliates (groups aligned with it), and its adherents (individuals linked to or inspired by the terrorist group). John Brennan, President Obama's top counterterrorism advisor, publicly described the strategy as the first one, "that designates the homeland as a primary area of emphasis in our counterterrorism efforts." The Strategy states:

We know al-Qa'ida and its affiliates continue to try to identify operatives overseas and develop new methods of attack that can evade U.S. defensive measures. At the same time, plots directed and planned from overseas are not the only sort of terrorist threat we face. Individuals inspired by but not directly connected to al-Qa'ida have engaged in terrorism in the U.S. Homeland. Others are likely to try to follow their example, and so we must remain vigilant.

The spate of recent arrests and other counterterrorism successes should not obscure the challenges facing law enforcement in disrupting homegrown terrorist plotting. Counterterrorism efforts exist within two broad contexts. Many of the legal behaviors associated with radicalization occur in the open marketplace of ideas where consumers weigh competing ideologies within the context of free speech. Conversely, the operational aspects of violent jihadist plots largely involve illegal activity. In this secretive realm involving criminality, law enforcement pursues terrorists in a real-world version of hide-and-seek.

The divergent nature of these two contexts may imply a distinct wall between the public realm and the secretive operational realm. In reality, the barrier is far from distinct. What happens operationally has significant impacts in the marketplace of ideas (Figure 1). The success of terrorist plots may spur radicalization, while effective policing may make terrorism a less popular option for radicals. High levels of radicalization may expand the potential pool of terrorist recruits.

Intelligence Approaches

A group of intelligence and terrorism experts argues that "to infiltrate terrorist conspiracies, identify and head off future terrorist attacks, and build the knowledge base required to rapidly investigate when terrorist incidents do occur requires human intelligence." The DOJ and FBI operate 103 Joint Terrorism Task Forces (JTTF) in the United States—71 created since 2001. These interagency entities include more than 4,000 federal, state, and local law enforcement officers and agents who "investigate acts of terrorism that affect the U.S., its interests, property and citizens, including those employed by the U.S. and military personnel overseas." As this suggests, their operations are highly tactical and focus on investigations, developing human sources (informants), and gathering intelligence to thwart terrorist plots.

JTTFs offer an important conduit for the sharing of intelligence developed from FBI-led counterterrorism investigations with outside agencies. These task forces also connect state and local law enforcement with the U.S. Intelligence Community on terrorism-related matters. To help facilitate this, especially as the threat of homegrown jihadists has emerged, the number of top-secret security clearances issued to local police working on JTTFs increased from 125 to 878 between 2007 and 2009.

A significant dilemma for law enforcement and intelligence officials who straddle the public realm of ideas and the secretive realm of terrorist operations is how to sift the law-abiding, non-violent radical attracted to jihadist rhetoric from the would-be terrorist who merits targeting. The vast amount of terrorist-related material available on the Internet in a relatively anonymous setting attracts homegrown individuals open to radicalization. Many of these individuals may show great interest in radical content, engage in radical discourse, but not become terrorists. A growing pool of those who view jihadism as "cool" and engage in online "talk" may make it harder for police to identify actual terrorists.

Preventive Policing

Since the 9/11 attacks, law enforcement has taken a more

proactive, intelligence-driven posture in its investigations. While serving as Deputy Attorney General, Paul McNulty described the Justice Department's aggressive, proactive, and preventative course as the only acceptable response from a department of government charged with enforcing our laws and protecting the American people. Awaiting an attack is not an option. That is why the Department of Justice is doing everything in its power to identify risks to our Nation's security at the earliest stage possible and to respond with forward-leaning—preventative— prosecutions.

One observer has described intelligence gathering in this context as "driven by a theory of preventive policing: in order to anticipate the next terror attack, authorities need to track legal activities.... It focuses not on crime, but on the possibility that a crime might be committed at some future date."

The FBI and DOJ also emphasized their forward-leaning approach with the September 29, 2008, revision of the Attorney General's Guidelines for Domestic FBI Operations, which they claim "make the FBI's operations in the United States more effective by providing simpler, clearer, and more uniform standards and procedures." Referred to as the "Mukasey Guidelines" after Michael B. Mukasey, who was Attorney General at the time of their release, this is the latest in a series of guidelines stretching back to 1976 that govern the FBI's investigative activities. The Mukasey Guidelines went into effect on December 1, 2008. In large part, these guidelines sprang from the post-9/11 national security context, in which the FBI surmised that it could not simply react to crimes. It had to preemptively search for criminal, counterintelligence, and terrorist threats to the homeland. As the FBI's General Counsel stated in congressional testimony:

We believe that this will allow the FBI to take additional necessary steps to becoming a more proactive organization. One of the key issues that we think the FBI needs to be able to do is assess potential risks and vulnerabilities. Having these additional techniques available at the assessment level, we think, will be key to the FBI's ability to efficiently and effectively answer those questions and assess risks.

The 2008 revision to the guidelines represents a consolidation of several other previously stand-alone documents that had governed FBI investigations. The 2008 Domestic Investigations and Operations Guide (DIOG)—the FBI's document governing the agency's implementation of the Mukasey Guidelines, which the FBI modified in 2011—reflects these changes as well.

The most prominent changes in the Mukasey Guidelines and the DIOG concern "assessments." Agents and analysts may now use assessments outside of the more traditional preliminary and full investigations, which require some level of factual predication. Preliminary investigations can be opened with "any 'allegation or information' indicative of possible criminal activity or threats to the national security." Opening a full investigation requires an "'articulable factual basis' of possible criminal or national threat activity." On the other hand, opening an assessment does not require particular factual predication. Instead, assessments are to follow specifically articulated purposes, of which there are five:

- Seek information, proactively or in response to investigative leads, relating to activities—or the involvement or role of individuals, groups, or organizations relating to those activities— constituting violations of federal criminal law or threats to the national security;
- Identify, obtain, and utilize information about actual or potential national security threats or federal criminal activities, or the vulnerability to such threats or activities;
- Obtain and retain information to inform or facilitate intelligence analysis and planning;
- Seek information to identify potential human sources, assess their suitability, credibility, or value of individuals as human sources; and
- Seek information, proactively or in response to investigative leads, relating to matters of foreign intelligence interest responsive to foreign intelligence requirements.

Assessments are not to be "pursued for frivolous or improper purposes and are not based solely on First Amendment activity or on the race, ethnicity, national origin, or religion of the subject of the assessment, or a combination of only such factors."

Assessments offer terrorism investigators a variety of techniques, including public surveillance and the use of confidential informants to penetrate conspiracies.

Civil libertarians and Muslim community organizations have voiced broad concerns about the new guidelines. According to media reporting, Farhad Khera, executive director of the nonprofit Muslim Advocates, has suggested that the Attorney General Guidelines are invasive and based on "generalized suspicion and fear on the part of law enforcement, not on individualized evidence of criminal activity." The American Civil Liberties Union (ACLU) has criticized the FBI's amassing of racial and ethnic data based on the new guidelines. As written, the guidelines allow for the collection of information about ethnic or racial communities and justify the gathering of such information for proactive purposes. The guidelines state that it should be done if it "will reasonably aid the analysis of potential threats and vulnerabilities, and, overall, assist domain awareness for the purpose of performing intelligence analysis." One ACLU official has described this as "racial profiling of entire communities."

DETECTING THE SHIFT FROM RADICAL TO VIOLENT JIHADIST

A major challenge for law enforcement is to gauge how quickly and at what point individuals move from radicalized beliefs to violence. Because not all terrorist suspects follow a single radicalization roadmap on their way to executing plots, U.S. law enforcement also faces the task of discerning exactly when radicalized individuals become real threats.

Among the tools employed by law enforcement is the monitoring of Internet and social networking sites. The USA PATRIOT Act (P.L. 107-56) authorizes the FBI to use National Security Letters to obtain a range of information including data pertaining to e-mail and Internet use from Internet Service Providers. In addition, according to an internal Justice Department document obtained under the Freedom of Information Act by the Electronic Frontier Foundation, law enforcement agents may also go undercover into social networking sites with false online profiles to exchange messages with suspects, identify a target's friends or relatives, and browse private information such as postings, personal photographs and video clips. The Obama Administration has sought approval from Congress to expand FBI authority to obtain records related to the context of e-mails and other Internet-based communications without first obtaining a warrant from a judge. "The proposal would add 'electronic communication transaction records'—like e-mail addresses used in correspondence and Web pages visited—to a list of the categories of information that FBI agents can demand."

A review of criminal complaints and indictments in terrorism cases reveal that the FBI has exploited the Internet activity of suspects and/or their e-mail communications to build cases against defendants in at least 28 of the post-9/11 cases studied in this report. Although much is said about terrorist use of the Internet for recruitment, training, and communications, these cases suggest that terrorists and aspiring terrorists will not find the Internet a uniformly permissive environment.

The case involving Mohamed Alessa and Carlos Almonte highlights the complexities in detecting transitions from radicalization to violent extremism. Investigators arrested the duo on June 5, 2010, at John F. Kennedy Airport (JFK) in New York as they allegedly tried to fly to Egypt. They hoped to eventually link up with the Somali terrorist organization, al-Shabaab. The case started with an e-mail tip to the FBI on October 9, 2006, which stated, [e]very time [Alessa and Almonte] access the Internet all they look for is all those terrorist videos about the Islam holly [sic] war and where they kill US soldiers and other terrible things.... They keep saying that Americans are their enemies, that everybody other than Islamic followers are their enemies ... and they all must be killed.

This statement suggests that in 2006, the two young men engaged in radical behavior, perusing jihadist websites and discussing terrorist activity. Between 2006 and 2010, investigators monitored the duo's actions as their beliefs arguably morphed into something more dangerous. Initially it was unclear whether the pair was just engaged in radical talk or actually planning for violent jihad. In 2006 and 2007, investigators debated the level of threat posed by Alessa and Almonte. A key shift occurred when law enforcement discovered after the fact that the duo had travelled to Jordan in 2007 but failed to get recruited as mujahedeen fighters. This helped convince authorities of the two plotters' actual intent to do harm. By 2009, the case included an undercover investigator from the NYPD interacting with thc two suspects.

The U.S. government's criminal complaint against Alessa and Almonte lays out the alleged overt activities marking the duo's change from radicals to terrorist suspects worthy of arrest. Back in New Jersey, Alessa and Almonte supposedly trained for jihad by lifting weights and rehearsing combat techniques using paintball guns. The government claims that they gathered equipment, including tactical-brand flashlights and combat boots. The pair also purportedly saved over $7,000 to fund their foreign violent jihad. The criminal complaint describes how the two discussed violent jihad and downloaded jihadist rhetoric. For example, Almonte is said to have kept a lecture by radical cleric Anwar al-Awlaki on his cell phone. The U.S. government contends that Alessa viewed a video including scenes of Al-Qaeda spokesperson Adam Gadahn praising Nidal Hasan, the alleged Ft. Hood shooter. Also, according to the criminal complaint, Almonte possessed computer files of violent jihadist documents authored by Osama Bin Laden and his second-in-command Ayman al-Zawahiri. For the government, Alessa and Almonte's transformation from radicals to terrorists likely culminated when the two allegedly booked reservations for separate flights to Egypt scheduled for June 5, 2010.

Two successful plots emphasize the difficulty of discerning when radicals become terrorist threats. Even if a suspect comes to the attention of law enforcement, evaluating the person's intent and capability remains challenging. Prior to the Fort Hood shooting, over the course of several months, Nidal Hasan allegedly sent a number of e-mails to Awlaki (who reportedly replied to only two of them). The e-mail exchange was assessed by investigators to be in line with the psychiatrist's research into Muslim U.S. soldiers' reactions to the wars in Iraq and

Afghanistan, thus, presumably protected speech. In retrospect it appears Hasan's intentions were far more menacing. Prior to Abdulhakim Muhammad's arrest for the June 1, 2009, shooting incident in Little Rock, Arkansas, the FBI interviewed him on several occasions. Muhammad spent 16 months in Yemen starting in the fall of 2007. While there, he married a woman from the southern part of the country. He allegedly taught English and learned Arabic during his time in the country. Yemeni officials imprisoned him in November 2008 on a visa overstay. He also supposedly possessed a fraudulent Somali visa. Yemen deported him to the United States in January 2009. The FBI is reported to have interviewed him before the shooting, including while he was in prison in Yemen and then again in Nashville soon after he returned. According to law enforcement officials, the episode in Yemen prompted a preliminary investigation by the FBI and other American law enforcement agencies into whether he had ties to extremist groups. But that investigation was inconclusive, leaving the FBI with insufficient evidence to wiretap his phone or put him under surveillance.

THE ROLE OF STATE AND LOCAL LAW ENFORCEMENT

A terrorist attack in the United States, whether committed by homegrown or foreign terrorists, will occur in a community within a state or tribal area. Since the plotting and preparation for domestic terrorist attacks (such as surveillance of a target, acquisition and transport of weapons or explosives, and even the recruitment of participants) will also occur within local communities, preventing such attacks is not only a federal responsibility but also a state, local, and tribal one. In 2010 testimony to Congress, Brian Michael Jenkins says that The diffuse nature of today's terrorism threat and the emphasis on do-it-yourself terrorism challenge the presumption that knowledge of terrorist plots will come first to federal authorities, who will then share this information with state and local authorities. It is just as likely—perhaps more likely—that local law enforcement could be the first to pick up clues of future conspiracies.

Every day, officers at over 17,000 state and local law enforcement agencies collect and document information regarding behaviors, incidents, and other suspicious activity associated with crime including terrorism. A joint study by the Departments of Justice and Homeland Security, and senior law enforcement officials concluded that "[t]he gathering, processing, reporting, analyzing, and sharing of suspicious activity is critical to preventing crimes, including those associated with domestic and international terrorism." A former police chief observed that, On the beat or mobile, cops are sensitive to things that do not look right or do not sound right ... [r]emember, it was a rookie cop on a routine check that resulted in the arrest of Eric Robert Rudolph in North Carolina despite the enormous commitment of federal resources.

Another example is the case of Oklahoma City bomber Timothy McVeigh. He was arrested after a traffic stop when Oklahoma State Trooper Charles J. Hanger noticed that McVeigh's yellow 1977 Mercury Marquis had no license plate. Using his home state as an example, a former U.S. Attorney maintains that "evidence of a potential terrorist threat or organized criminal enterprise is far more likely to be found in the incidental contact with the 10,000 police officers in the state of Washington than by the less than 150 FBI agents assigned to the Seattle Field Division."

The role of state, local, and tribal law enforcement in detecting nascent terrorist plotting is particularly important considering the challenges noted elsewhere in this report in detecting terrorist lone wolves. The four successful homegrown jihadist terrorist attacks that have occurred since 9/11 were all committed by lone wolves. Jenkins believes that preventing future terrorist attacks requires effective domestic intelligence collection that is best accomplished by local authorities.

Integrating state, local, and tribal law enforcement into the national counterterrorism effort continues to be an abiding concern of policymakers. After the National Commission on Terrorist Attacks Upon the United States (9/11 Commission) cited breakdowns in information sharing and the failure to fuse pertinent intelligence (i.e., "connecting the dots") as key factors in the failure to prevent the 9/11 attacks several efforts were made to improve the sharing of terrorism information between federal, state, local, and tribal law enforcement agencies:

- States and major urban areas established intelligence fusion centers. Congress has defined fusion centers as a "collaborative effort of two or more Federal, state, local, or tribal government agencies that combines resources, expertise, or information with the goal of maximizing the ability of such agencies to detect, prevent, investigate, apprehend, and respond to criminal or terrorist activity." By 2012, there were 77 federally recognized fusion centers.
- In the 2004 Intelligence Reform and Terrorism Prevention Act (P.L. 108-458), Congress mandated the creation of an Information Sharing Environment (commonly known as the "ISE") to provide and facilitate the means of sharing terrorism information among all appropriate federal, state, local, and tribal entities, and the private sector through the use of policy guidelines and technologies.
- Congress made information sharing a priority of the new DHS intelligence organization, requiring it "to disseminate, as appropriate, information analyzed by the Department within the Department, to other agencies of the Federal government with responsibilities related to homeland security, and to agencies of State and local government and private sector entities, with such responsibilities in order to assist in the deterrence, prevention, preemption of, or response to, terrorist attacks against the United States."
- Congress mandated that DHS support fusion centers in the Implementing Recommendations of the 9/11 Commission Act of 2007 (P.L. 110-53). DHS supports these centers through its State, Local, and Regional Fusion Center Initiative by providing operational, analytic, reporting, and management advice and assistance; training; information technology systems and connectivity; and intelligence officers and analysts.

The Nationwide Suspicious Activity Report Initiative (NSI) is a program to push terrorism-related information generated locally between and among federal, state, local, and tribal levels. Specifically, it is a framework to support the reporting of suspicious activity—from the point of initial observation to the point where the information is available in the information sharing environment. It is a standardized, integrated approach to gathering, documenting, processing, analyzing, and sharing information about suspicious activity that is potentially terrorism-related while protecting the privacy and civil liberties of Americans. The intent is for this locally generated suspicious activity reporting to be combined in a systematic way with other sources of intelligence at the federal level to uncover criminal activity, including terrorism.

Investigative Approaches

To counter violent jihadist plots, U.S. law enforcement has employed two tactics that have been described by one scholar as the "Al Capone" approach and the use of "agent provocateurs." The Capone approach involves apprehending individuals linked to terrorist plots on lesser, non-terrorism-related offenses such as immigration violations. In agent provocateur cases—often called sting operations—government undercover operatives befriend suspects and offer to facilitate their activities. As the "Al Capone," moniker suggests, historically, these tactics have been employed against many types of targets such as mafia bosses, white-collar criminals, and corrupt public servants. While these techniques combined with the cultivation of informants as well as surveillance (especially in and around mosques) may be effective in stymieing rapidly developing terrorist plots, their use has fostered concern within U.S. Muslim communities.

The Capone Approach

As mentioned, the Capone approach involves apprehending individuals linked to terrorist plots on lesser, non-terrorism-related offenses such as immigration violations. This approach fits within a preventative mode of counterterrorism prosecution and has received media scrutiny. Experts have noted that immediately after 9/11, DOJ often leveled lesser charges against terrorist suspects to preemptively squelch potential attacks. However, according to the Center on Law and Security at New York University School of Law, DOJ has moved toward trying suspected terrorists as terrorists instead of leaning heavily on lesser charges. In 2001 and 2002, 8% of defendants labeled as terrorists in the media were charged under terrorism statutes, this figure rose to 47% by 2006 and 2007. Regardless, the Capone approach is still used in terrorism cases.

Lying to an FBI Special Agent is one of the violations reminiscent of the Capone approach. A recent example stands out. On July 21, 2010, Paul Rockwood, Jr., a U.S. citizen and Muslim convert, pled guilty to making false statements to the FBI. Rockwood's wife, Nadia Rockwood, also pled guilty to making false statements related to her husband's case. By early 2010, while living in King Salmon, Alaska, Paul Rockwood had developed a list of 15 people he planned to kill, believing that they had desecrated Islam. He had also researched explosives and shared with others ideas about mail bombs or using firearms to kill his targets. It appears that prosecutors could not pursue a case based on more substantive terrorism charges and opted to neutralize a threat—someone apparently preparing to kill people—by using the Capone approach.

The utility of this preventative technique coupled with actual terrorism charges was exhibited by the FBI in its case against Najibullah Zazi. Zazi arrived in New York on September 10, 2009, with explosive material and plans to detonate bombs in New York's subway system. Zazi feared authorities had caught up to him and returned to Denver on September 12. Between September 10 and 19, the FBI monitored his activities and bolstered its case with searches of a vehicle and locations linked to him in New York and Denver. Zazi also agreed to interviews with the FBI in Denver. On September 19, Special Agents first arrested Zazi in Aurora, Colorado, for knowingly and willfully lying to the FBI. Presumably this was done because he might flee. Four days later, a grand jury returned a more substantive one-count indictment against him on weapons of mass destruction charges.

DOJ used similar charges against Ahmad Wais Afzali, an imam from Queens. He was arrested for tipping off Zazi to the FBI's investigation. On March 4, 2010, Afzali pled guilty to lying to federal officials. He admitted that he warned Zazi that the FBI had asked about him. Afzali also stated that during the phone conversation he simply cautioned Zazi not to "get involved in

Afghanistan garbage." He stated in court that he misled the FBI about a telephone conversation he had with Zazi. Afzali claimed that by lying to investigators he had hoped to protect himself, not Zazi. Afzali had been a source of information for federal and New York City investigators in the past.

In another instance of the Capone approach, in 2008 the federal government charged Tarek Mehanna for lying to FBI agents regarding his relationship to Daniel Maldonado, subsequently convicted and jailed for terrorism-related offenses. Mehanna's 2008 arrest occurred at Boston's Logan International Airport as he was preparing to leave the country, according to news reports. He was subsequently released on bail. His defense attorney claimed that the FBI wanted Mehanna to become an informant, and his refusal precipitated his 2009 indictment and re-arrest on terrorism charges.

Agent Provocateur Cases

Agent provocateur cases rely on expert determination by law enforcement that a specific individual or group is likely to move beyond radicalized talk and engage in violent jihad. The ultimate goal is to catch a suspect committing an overt criminal act such as pulling the proverbial trigger but on a dud weapon. By engaging in such strategy, investigators hope to obtain ironclad evidence against suspects.

Three FBI investigations exemplify the utility of this approach. On November 26, 2010, Mohamed Osman Mohamud was arrested after he attempted to set off what he believed was a vehicle bomb at an annual Christmas tree lighting ceremony in Portland, Oregon. Mohamud thought he had plotted with terrorists to detonate the bomb. In actuality the device was a dud assembled by his co-conspirators, FBI undercover operatives. Mohamud offered the target for the strike, provided components for assembly of the device, gave instructions for the operation, and mailed passport photographs for his getaway plan to FBI undercover operatives.

On September 24, 2009, a Jordanian immigrant named Hosam Smadi was arrested for attempting to detonate what he thought was a car bomb in the parking lot of a 60-story skyscraper in Dallas, Texas. On May 26, 2010, he pled guilty to one count of attempted use of a weapon of mass destruction. Smadi's apprehension resulted from an FBI operation including at least three undercover employees. The operation duped Smadi into believing he was planning an attack with Al Qaeda operatives. It ended with Smadi driving a truck he believed to contain a live bomb into the underground garage of 60-story Fountain Place in Dallas, Texas. He used a cell phone to try and trigger the dud.

The same day of Smadi's arrest, the FBI apprehended Michael C. Finton in Springfield, IL, on similar but unrelated charges. Finton's case also relied heavily on undercover FBI personnel. Allegedly they supplied him with a van Finton believed contained almost one ton of high explosives. According to the DOJ, he drove and parked the van near the Paul Findley Federal Building and Courthouse in downtown Springfield. FBI Special Agents arrested Finton after he tried to detonate the bogus bomb using a cell phone.

Initially, the FBI appears to have just tracked the activities of Finton and Smadi. How Mohamud's case played out is less certain, based on publicly available information. However, the investigations—particularly the Finton and Smadi cases—likely reached tipping points encouraging the Bureau to initiate much more proactive agent provocateur-type operations.

Finton had converted to Islam while in prison on aggravated robbery and battery charges. According to court documents, he was released in 2006 but in 2007 was re-arrested and returned to prison because of a parole violation. At the time, a search of Finton's vehicle revealed passages he wrote that championed martyrdom as well as attempted correspondence with John Walker Lindh, a U.S. citizen who pled guilty in federal court to serving in the Taliban army and carrying weapons. In 2008, after Finton was released from prison for his parole violation, members of the FBI's Springfield JTTF interviewed him. The JTTF also used an informant to monitor Finton, who engaged in radical rhetoric after his release. In January 2009, the informant reported that Finton planned to travel to the Gaza strip to fight Israelis. At this juncture in the investigation, the FBI allegedly initiated its agent provocateur strategy to nab Finton.

The tipping point in the Smadi investigation is a little less specific. He allegedly had come to the agency's attention because the jihadist sentiment he displayed among an online group of extremists supposedly "stood out." Investigators claim Smadi exhibited "vehement intention to conduct terror attacks in the United States and ... zealous devotion to Osama Bin Laden and Al Qaeda." As a result, an FBI undercover employee communicated with Smadi. More than 10 exchanges between the two emphasized Smadi's desire to conduct violent jihad on behalf of Al Qaeda. Thus, the FBI determined he was a "legitimate threat," introduced him to another undercover employee who posed as a senior member of an Al Qaeda sleeper cell, and ostensibly set the sting in motion.

The tipping point in the Mohamud investigation is even less clear due to ambiguity in the publicly available information regarding the timeline of the case. At some point, someone from the local Muslim community alerted the FBI to Mohamud, a 19-year-old Somali-born naturalized U.S. citizen. Media reports have suggested that a family member, perhaps Mohamud's father, relayed concerns about the young man to officials. According to DOJ, in December 2009 Mohamud communicated with an individual the U.S. government believed to be a terrorist located in Pakistan. The duo allegedly discussed Mohamud traveling to Pakistan to prepare for violent jihad. When exactly the FBI learned this information is unknown. However, after Mohamud was not allowed to board a flight from Portland to Kodiak, Alaska, on June 14, 2010, the FBI interviewed him. He purportedly told the FBI that he planned to take a fishing job in Alaska for the summer and that he had previously wanted to travel to Yemen but had neither purchased tickets nor obtained a visa. According to court documents, shortly thereafter, on June 23, an FBI undercover employee professing to be an associate of the Pakistan-based terrorist e-mailed Mohamud. It is unclear whether or not Mohamud's attempt to travel to Alaska and his interview precipitated the undercover operation.

Court documents in the Smadi, Finton, and Mohamud cases allege that FBI undercover employees tested the suspects to ascertain the depth of their intent to do harm. The FBI evaluated Mohamud's resolve on a number of occasions. Two stand out. Mohamud's first meeting with an undercover FBI operative entailed a discussion in which the would-be violent jihadist was told that he could help "the cause" in "a number of ways ... ranging from simply praying five times a day to becoming a martyr." The young man responded, saying that he wanted to become "operational" and needed help in staging an attack. When in a following meeting Mohamud suggested the Christmas tree lighting ceremony as his intended target, an FBI undercover employee noted that children attend such events. Mohamud responded by saying that he wanted a large crowd "that will ... be attacked in their own element with their families celebrating the holidays."

In the Smadi and Finton cases, the suspects received reassurances that if they quit the schemes, they would face no repercussions from their fellow (sham) plotters. FBI undercover operatives repeatedly tried to discourage Smadi's violent jihadist sentiments. In July 2009, an undercover employee (the fictitious senior member of an Al Qaeda sleeper cell), offered Smadi a way out of the plot. The mock Al Qaeda operative counseled Smadi by saying that different types of jihad existed, and he did not have to follow through on the plot if he was uncomfortable with it. He reassured Smadi by stressing that if he backed out, he would remain part of Al Qaeda's "brotherhood." Regardless, Smadi steadfastly believed in the plot and refused to quit. Like Smadi, Finton was given at least one opportunity to abandon his scheme. He allegedly understood that, "anytime he felt uncomfortable, he could walk out the door and still be a brother."

The "Bind" for Law Enforcement

Not all agent provocateur cases appear as thorough in their efforts to reveal the harmful intent of suspects. Some cases have raised controversy about the extent to which government informants or agents have entrapped suspects and/or supported or pushed along terrorist plots. These instances illustrate what Philadelphia Inquirer reporter and author, Stephan Salisbury, describes as the "bind" the FBI finds itself in. "On one hand it is being charged by the Justice Department to go out and stop this stuff [terrorism] before it happens. But on the other, it is getting criticized for the techniques it is using to do that." The 2008 Attorney General's Guidelines for Domestic FBI Operations address the same competing forces, and as mentioned their implementation has spurred concerns among civil liberties groups.

Investigations of the so-called Newburgh Four and Liberty City Seven plots illustrate this bind. In each, law enforcement has been criticized for its use of undercover informants. To counter this, in both cases, officials emphasized the importance of prevention—neutralizing threats posed by the groups involved. For example, in a press conference related to the Newburgh plot, New York City Mayor Michael Bloomberg reassured the public by stating that the plotters did not have ties to a larger terrorist organization. However, he went on to stress the preemptive aspects of the case, "I've always thought of our police department's primary job, not as first responders but as first preventers." Cognizant of criticisms that the Liberty City men neither were competent nor their plotting viable, former Attorney General Gonzalez cautioned that our philosophy here is that we try to identify plots in the earliest stages possible, because we don't know what we don't know about a terrorist plot ... it's dangerous for us to make an evaluation case by case ... well, this is a really dangerous group, this is really not a dangerous group. And we felt that the combination of the planning and the overt acts taken were sufficient to support this prosecution.

Newburgh Four

The Newburgh Four case has kindled controversy regarding the use of an agent provocateur. In the investigation, an FBI informant allegedly offered plotters $250,000 and a luxury car, among other inducements to trigger explosives near a synagogue and to shoot down military aircraft. On June 14, 2010, the federal judge hearing the trial delayed its start, because prosecutors may have failed to provide to defense attorneys relevant case information. Days earlier the defense received an FBI document suggesting that the lead plotter, James Cromitie, was not a threat. News accounts suggest the plotters may have been heavily influenced by the FBI's informant. They have also raised questions about the informant in the case, alleged to be a man named Shahed Hussain. According to the Village Voice, Hussain duped the Newburgh Four into their plot. The Voice suggested that the quartet of smalltime felons had no grand terrorist ambitions, and Hussain had plied them with cash and suggestions.

The Newburgh Four were arrested in May 2009. They purportedly had attempted to detonate explosives near a synagogue in the Riverdale section of the Bronx in New York City. The federal government asserts the plotters also planned to shoot down military airplanes at the New York Air National Guard Base at Stewart Airport in Newburgh, New York. Hussain allegedly passed himself off as a member of a Pakistani terrorist organization, Jaish-e-Mohammed, and provided the four suspects with inert C-4 explosives and an inactive Stinger surface-to-air missile. The Newburgh Four were found guilty of the plot on October 18, 2010.

According to other news reports, Hussain, a Pakistani immigrant, became an FBI informant in 2002 to win leniency and avoid deportation on fraud charges. They stemmed from when he worked as a translator for the New York Department of Motor Vehicles. Hussain pled guilty to production and transfer of false government identification documents—illegally helping immigrants obtain licenses. He had also served as the key informant in the 2003 and 2004 FBI sting operation implicating Mohammed Hossain and Yassin Aref in a plot to launder money related to the sham sale of surface to air missiles to terrorists.

Liberty City Seven

Like the Newburgh Four case, the Liberty City Seven investigation also generated questions regarding informant use by the FBI. Seven Miami-area men were arrested in 2006 for allegedly plotting to blow up the Sears Tower (now called Willis Tower) in Chicago, the FBI building in North Miami Beach, and other government buildings in Miami-Dade County. Defense attorneys called the case an outrageous example of government entrapment claiming that the men had neither the will nor the means to carry out the crimes. An FBI informant posing as an Al Qaeda member in the case, offered the men $50,000 as part of their plot. He also obtained warehouse space for the group's activities, led a ceremony in which the conspirators swore allegiance to Al Qaeda, gave the group video cameras for surveillance activities, and suggested targeting Miami's FBI offices.

One of the two FBI informants in the investigation, Abbas al-Saidi, was jailed after reportedly having extorted $7,000 from a friend who raped his girlfriend and then, after accepting the money, beat her up. The other informant, Elie Assad, also had a domestic battery charge on his record. According to FBI agents, Assad failed a polygraph test administered while he was working for them on a previous case in Chicago. A 35-year veteran of the FBI, who was hired as an expert witness by the Liberty City defense team, stated that Assad never should have been authorized to work on the [Liberty City] case at all. However, at trial, the former FBI agent was not allowed to testify nor did the judge permit the testimony about Assad's failed polygraph test. After juries in the first two trials failed to reach a verdict, six of the seven Liberty City men were convicted at a third trial and sentenced to long prison sentences.

7

Al-Qaeda Unique among Terrorist Organizations

Four characteristics distinguish al-Qaeda from its predecessors in either nature or degree: its ºuid organization, recruitment methods, funding, and means of communication.

FLUID ORGANIZATION

The al-Qaeda of September 2001 no longer exists. As a result of the war on terrorism, it has evolved into an increasingly diffuse network of affiliated groups, driven by the worldview that al-Qaeda represents. In deciding in 1996 to be, essentially, a "visible" organization, running training camps and occupying territory in Afghanistan, al-Qaeda may have made an important tactical error; this, in part, explains the immediate success of the U.S.-led coalition's war in Afghanistan.

Since then, it has begun to resemble more closely a "global jihad movement," increasingly consisting of web-directed and cyber-linked groups and ad hoc cells. In its evolution, al-Qaeda has demonstrated an unusual resilience and international reach. It has become, in the words of Porter Goss, "only one facet of the threat from a broader Sunni jihadist movement." No previous terrorist organization has exhibited the complexity, agility, and global reach of al-Qaeda, with its ºuid operational style based increasingly on a common mission statement and objectives, rather than on standard operating procedures and an organizational structure.

Al-Qaeda has been the focal point of a hybrid terrorist coalition for some time, with ties to inspired freelancers and other terrorist organizations both old and new. Some observers argue that considering al-Qaeda an organization is misleading; rather it is more like a nebula of independent entities (including loosely associated individuals) that share an ideology and cooperate with each other.

The original umbrella group, the International Islamic Front for Jihad against Jews and Crusaders, formed in 1998, included not only al-Qaeda but also groups from Algeria, Bangladesh, Egypt, and Pakistan. A sampling of groups that are connected in some way includes the Moro Islamic Liberation Front (Philippines), Jemaah Islamiyah (Southeast Asia), Egyptian Islamic Jihad (which merged with al-Qaeda in 2001), al-Ansar Mujahidin (Chechnya), al-Gama'a al-Islamiyya (primarily Egypt, but has a worldwide presence), Abu Sayyaf (Philippines), the Islamic Movement of Uzbekistan, the Salafist Group for Call and Combat (Algeria), and Harakat ul-Mujahidin (Pakistan/Kashmir). Some experts see al-Qaeda's increased reliance on connections to other groups as a sign of weakness; others see it as a worrisome indicator of growing strength, especially with groups that formerly focused on local issues and now display evidence of convergence on al-Qaeda's Salafist, anti-U.S., anti-West agenda.

The nature, size, structure, and reach of the coalition have long been subject to debate. Despite claims of some Western experts, no one knows how many members al-Qaeda has currently or had in the past. U.S. intelligence sources place the number of individuals who underwent training in camps in Afghanistan from 1996 through the fall of 2001 at between 10,000 and 20,000; the figure is inexact, in part, because of disagreement over the total number of such camps and because not all attendees became members. The International Institute for Strategic Studies in 2004 estimated that 2,000 al-Qaeda operatives had been captured or killed and that a pool of 18,000 potential al-Qaeda operatives remained. These numbers can be misleading, however: it would be a mistake to think of al-Qaeda as a conventional force, because even a few trained fighters can mobilize many willing foot soldiers as martyrs.

Methods of Recruitment

The staying power of al-Qaeda is at least in part related to the way the group has perpetuated itself; in many senses, al-Qaeda is closer to a social movement than a terrorist group. Involvement in the movement has come not from pressure by senior al-Qaeda members but mainly from local volunteers competing to win a chance to train or participate in some fashion.

The process seems to be more a matter of "joining" than being recruited, and thus the traditional organizational approach to analyzing this group is misguided.

But the draw of al-Qaeda should also not be overstated: in the evolving pattern of associations, attraction to the mission or ideology seems to have been a necessary but not sufficient condition. Exposure to an ideology is not enough, as reflected in the general failure of al-Qaeda to recruit members in Afghanistan and Sudan, where its headquarters were once located. As psychiatrist Marc Sageman illustrates, social bonds, not ideology, apparently play a more important role in al-Qaeda's patterns of global organization.

Sageman's study of established links among identified al-Qaeda operatives indicates that they joined the organization mainly because of ties of kinship and friendship, facilitated by what he calls a "bridging person" or entry point, perpetuated in a series of local clusters in the Maghreb and Southeast Asia, for example. In recent years, operatives have been connected to al-Qaeda and its agenda in an even more informal way, having apparently not gone to camps or had much formal training: examples include those engaged in the London bombings of July 7 and 21, 2005, the Istanbul attacks of November 15 and 20, 2003, and the Casablanca attacks of May 16, 2003.

This loose connectedness is not an accident: bin Laden describes al-Qaeda as "the vanguard of the Muslim nation" and does not claim to exercise command and control over his followers. Although many groups boast of a connection to al-Qaeda's ideology, there are often no logistical trails and thus no links for traditional intelligence methods to examine. This explains, for example, the tremendous difficulty in establishing connections between a radical mosque, bombers, bomb makers, supporters, and al-Qaeda in advance of an attack (not to mention after an attack).

Another concern has been the parallel development of Salatist networks apparently drawing European Muslims into combat against Western forces in Iraq. The European Union's counterterrorism coordinator, Gijs de Vries, for example, has cautioned that these battle-hardened veterans of the Iraq conflict will return to attack Western targets in Europe.

The Ansar al-Islam plot to attack the 2004 NATO summit in Turkey was, according to Turkish sources, developed in part by operatives who had fought in Iraq. A proportion of those recently drawn to the al-Qaeda movement joined after receiving a Salafist message disseminated over the internet. Such direct messages normally do not pass through the traditional process of vetting by an imam. European counterterrorism officials thus worry about members of an alienated diaspora— sometimes second-and third-generation immigrants—who may be vulnerable to the message because they are not thoroughly trained in fundamental concepts of Islam, are alienated from their parents, and feel isolated in the communities in which they find themselves. The impulse to join the movement arises from a desire to belong to a group in a context where the operative is excluded from, repulsed by, or incapable of successful integration into a Western community.

Thus, with al-Qaeda, the twentieth-century focus on structure and function is neither timely nor sufficient. Tracing the command and control relationships in such a dramatically changing movement is enormously difficult, which makes comparisons with earlier, more traditional terrorist groups harder but by no means impossible; one detects parallels, for example, between al-Qaeda and the global terrorist movements that developed in the late nineteenth century, including anarchist and social revolutionary groups.

Means of Support

Financial support of al-Qaeda has ranged from money channelled through charitable organizations to grants given to local terrorist groups that present promising plans for attacks that serve al-Qaeda's general goals. The majority of its operations have relied at most on a small amount of seed money provided by the organization, supplemented by operatives engaged in petty crime and fraud. Indeed, beginning in 2003, many terrorism experts agreed that al-Qaeda could best be described as a franchise organization with a marketable "brand." Relatively little money is required for most al-Qaedaassociated attacks. As the International Institute for Strategic Studies points out, the 2002 Bali bombing cost less than $35,000, the 2000 USS *Cole* operation about $50,000, and the September 11 attacks less than $500,000. Another element of support has been the many autonomous businesses owned or controlled by al-Qaeda; at one point, bin Laden was reputed to own or control approximately eighty companies around the world. Many of these legitimately continue to earn a profit, providing a self-sustaining source for the movement. International counterterrorism efforts to control al-Qaeda financing have reaped at least $147 million in frozen assets. Still, cutting the financial lifeline of an agile and low-cost movement that has reportedly amassed billions of dollars and needs few resources to carry out attacks remains a formidable undertaking.

Choking off funds destined for al-Qaeda through regulatory oversight confronts numerous challenges. Formal banking channels are not necessary for many transfers, which instead can occur through informal channels known as "alternative remittance systems," "informal value transfer systems," "parallel banking," or "underground banking." Examples include the much-discussed *hawala* or *hundi* transfer networks and the Black Market Peso Exchange that operate through family ties or unofficial reciprocal arrangements. Value can be stored in commodities such as diamonds and gold that are moved through areas with partial or problematical state sovereignty. Al-Qaeda has also used charities to raise and move funds, with a relatively small proportion of gifts being siphoned off for illegitimate purposes, often without the knowledge of donors. Yet efforts to cut off charitable ºows to impoverished areas may harm many genuinely needy recipients and could result in heightened resentment, which in turn may generate additional political support for the movement. Al-Qaeda's fiscal autonomy makes the network more autonomous than its late-twentieth-century state-sponsored predecessors.

Means of Communication

The al-Qaeda movement has successfully used the tools of globalization to enable it to communicate with multiple audiences, including potential new members, new recruits, active supporters, passive sympathizers, neutral observers, enemy governments, and potential victims. These tools include mobile phones, text messaging, instant messaging, and especially websites, email, blogs, and chat rooms, which can be used for administrative tasks, fund-raising, research, and logistical coordination of attacks. Although al-Qaeda is not the only terrorist group to exploit these means, it is especially adept at doing so.

A crucial facilitator for the perpetuation of the movement is the use of websites both to convey messages, *fatwas,* claims of attacks, and warnings to the American public, as well as to educate future participants, embed instructions to operatives, and rally sympathizers to the cause. The internet is an important factor in building and perpetuating the image of al-Qaeda and in maintaining the organization's reputation. It provides easy access to the media, which facilitates al-Qaeda's psychological warfare against the West. Indoctrinating and teaching new recruits is facilitated by the internet, notably through the dissemination of al-Qaeda's widely publicized training manual (nicknamed "The Encyclopedia of Jihad") that explains how to organize and run a cell, as well as carry out attacks. Websites and chat rooms are used to offer practical advice and facilitate the fraternal bonds that are crucial to al-Qaeda. In a sense, members of the movement no longer need to join an organization at all, for the individual can participate with the stroke of a few keys. The debate over the size, structure, and membership of al-Qaeda may be a quaint relic of the twentieth century, displaced by the leveling effects of twenty-first-century technology. The new means of communication also offer practical advantages. Members of al-Qaeda use the web as a vast source of research and data mining to scope out future attack sites or develop new weapons technology at a low cost and a high level of sophistication. On January 15, 2003, for example,

U.S. Secretary of Defence Donald Rumsfeld quoted an al-Qaeda training manual retrieved by American troops in Afghanistan that advised trainees that at least 80 percent of the information needed about the enemy could be collected from open, legal sources.

AL QAEDA'S LEADERSHIP AND EXTREMIST MUSLIM IDEOLOGY

In looking at the dominant characteristics of a belligerent, Clausewitz indicated that a center of gravity in a popular uprising is the "personalities of the leaders and public opinion." Al Qaeda's leader, Osama Bin Laden, fits the Clausewitzian definition of a personality leading a popular uprising. Only today, this uprising is on a global scale with the objective of overthrowing the world order. Bin Laden rallies Muslim extremists. His charisma, vision, wealth, and leadership abilities are the reasons Al Qaeda is an effective terrorist organization striking fear across the globe while winning admiration among many in the Muslim world. Author Rohan Gunaratna in describing Bin Laden's capabilities:

In the spectrum of contemporary terrorist leaders Osama bin Laden *has no equal*. As a leader who has employed violence in pursuit of his political aims and objectives, he stands out in many ways. First, he is the only leader to have built a truly multinational terrorist group that can strike anywhere in the world. For over a decade *Osama has inspired, instigated and supported Islamist guerrillas and terrorists*, bringing about many deaths and much human suffering. In the World Trade Centre attack alone, the victims were from nearly 100 different nationalities. Second, *he has built a popular following throughout the Islamic world, being almost revered* in Muslim circles in Asia, Africa and the Middle East and among the first- and second-generation migrants in North America, Europe and Australia. *Nor has his popularity waned* despite evidence that he masterminded the worst terrorist attack in history. *He continues to be regarded as the supreme symbol of resistance to US imperialism.* Third, Osama's disposition towards his enemies has not mellowed in the face of the imminent threat to his own life and to his organisation. Even after the US cruise missile attacks in 1998 and intervention in Afghanistan in late 2001, the tone of his statements has remained constant, if not more strident. To his admirers *he sets an example of fearlessness; he is unrelenting; neither he nor Al Qaeda will compromise.*

It is interesting to note that Clausewitz connected leaders of popular uprisings with public opinion. He did not expand on this idea in his book *On War,* but, his phrasing of "personalities of leaders and public opinion," clearly links these two elements as a single center of gravity candidate. Although Clausewitz never could have imagined the world as it exists today, his observations and words still resonate by relating to the Gunaratna's description above of Bin Laden and that segment of the Muslim population that supports his extremist Muslim ideology. Thus, with Bin Laden, coupled with extremist ideology, as the strategic center of gravity for Al Qaeda, the United States must "direct its energies" at both. Echevarria offers the counter to this by saying: ... the avowed "hatred of apostasy," rooted in a radical brand of Islam – rather than Osama bin Laden or another individual leader—probably serves as the group's COG. Admittedly, bin Laden laid much of the groundwork to establish Al Qaeda, but it does not appear that his removal will cause his organization to collapse. Most analysts and intelligences sources claim that *if bin Laden were captured or killed, another leader would simply take his place.* That leader can only turn out to be either more or less effective than bin Laden. Thus, Al Qaeda's leadership really amounts to a center of critical capability—something we want to neutralize but not something, in itself, that will end the war.

In my opinion, Bin Laden is not replaceable—another leader cannot "simply take his place." Bin Laden possesses characteristics of a successful commander who not only knows the rules of the game, but he is "the one who through his genius created them." Neutralizing this "genius," who is clearly a talented yet ruthless and evil leader, will achieve "significant" results that will commence the unraveling of Al Qaeda. The author Peter Bergen, CNN's terrorism analyst, notes that if Bin Laden is captured or killed, Al Qaeda will be dealt a blow. Bergen goes on to say:

Others down the chain of command might hate the United States as much or more, but it was bin Laden's charisma and organizational skills that created his transnational terrorist concern.

In death bin Laden will certainly become a martyr for his immediate followers. But the most obvious statement you can make about martyrs is that they are dead, and that would immediately make bin Laden less potent. Bin Laden's al-Qaeda occupies the space that exists somewhere in between a cult and a genuine mass movement. Cults usually disappear with the deaths of their leaders: think of Jim Jones or David Koresh. So too will "bin Ladenism" eventually join what President Bush has called "history's unmarked grave of discarded lies." In identifying the "hatred of apostasy" as the possible center of gravity, Echevarria suggests that the strategy to defeat Al Qaeda "will mean employing the diplomatic and informational elements of national power as deliberately, if not more so, as the military one." The United States will need to employ these two elements of power as well as the economic element of power to effect the Islamist attitude and defiance. But, identifying the "hatred of apostasy" as the sole center of gravity seems to be an intangible thing to attack. In my strategic judgment, other way around.

Neutralizing the Al Qaeda leadership should be the first priority and the "hub of all power and movement at which our energies should be directed." To effect defeat of Al Qaeda by concentrating on influencing the will of disaffected Islamists may take a generation or longer to accomplish. We have a more immediate need to conduct moral and physical harm on the Al Qaeda leadership now before they can orchestrate more hate and another major attack on us.

As Bin Laden provides the motivation of "hatred of apostasy," fuelling a worldwide uprising, his critical requirements include his personal safety and that of key Al Qaeda deputies within the command and control element, his ability to periodically communicate direction and targets for terrorists cells, and his ability to communicate his Islamist message to the world and gain support for his movement. Bin Laden also requires resources (financing, weapons, etc.) and a place to hide. Al Qaeda's operations are also enhanced by the cooperation of other terrorist groups and entities sympathetic to Bin Laden's cause through material assistance and shared information and intelligence. Bin Laden is vulnerable to U.S. or allied surveillance and attack if he can be located. He also could be rendered irrelevant if the Islamist movement that supports him could be thwarted. If Bin Laden is killed, his martyrdom would probably not last because martyrs do not feed or take care of people. On the other hand, martyrs can become powerful images; an information campaign would be necessary to counter this. If he is captured alive, he should be taken out of the limelight and tried in front of a tribunal without public access and media coverage.

The critical requirement for a "popular uprising" as in Al Qaeda's Islamist movement, is a charismatic and visionary leader like Bin Laden. In addition, the movement requires something to hate (like Western culture) and is further fuelled by repression and poverty and the lack of opportunity.

The movement is further organized by the effort to educate and institutionalize the radical form of Islam through a "network of fundamentalist schools (*madrassas*), some of which radicalize and recruit youngsters for entrance into terrorists networks. Funded through Islamic charities and often espousing extreme views, *madrassas* will remain a key source of trouble in the years ahead."

The movement and its ideology are vulnerable to "fighting an idea with a better idea."

And, these ideas would include improved human rights, democratization of all nations in the Middle East, resolution of the Israeli/Palestian issue, and stabilization of the Middle East region and economic development. It will take a generation or longer, but the United States must lead this effort.

ORGANIZATION STRUCTURE OF AL-QAEDA

Though the current structure of al-Qaeda is unknown, information mostly acquired from Jamal al-Fadl provided American authorities with a rough picture of how the group was organized. While the veracity of the information provided by al-Fadl and the motivation for his cooperation are both disputed, American authorities base much of their current knowledge of al-Qaeda on his testimony. Osama bin Laden is the emir and Senior Operations Chief of al-Qaeda (although originally this role may have been filled by Abu Ayoub al-Iraqi), advised by a Shura Council, which consists of senior al-Qaeda members, estimated by Western officials at about twenty to thirty people. Ayman al-Zawahiri is al-Qaeda's Deputy Operations Chief and Abu Ayyub al-Masri is possibly the senior leader of al-Qaeda in Iraq.

- The Military Committee is responsible for training operatives, acquiring weapons, and planning attacks.
- The Money/Business Committee runs business operations, provides air tickets and false passports, pays al-Qaeda members, and oversees profit-driven businesses. In the 9/11 Commission Report, it is estimated that al-Qaeda requires $30,000,000 USD per year to conduct its operations.
- The Law Committee reviews Islamic law and decides if particular courses of action conform to the law.
- The Islamic Study/Fatwah Committee issues religious edicts, such as an edict in 1998 telling Muslims to kill Americans.
- In the late 1990s there was a publicly known Media Committee, which ran the now-defunct newspaper *Nashrat al Akhbar (Newscast)* and handled public relations.
- In 2005, al Qaeda formed As-Sahab, a media production house, to supply its video and audio materials.

The number of individuals belonging to the organization is also unknown. According to the controversial BBC documentary *The Power of Nightmares*, al-Qaeda is so weakly linked together that it is hard to say it exists apart from Osama bin Laden and a small clique of close associates. The lack of any significant numbers of convicted al-Qaeda members despite a large number of arrests on terrorism charges is cited by the documentary as a reason to doubt whether a widespread entity that meets the description of al-Qaeda exists at all. Therefore the extent and nature of al-Qaeda remains a topic of dispute.

Its rank and file has been described as changing from being "predominantly Arab," in its first years of operation, to "largely Pakistani," as of 2007. It has been estimated that 62% of al-Qaeda members have university education.

Organization v. Concept

When asked about the possibility of Al Qaeda's connection to the 7 July 2005 London bombings in 2005, Metropolitan Police Commissioner Sir Ian Blair said: "Al Qaeda is not an organization. Al Qaeda is a way of working... but this has the hallmark of that approach.... Al Qaeda clearly has the ability to provide training... to provide expertise... and I think that is what has occurred here."

What exactly al-Qaeda is, or was, remains in dispute. In the BBC documentary *The Power of Nightmares,* writer and journalist Adam Curtis contends that the idea of al-Qaeda as a formal organization is primarily an American invention. Curtis contends the name "al-Qaeda" was first brought to the attention of the public in the 2001 trial of Osama bin Laden and the four men accused of the 1998 United States embassy bombings in East Africa. As a matter of law, the U.S. Department of Justice needed to show that Osama bin Laden was the leader of a criminal organization in order to charge him *in absentia* under the Racketeer Influenced and Corrupt Organizations Act, also known as the RICO statutes. The name of the organization and details of its structure were provided in the testimony of Jamal al-Fadl, who claimed to be a founding member of the organization and a former employee of Osama bin Laden. To quote the documentary directly:

The reality was that bin Laden and Ayman Zawahiri had become the focus of a loose association of disillusioned Islamist militants who were attracted by the new strategy. But there was no organization. These were militants who mostly planned their own operations and looked to bin Laden for funding and assistance. He was not their commander. There is also no evidence that bin Laden used the term "al-Qaeda" to refer to the name of a group until after September the 11th, when he realized that this was the term the Americans had given it.

Questions about the reliability of al-Fadl's testimony have been raised by a number of sources because of his history of dishonesty and because he was delivering it as part of a plea bargain agreement after being convicted of conspiring to attack U.S. military establishments. Sam Schmidt, a defence lawyer from the trial, had the following to say about al-Fadl's testimony:

IDEOLOGY OF ISLAMIST MOVEMENT

The radical Islamist movement in general and al-Qaeda in particular developed during the Islamic revival and Islamist movement of the last three decades of the 20th century along with less extreme movements. Some have argued that "without the writings" of Islamic author and thinker Sayyid Qutb "al-Qaeda would not have existed."

Qutb preached that because of the lack of sharia law the Muslim world was no longer Muslim, having reverted to pre-Islamic ignorance known as jahiliyyah. To restore Islam, a vanguard movement of righteous Muslims was needed to implement Sharia and rid the Muslim world of any non-Muslim influences, such as concepts like socialism or nationalism.

Enemies of Islam included "treacherous Orientalists" and "world Jewry", who plotted "conspiracies" and "wicked[ly]" opposed Islam. In the words of Mohammed Jamal Khalia, a close college friend of Osama bin Laden: *Islam is different from any other religion; it's a way of life. We [Khalia and bin Laden] were trying to understand what Islam has to say about how we eat, who we marry, how we talk. We read Sayyid Qutb. He was the one who most affected our generation.* Qutb had an even greater influence on Osama bin Laden's mentor and another leading member of al-Qaeda, Ayman al-Zawahiri. Zawahiri's uncle and maternal family patriarch, Mafouz Azzam, was Qutb's student, then protégé, then personal lawyer and finally executor of his estate-one of the last people to see Qutb before his execution.

"Young Ayman al-Zawahiri heard again and again from his beloved uncle Mahfouz about the purity of Qutb's character and the torment he had endured in prison." Zawahiri paid homage to Qutb in his work *Knights under the Prophet's Banner.* One of the most powerful effects of Qutb's ideas was the idea that many who said they were Muslims were not, i.e. they were apostates, which not only gave jihadists "a legal loophole around the prohibition of killing another Muslim," but made "it a religious obligation to execute" the self-professed Muslim. These alleged apostates included leaders of Muslims countries since they failed to enforce sharia law.

ATTACKS

1992

On December 29, 1992, al-Qaeda's first terrorist attack took place as two bombs were detonated in Aden, Yemen. The first target was the Movenpick Hotel and the second was the parking lot of the Goldmohur Hotel.

The bombings were an attempt to eliminate American soldiers on their way to Somalia to take part in the international famine relief effort, Operation Restore Hope.

Internally, al-Qaeda considered the bombing a victory that frightened the Americans away, but in the United States the attack was barely noticed. No Americans were killed because the soldiers were staying in a different hotel altogether, and they went on to Somalia as scheduled. However little noticed, the attack was pivotal as it was the beginning of al-Qaeda's change in direction, from fighting armies to killing civilians. Two people were killed in the bombing, an Australian tourist and a Yemeni hotel worker. Seven others, mostly Yemenis, were severely injured.

Two *fatwa* are said to have been appointed by the most theologically knowledgeable of al-Qaeda's members, Mamdouh Mahmud Salim, aka Abu Hajer al Iraqi, to justify the killings according to Islamic law. Mamdouh Mahmud Salim referred to the thirteenth-century scholar Ibn Taymiyyah, much admired by Wahhabis.

In a famous fatwa, Ibn Tamiyyah had ruled that Muslims should kill the invading Mongols, and so too Salim said al-Qaeda should kill American soldiers. The second fatwa followed another of Ibn Tamiyyah's, that Muslims should not only kill Mongols but anyone who aided the Mongols, who bought goods from them or sold to them. In addition the killing of someone merely standing near a Mongol was justified as well. He ruled these killings just because any innocent bystander, like the Yemenite hotel worker, would find their proper reward in death, going to Paradise if they were good Muslims and to hell if they were bad. This became al-Qaeda's justification for killing civilians.

1993 WORLD TRADE CENTER BOMBING

In 1993, Ramzi Yousef used a truck bomb to attack the World Trade Center in New York City. The attack was intended to break the foundation of Tower One knocking it into Tower Two, bringing the entire complex down. Yousef hoped this would kill 250,000 people. The towers shook and swayed but the foundation held and he succeeded in killing only six people (although he injured 1,042 others and caused nearly $300 million in property damage). After the attack, Yousef fled to Pakistan and later moved to Manila. There he began developing the Bojinka Plot plans to blow up a dozen American airliners simultaneously, to assassinate Pope John Paul II and President Bill Clinton, and to crash a private plane into CIA headquarters. He was later captured in Pakistan. None of the U.S. government's indictments against Osama bin Laden have suggested that he had any connection with this bombing, but Ramzi Yousef is known to have attended a terrorist training camp in Afghanistan. After his capture, Yousef declared that his primary justification for the attack was to punish the United States for its support for the Israeli occupation of Palestinian territories and made no mention of any religious motivations.

Late 1990s

On November 13, 1995, a van containing a hundred pounds of Semtex explosive blew up near the communications center for the Saudi National Guard in downtown Riyadh, Saudi Arabia, where some American military contractors and Army officers had been training the Saudi National Guard. Seven people were killed, and sixty people were injured. The Saudi government arrested four men, "torturing confessions" out of them that they had been inspired by bin Laden's speeches and trained at al-Qaeda's camp in Afghanistan, and quickly executed them. It is unclear if they had anything to do with the crime. As with many bombings suspected to be the work of al-Qaeda, bin Laden praised the attacks but denied authorizing the attack or training the bombers.

The U.S. embassy bombings in East Africa, resulting in upward of 300 deaths, mostly locals. A barrage of cruise missiles launched by the U.S. military in response devastated an al-Qaeda base in

Khost, Afghanistan, but the network's capacity was unharmed. Bin Laden then turned his sights towards the United States Navy. In October 2000, al-Qaeda militants in Yemen bombed the missile destroyer U.S.S. Cole in a suicide attack, killing 17 U.S. servicemen and damaging the vessel while it lay offshore. Inspired by the success of such a brazen attack, al-Qaeda's command core began to prepare for an attack on the United States itself.

September 11 Attacks

The September 11 attacks were the most devastating terrorist acts in American and world history, killing approximately 3,000 people. Two commercial airliners were deliberately flown into the World Trade Center towers, a third into The Pentagon, a fourth, originally intended to target the United States Capitol crashed in Pennsylvania. The attacks were conducted by al-Qaeda, acting in accord with the 1998 *fatwa* issued against the United States and its allies by military forces under the command of bin Laden, al-Zawahiri, and others. Evidence points to suicide squads led by al-Qaeda military commander Mohamed Atta as the culprits of the attacks, with bin Laden, Ayman al-Zawahiri, Khalid Shaikh Mohammed, and Hambali as the key planners and part of the political and military command. Messages issued by bin Laden after September 11, 2001 praised the attacks, and explained their motivation while denying any involvement. Bin Laden legitimized the attacks by identifying grievances felt by both mainstream and Islamist Muslims, such as the general perception that the United States was actively oppressing Muslims. Bin Laden asserted that America was massacring Muslims in 'Palestine, Chechnya, Kashmir and Iraq' and that Muslims should retain the 'right to attack in reprisal'. He also claimed the 9/11 attacks were not targeted at women and children, but 'America's icons of military and economic power'. Evidence has since come to light that the original targets for the attack may have been nuclear power stations on the east coast of the U.S. The targets were later altered by al-Qaeda, as it was feared that such an attack "might get out of hand".

AL QAEDA UNDER ATTACK

In recent years, al Qaeda has come under attack by leading

Muslim voices in the form of criticism of its theological, jurisprudential, and strategic reasoning. The criticism has been particularly strident regarding al Qaeda's violence against fellow Muslims. Among the harshest attacks coming from outside the salafi-jihadi movement are those from Saudi cleric Salman al-Awda and Egyptian cleric Yusuf al-Qaradawi. In a September 14, 2007, open letter titled "A Ramadan Letter to Osama bin Laden," al-Awda asked bin Laden: "How much blood has been spilled? How many innocent children, women, and old people have been killed, maimed, and expelled from their homes in the name of 'al Qaeda'?"6 Al-Awda reportedly had been an important early influence on bin Laden's religious views. In June 2009, al-Qaradawi, a highly influential Qatar-based cleric who is chairman of the International Federation of Muslim Scholars, published a book in which he repudiated al Qaeda's concept of jihad as a "mad declaration of war upon the world." This work, by a popular, mainstream Islamic cleric who has a weekly program on al-Jazeera television and who retains a storied ability to serve as a barometer of broader mainstream Muslim opinion, suggested that the mainstream tide might have turned against al Qaeda.

In many ways, the attacks on al Qaeda and "revisions" of jihadi doctrine from within the salafi-jihadi movement have been even more scathing, and there should be little doubt that these high-profile defections from the movement have raised doubts about al Qaeda among its cadres and sympathizers. In April 2007, the Kuwaiti salafi-jihadi scholar Hamid al-Ali issued a *fatwa* (religious ruling) against the establishment of the Islamic State of Iraq, implicitly criticizing al Qaeda's affiliate in Iraq for its violence. "The spreading of bigotry and rancor, even if wrapped in the cloak of religion, is the work of the devil and of people who follow their own caprice. It must be avoided. Everyone must keep distance from such a dangerous path," wrote al-Ali. Late 2007 saw the release of a book by Sayyid Imam Abd al-Aziz al-Sharif, the former Egyptian Islamic Jihad Organization ideologue and author of a classic jihadi manual. In his book, Sayyid Imam extensively revised his earlier positions on the jurisprudence of jihad, making violent jihad impermissible under most circumstances. This was an especially important attack from within the salafi-jihadi camp, as

Sayyid Imam had formerly been the ideological mentor to Ayman al-Zawahiri. Sayyid Imam's *volte-face* on the permissibility of jihad sent shock waves through the salafi-jihadi community and led to a public dispute with al-Zawahiri. Also in late 2007, former Libyan Islamic Fighting Group leader Nu'man Bin 'Uthman issued his opening salvo against al Qaeda, framing his criticisms in both strategic and jurisprudential terms.

In January 2009, the Egyptian Islamic Group—a prominent former jihadi group, most of whose leadership declared a unilateral cease-fire in the late 1990s and formally renounced violence in March 2002—issued a statement urging al Qaeda to observe a cease-fire until it could assess the intentions of the recently elected Obama administration. 15 In September 2009, the Libyan Islamic Fighting Group released a new "code" for jihad in the form of a 417-page religious document that served as an extended critique and recantation of al Qaeda's reading of the jurisprudence of jihad.

In November 2010, former al Qaeda spokesman Suleman Abu Ghaith released a book that constituted another damning indictment of al Qaeda from a former insider. Echoing other critics, Abu Ghaith emphasized that after having pledged allegiance to Taliban leader Mullah Mohammed Omar while in Afghanistan, bin Laden violated Islamic law by failing to abide by Omar's instructions not to attack the United States. This violation, according to Abu Ghaith and others, made bin Laden an unfit leader who deserved punishment.

Finally, in late 2010, al Qaeda's former military planner Sayf al-Adl wrote a number of letters calling upon al Qaeda's leaders to conduct a comprehensive review of their operations, including the 9/11 attacks, for the purpose of "assessing the past stage, learning the lessons, and drawing up a strategy for the future." The letters were highly critical of al Qaeda's past mistakes, but it is also alarming that al-Adl appeared to be advocating that the group emphasize a strategy focused on attacking the United States rather than local Muslim regimes. In the wake of bin Laden's death, al-Adl was appointed al Qaeda Central's acting chief until al Qaeda's Shura Council could choose a more permanent successor.
Implications for U.S. Strategy and Policy

Suspicions of U.S. intentions run deep in many parts of the Muslim world, and it can be difficult to overcome the undercurrent of sheer resentment of U.S. superpower status, whatever Washington does, but al Qaeda's current situation nonetheless presents opportunities, especially now, given the death of the charismatic and organizationally adept bin Laden and the opening of political space in some Muslim countries as a result of the Arab Spring. With al Qaeda already under considerable pressure from within the Muslim community, what, if any, fruitful role can the United States play in what is essentially an intra-Muslim debate about the nature of Islam and the permissibility of violent jihad? In short, U.S. strategy and policy should take the long view, which means focusing on three objectives: (1) reducing or eliminating the irritants that fuel support for al Qaeda, (2) promoting universal democratic and humanitarian values, and (3) avoiding actions and rhetorical missteps that reinforce al Qaeda's narrative.

Reducing or eliminating the irritants that fuel support for al Qaeda. Al Qaeda's grand strategy is based on the dual assumptions that attacks on the United States can lure it into intervening militarily in Muslim lands and that Muslims can then more easily be mobilized into jihad beneath al Qaeda's banner. With a withdrawal of U.S. military forces from Iraq by the end of 2011 and substantial reductions of forces in Afghanistan envisioned to begin by the end of 2014, this irritant will diminish, and al Qaeda will find it increasingly difficult to exploit this issue in mobilizing jihadists. It bears mentioning that bin Laden's own radicalization appears to have been fuelled by the 1991 Gulf War, the deprivations experienced by Iraqis in the war's aftermath, and the prolonged presence of U.S. troops in Saudi Arabia following that war.

Future decisions to deploy or permanently station U.S. military forces in Muslim lands must be carefully weighed against their potential consequences for fuelling recruitment and mobilization into al Qaeda extremism. In a similar vein, the United States can weaken al Qaeda's ability to exploit the Palestinian issue by continuing efforts to expand the writ and influence of the Palestinian Authority and to promote a broader settlement between Israel and the Palestinians. Al Qaeda has judged that the Israeli occupation of Palestine is the issue that is most salient to Muslims worldwide—and the most easily exploited in its propaganda and recruitment efforts. Thus, despite the current impasse in Israeli-Palestinian negotiations, it is crucial that the United States continue its decades-long effort to promote a broader settlement.

Promoting universal democratic and humanitarian values. By promoting and supporting democratic reform in the Muslim world, the United States aligns itself with the aspirations of most ordinary Muslims and is better positioned to marginalize al Qaeda because of the organization's outright rejection of democracy and peaceful political competition.

The overthrow of corrupt and despotic leaders and the opening of political space, as occurred in the recent revolutions in Tunisia, Egypt, and Libya, can help sap support for al Qaeda's extremism and channel energies toward peaceful political competition. Efforts by the United States to secure the release of political prisoners also can provide tangible signs of the U.S. commitment to democratic values. Finally, by providing humanitarian assistance and disaster relief, as it did following the December 2004 Indian Ocean tsunami that struck Indonesia and other nations in the region and the October 2005 earthquake that struck Pakistan, the United States can soften its image abroad, build goodwill in Muslim nations, and help to inoculate their populations against al Qaeda propaganda and rhetoric promoting violence against America. Avoiding actions and rhetorical missteps that reinforce al Qaeda's narrative. U.S. efforts to directly influence intra-Muslim debates over the nature of Islam and the permissibility of violent jihad seem highly unlikely to be effective. The theological and jurisprudential conditions and constraints that bear on the conduct of violent jihad are complex and subtle, and official U.S. efforts to opine on or influence such matters carry grave risks of both alienating potential friends and allies within the Muslim world and reinforcing al Qaeda's narrative that the United States aims to refashion Islam into a moderate or even secular form. U.S. deeds of the types outlined above matter far more than words, but U.S. words can also cause great harm. Characterizing U.S. efforts against al Qaeda as part of a "crusade" or clash of civilizations may play well with some domestic audiences, but ultimately, it is likely to reinforce al Qaeda's narrative of an Islam that is under attack by the non-Muslim world.

This is clearly not a strategy for quick, short-term results. Rather, as was the case with the earlier U.S. sustained effort to promote democracy, markets, and individual freedom over totalitarian communism, it is a strategy that is likely to require decades or generations of effort. However, only by taking the long view will the United States be able to establish conditions that favour the triumph of a merciful, compassionate, and tolerant Islam over the violent nihilism of al Qaeda and its fellow travellers. A Psychological Triumph. There is very little concrete evidence upon which to base such dire forecasts. The threat of nuclear terror floats far above the world of known facts. How has al Qaeda managed to pull off this stunning feat of psychological legerdemain?

The dramatic impact of terrorism provides part of the answer. What distinguishes terrorism from other modes of armed conflict is the separation between the actual targets of terrorist violence and the targets of the psychological terror. Because terrorists cannot hope to defeat their foes in open battle, they deliberately aim spectacular attacks at vulnerable civilian targets, hoping to create an atmosphere of terror, which will induce the public audience to exaggerate the terrorists' strength and dissuade governments from pursuing policies opposed by the terrorists because of the perceived price. Terrorist attacks also create political crises, provoking overreaction and compelling governments to divert vast resources to security in order to maintain public confidence that they will be protected, even while knowing that absolute security is not possible. This is the very essence of terrorism. And it often works. The trajectory of contemporary terrorist violence also has contributed to fears of mass destruction.

As war has become less lethal, terrorism has become more lethal. In the decades since World War II, military power has moved away from the industrial-scale slaughter of total war, placing greater emphasis on reducing collateral casualties to a minimum. The development of increasingly precise weapons has facilitated this effort. Domestic genocide, particularly the targeting of specific ethnic groups, has been the exception to this rule. Meanwhile, contemporary terrorists have moved in the opposite direction, toward large-scale indiscriminate violence, escalating from small, mostly symbolic bombings involving few casualties in the 1970s to truck bombs aimed at killing hundreds in the 1980s and 1990s to the attacks on September 11, 2001, that killed thousands. From this cataclysmic event, it was easy to extrapolate the idea of Osama bin Laden using a nuclear weapon if he had one. The 9/11 terrorist attacks fundamentally altered perceptions of plausibility. With box cutters and mace, terrorists turned commercial airliners into guided missiles that brought down skyscrapers. People feared that al Qaeda would try to launch more 9/11-scale attacks if it could, or perhaps even more-ambitious attacks. Terrorist scenarios that had been deemed far-fetched before 9/11 became operative presumptions after 9/11. In this environment, no terrorist scheme could be dismissed. Nuclear terrorism ascended to a clear and present danger.

There are vast differences between chemical, biological, radiological, and nuclear weapons. In its final report, written before 9/11, the National Commission on Terrorism chose wisely to avoid the collective term "weapons of mass destruction." Aggregating such weapons confuses a low threshold for occurrence—terrorists already have employed chemical and biological weapons, with modest results—with a high potential for theoretical casualties, thereby exaggerating both probability and likely consequences. Realistically, only biological and nuclear weapons have a capacity for true mass destruction. And nuclear weapons differ from biological weapons in that biological weapons also may be used to kill just a few, as the anthrax letters did. It is hard to imagine a minor nuclear attack. Absence of Warning

Paradoxically, the absence of evidence heightens the threat. Many believe that the public will have no warning of an impending terrorist nuclear attack. Although there are two diametrically opposite views of U.S. intelligence capabilities, both fuel nuclear terror. The first view of U.S. intelligence credits it with omniscience but remains suspicious that Washington is deliberately withholding information to avoid causing public panic. This is a popular theme among conspiracy-driven books and articles on nuclear terrorism that promise to tell the reader what the government will not. In fact, since 9/11, the government has routinely passed threat information—some of it vague, even dubious—on to the public. Yet it is also true that since the 1970s, there have been scores of undisclosed nuclear threats to American cities. The Federal Bureau of Investigation (FBI) and U.S. Department of Energy nuclear emergency teams have mobilized to conduct secret searches. All of the threats were found to be apparent hoaxes, but none of this was published at the time. As an example, just after 9/11, the CIA received intelligence from a source appropriately code-named Dragonfire that terrorists had planted a nuclear device in New York City. The federal government initiated a search without informing the public or local authorities. Nothing was found—the source was mistaken. But given this record, it is conceivable that if the government received credible intelligence that al Qaeda or another terrorist organization had acquired a nuclear weapon, it might not reveal it.

The second view of U.S. intelligence is that it cannot be depended upon to provide advance warning of a terrorist nuclear attack. We will know it only when we see the bright yellow flash. After all, American intelligence officials were surprised to discover in 1991 that Iraq had come closer to developing nuclear weapons than they had imagined. U.S. intelligence did not foresee 9/11. It failed to predict the testing of nuclear weapons by India, Pakistan, and North Korea, but prior to the Iraq War, it reported with confidence that Iraq had weapons of mass destruction when it had none. While this recitation is not entirely fair to the intelligence community, perceived past failures of intelligence do not inspire confidence.

Lacking hard evidence that terrorists have nuclear weapons or material, intelligence analysts instead pore over al Qaeda's public statements for warnings or other clues about its interest in nuclear weapons. They argue over whether *fatwas*—religious rulings—authorizing al Qaeda to kill millions should be interpreted as the obligatory warning required by Islamic concepts of warfare.

They debate whether terrorists might be deterred from acquiring or using nuclear weapons. These are legitimate lines of inquiry, but they also reify the threat, treating a hypothetical—al Qaeda's or any terrorists' possession of nuclear weapons—as if it were a concrete fact, or at least an inevitable development. Spinning Nuclear Fantasies

Al Qaeda's efforts to obtain nuclear weapons were accompanied by an active communications effort, which implied that the terrorist group was further along in its quest than it actually was. This public communications campaign intensified as al Qaeda's central leadership came under increasing pressure after 9/11. In earlier interviews, Osama bin Laden, when asked by reporters about weapons of mass destruction, coyly responded that their acquisition was a religious duty. But in an interview with a Pakistani reporter in November 2001, as the Taliban and al Qaeda were being bombed by American warplanes, bin Laden and Ayman al-Zawahiri were said to have claimed that al Qaeda had chemical and nuclear weapons, although the reporting of this interview raised doubts. The first published version had bin Laden saying only that al Qaeda would survive even if the United States used chemical or nuclear weapons against it; subsequent versions of the same interview introduced the claim that al Qaeda itself already had such weapons.

Neither of al Qaeda's two top leaders made many public mentions of nuclear weapons after the 2001 interview, but in 2002, an al Qaeda spokesman posted a message on the Internet claiming that because the United States was responsible for the deaths of millions of Muslims, al Qaeda, in accordance with Islamic law, had the right to kill 4 million Americans. This was amended by a fugitive Saudi cleric who issued a religious ruling in 2003 authorizing al Qaeda to kill 10 million Americans.

Exactly why al Qaeda elicited the two statements about killing millions of Americans is not known, but the statements excited the organization's followers and alarmed analysts in the United States. The two communications prompted a lively discourse among jihadists about al Qaeda's nuclear posture and strategy, as if its possession of nuclear weapons were real. Analysts in the

United States, meanwhile, interpreted the two statements as providing the necessary warning before attack required by the Islamic code of warfare. They noted that the only way al Qaeda could achieve this magnitude of casualties was with nuclear, or possibly biological, weapons. It was seen as a signal. Al Qaeda's communications campaign was not a centrally directed effort but, rather, a distributed project, a new phenomenon made possible by the Internet. A chorus of online jihadists carried on the campaign, issuing threats and adding lurid landscapes of fireballs and mushroom clouds over Manhattan and Washington. These were the fantasies of the powerless, vicarious participation in al Qaeda's terrorist campaign. Psychologically satisfying to their jihadist authors, they kept Western government officials on edge.

THE TROUBLING EFFECTIVENESS OF AL-QAEDA'S PSYOP ON THE PAKISTANI ARMY

Going forward in the global conflict before us, it is important to acknowledge and understand that al-Qaeda is currently engaged in an Information Operation (IO) campaign inside Pakistan. This is in addition to its efforts to gain influence outside of Pakistan, particularly with Muslims in Europe, the Middle East and in the US. The primary target of the Pakistan campaign is the Pakistani military and it is driven by al-Qaeda's accelerating insurgency inside Pakistan. Understanding how and why al-Qaeda has undertaken this effort allows decision makers greater understanding of al-Qaeda's aims and equips them with a 'lay of the land' required to counter al-Qaeda's message and objectives.

Usama bin Laden's latest recorded message is the third in just two weeks following three years of virtual silence from the al-Qaeda leader. In it, bin Laden calls on Pakistani Muslims to acknowledge that Musharraf's actions are examples of his loyalty to the United States and representative of his unbelief. For bin Laden and his compatriots, such unbelief marks Musharraf as 'kufr' and places the requirement on believers to make "armed rebellion against him." The misguided understanding that bin Laden and al-Qaeda have of Islam makes it obligatory to fight against those who rule outside of their interpretation of Islam, and its overly broad application of tawhid. Yet bin Laden crafts a different message for the Pakistani Army, whom he advises to "resign" from their jobs, "disassociate yourself from Pervez and his Shirk (polytheism)" and "enter anew into Islam."

Ayman al-Zawahiri's latest video message and bin Laden's audio message, released on the same day, mark as-Sahab's 77th and 78th propaganda productions this year alone. There is a clear shifting of gears in the al-Qaeda Information Operations, most notably within Pakistan as well as their international efforts surrounding the 6th anniversary of the September 11th attacks.

Before looking further into the al-Qaeda Pakistani IO campaign, we must address the al-Qaeda-Taliban insurgency actively ongoing in Pakistan.

Al-Qaeda in Pakistan-From Terrorism to Insurgency

There is, of course, no single agreed upon definition of terrorism. Terrorism is defined in the US Code of Federal Regulations as "...the unlawful use of force and violence against persons or property to intimidate or coerce a government, the civilian population, or any segment thereof, in furtherance of political or social objectives." (28 C.F.R. Section 0.85) For instance, terrorism is – among other things-a tactic employed to increase support for a group through inspiration while also decreasing effective resistance to the group through intimidation. An example of this type of terrorism would be the beheading of those deemed to be 'spies' for the Americans in South Waziristan, the multiple car bomb and rocket attacks, or the anti-aircraft assassination attempts on Musharraf. Additionally, the bombings that took place after the Pakistani government raid on Lal Masjid (the Red Mosque) are an example of the use of terror to gain influence. No matter the definition of terrorism being applied, al-Qaeda has clearly been a terrorist organization in Pakistan.

Beyond Pakistan, Al-Qaeda seeks to – in part-influence American foreign policy through terrorist means. But within Pakistan, al-Qaeda has clearly and by specific design transformed from being simply a dangerous international terrorist group *within* Pakistan to a full-fledged internal insurgency *against* it. This transformation is represented through the efforts of al-Qaeda to acquire the armored assets of a state Army and its nuclear weapons, as well as the pursuit of land holdings to be integrated into the larger objective of creating an Islamic state to be ruled by a successor to the Prophet, a Khalifa or Caliph, nearly 1350 years after the last of the 'rightly guided' rulers.

An insurgency is a movement with specific governmental designs on the host country. In *Countering Evolved Insurgent Networks*, Col. Thomas X. Hammes (USMC, Ret.) quotes Bard O'Neill to define an insurgency. O'Neill wrote, "Insurgency may be defined as a struggle between a nonruling group and the ruling authorities in which the nonruling group consciously uses *political resources* (e.g., organizational expertise, propaganda, and demonstrations) and *violence* to destroy, reformulate, or sustain the basis of one or more aspects of politics."

In more accessible terms, Terrorism-Research.com offers that the ultimate goal of an insurgency "is to challenge the existing government for control of all or a portion of its territory, or force political concessions in sharing political power."

Both aptly describe al-Qaeda's actions, operations and aims within Pakistan, a ready-made nuclear power which the terrorist group seeks to wrest complete control.

Perhaps the best way to describe al-Qaeda's Pakistan insurgency is to call it a "Death by a Thousand Cuts." They have openly sought not only the assassination of Pervez Musharraf, but also the demise – or reconfiguration – of the Pakistani national government. In a strategy that has been executed with remarkable patience, al-Qaeda has gained acknowledged control of several sizable territories in Pakistan's Federally Administered Tribal Areas.

After defeating Pakistani forces on the battlefield, the Taliban-al-Qaeda alliance have secured various 'peace accords' replete with concessions from the Musharraf government. Effective control of North Waziristan, South Waziristan, Bajour and Swat have been ceded to them and Pakistani forces were – upon agreement – effectively withdrawn from the areas handed the Taliban-al-Qaeda alliance through the accords. The accords, no matter how presented by the Musharraf government, represented abject defeat.

Al-Qaeda Insurgency: Destination-Islamabad

Domination in these territories has allowed al-Qaeda the haven necessary to rebuild its training and planning infrastructure as well as replenish its human resources. After a few short weeks of basic military training, Taliban conscripts are sent in waves across the border to battle US and Coalition forces in Afghanistan.

However, al-Qaeda has no designs on investing in regaining that territory. There are no resources for them there – and a more formidable, if reduced, military force to be reckoned with. One whose defeat of the terrorist group drove them into Pakistan's border regions to begin with. Al-Qaeda's designs are not back towards the west, but rather onward deeper into the heart of Pakistan.

While al-Qaeda's Pakistan insurgency has been largely waged in the FATA region, it's territorial aims are by no means limited to it. Rather, al-Qaeda seeks control of all of Pakistan, including its military, weapons and economic capabilities. Al-Qaeda has been executing this strategy one territory, one victory at a time. And it now closes in on Islamabad.

Indeed, an analysis by the Pakistani Interior Ministry warned Pakistani President Pervez Musharraf of precisely this. The *New York Times* reported that the 15-page internal Pakistani document warned Musharraf that "the influence of the extremists is swiftly bleeding east and deeper into his own country, threatening areas like Peshawar, Nowshera and Kohat, which were considered to be safeguarded by Pakistani government forces." The Interior Ministry document said that Peshewar endures the "highest number of terrorist incidents, including attacks on local police," and that in Bannu and Tank regions, police are "patronizing the local Taliban and have abdicated the role of law and order." It is important to note that Peshewar is the capital of the North West Frontier Province (NWFP). Much of the Pakistani government, non-Islamist educators, officials and police forces live inside heavily armed and walled communities in the NWFP, where they are more safe from al-Qaeda attack. The NWFP borders the Federally Administered Tribal Areas under direct Taliban-al-Qaeda control on one side and the Pakistani capital of Islamabad on the other.

The rising violence is a clear indicator of the expansion of al-Qaeda's insurgency as it marches patiently but steadily toward Islamabad. As evidenced by bin Laden's latest message, that patience may be nearing an end.

Usama bin Laden's latest message implored the Pakistani public to take up arms against Musharraf and warned the army's soldiers to break ranks and fight Musharraf with al-Qaeda rather than serve him. This is a sign that al-Qaeda's patient approach to its Pakistan insurgency has run its course. There could be a maelstrom of events to follow in Pakistan.

AQ Targets Police for Violence and Army Soldiers for Influence

The al-Qaeda Information Operation (IO) is designed to support the insurgency's incremental march on Islamabad. The key to understanding the al-Qaeda IO and its insurgency goals is to understand how al-Qaeda primarily targets Pakistani Interior Ministry forces (police, constabularies and the Frontier Corps) for physical attack while targeting Pakistani regular army forces for influence and subversion.

The persistent mention of Pakistani police forces – rather than Pakistani Army forces – is expected in any Pakistani Interior Ministry report, as the Police forces fall under the Interior. But Pakistani police forces also decidedly bear the brunt of al-Qaeda's lethal attacks and not the Pakistani Army. It's not that al-Qaeda and their indigenous Taliban allies cannot attack the Pakistani Army with expectations of success. They most certainly can and have. With bin Laden's latest audio message delivering a combination invitation and ultimatum to Pakistani Army soldiers, al-Qaeda's designs for the Pakistani Army are more clearly visible. The reason for attacking Pakistani police forces is two-fold and – in this writer's view-also the most elusive and yet perhaps most important indicator of the ongoing al-Qaeda insurgency.

First, the Interior Ministry is widely regarded as the one segment of the Pakistani government with unwavering loyalty to Musharraf, whom al-Qaeda has sought to assassinate several times. Unlike the military and the military's intelligence arm (ISI), the

Pakistani police forces, constabularies and Frontier Corps of the Interior Ministry do not have historical ties to Islamist groups such as Lashkar-e-Taiba, al-Qaeda and the Taliban. Interior Ministry loyalty to Musharraf makes their ranks logical targets for the Islamists who seek to kill and replace Musharraf atop an Islamist-run Pakistani government.

Secondly, and most importantly, al-Qaeda at the same time seeks to avoid open bloody conflict with the Army. Not because it fears the deadly consequences of such a confrontation, but rather because al-Qaeda senior leadership wants the Pakistani military intact – for themselves. Ideally, they do not want to ultimately find Musharraf killed or oustered only to have the military splintered internally between pro-government and pro-al-Qaeda commanders. Al-Qaeda is executing an insurgency to gain control, not to touch off a civil war.

In the end, al-Qaeda's design is also to co-opt an intact military in order to gain command of a military force with the assets of a state (aircraft, armor, etc.) and direct control of Pakistan's nuclear arsenal. Recent reports of defections of Pakistani military elements since bin Laden's latest message to them indicates a level of success in the al-Qaeda IO campaign targeting them.

Measuring al-Qaeda's PSYOP Success

Three weeks ago, well over 200 Pakistani Army soldiers surrendered to a much smaller number of fighters from the Taliban-al-Qaeda alliance without a shot fired. But the al-Qaeda IO campaign primarily targeting the Pakistani regular army forces has a spillover effect on other forces-and the general populace-as well. It is reported in Pakistan that many soldiers in the Pakistani Army, Frontier Corps paramilitary and police forces are refusing to fight or putting up little fight against their own countrymen inside the Federally Administered Tribal Area. It is difficult to dispute the success of al-Qaeda's Psychological Warfare efforts inside Pakistan. The message has been consistent for several years and al-Qaeda's patience and restraint in seeing it through are significant qualities of the terrorist organization turned insurgent group. With every message and in all their forms, al-Qaeda has sought to convince the Army soldiers that they are not al-Qaeda's enemy, rather that they are simply being misled by Musharraf. In bin Laden's latest message, he said of the Pakistani Army, "we see the armies becoming tools and weapons in the hands of the Kuffaar [unbeliever, referencing Musharraf and the US] against the Muslims."

This message resonates, as many Pakistanis are reluctant to take up arms against other Pakistanis, whether those they would confront are Taliban or al-Qaeda or not. It must also be considered that upwards of 30% of the Pakistani Army are, like the Taliban, ethnic Pashtuns. The vast majority of them are enlisted foot soldiers, as very few ethnic Pashtuns hold leadership positions, largely due to internal social and educational dynamics.

Even among the Pakistani police forces in the North West Frontier Province, many are said to have requested leave or simply deserted when faced with the outlook of deadly confrontations with fellow Pakistanis among the Taliban-al-Qaeda alliance. In other instances, including the Interior Ministry's report that specifically cited the Bannu and Tank regions, police are "patronizing the local Taliban and have abdicated the role of law and order."

Where True Power Lies...And Grows

This is an indication that fear is also a prime motivator among Pakistanis. In the North West Frontier Province capital of Peshawar, al-Qaeda's black banner of jihad can be seen displayed in the widows of many shops and flying in various places. This does not necessarily mean that there is explicit support in the hearts and minds of all Pakistanis there – even among those flying the al-Qaeda banner.

Though Peshewar and the rest of the NWFP are technically under Pakistani state control, this indicates a reflection among the populace of where the true power lies – outside the walled communities where many government employees and 'moderate' citizens take refuge. In many cases, the al-Qaeda banner may well be flown simply out of self-protection to avoid attack on their particular shops.

The police cannot protect everyone all the time, but al-Qaeda and the Taliban can attack at their choosing. And from a local's perspective, this is where the true power lies. And as more and more Pakistanis in the police forces, the Frontier Corps and the regular army begin to show a reluctance to do battle, the al-Qaeda power in these region grows, both in measurable means on the ground and within the minds of the Pakistani populace.

Such are the tangible gains of effective, persistent and robust al-Qaeda information operations, a classic PSYOP directed at both the Pakistani population writ large and also expressly directed at the Pakistani Army. As a result, Pakistani forces are engaging al-Qaeda and the Taliban less and less. In fact, President Musharraf announced that in 2008, there will be no Pakistani Army activity at all in al-Qaeda-held territory, deferring engagement to the less capable and less effective Frontier Corps and Pakistani police and constabularies.

8

Lashkar-e-Taiba (Militant Islamist Organizations)

Lashkar-e-Taiba is one of the largest and most active militant Islamist organizations in South Asia, operating mainly from Pakistan. It was founded by Hafiz Muhammad Saeed, Abdullah Yusuf Azzam and Zafar Iqbal in Afghanistan. With its headquarters based in Muridke, near Lahore inPunjab province of Pakistan, the group operates several training camps in Pakistan-administered Kashmir.

Lashkar-e-Taiba has attacked civilian and military targets in India, most notably the 2001 Indian Parliament attack and the 2008 Mumbai attacks. Its stated objective is to introduce an Islamic state in South Asia and to "liberate" Muslims residing in Indian Kashmir. The organization is banned as a terrorist organization by India, Pakistan, the United States, the United Kingdom, the European Union, Russia and Australia. Some experts such as former French investigating magistrate Jean-Louis Bruguière andNew America Foundation president Steve Coll believe that Pakistan's main intelligence agency, the Inter-Services Intelligence (ISI), continues to give LeT intelligence help and protection.

OBJECTIVE

While the primary area of operations of the their militant activities is the Kashmir valley, their professed goal is not limited to challenging India's sovereignty over Jammu and Kashmir.

LeT sees the issue of Kashmir as part of a wider global struggle. The group has repeatedly claimed through its journals and websites that its main aim is to destroy the Indian republic and to annihilate Hinduism and Judaism.

LeT has declared Hindus and Jews to be the "enemies of Islam", as well as India and Israel to be the "enemies of Pakistan". In a pamphlet entitled "Why Are We Waging Jihad?"

The group defined its agenda as the restoration of Islamic rule over all parts of India and declared India, Israel and the United States as existential enemies of Islam.

The LeT believes that violent jihad is the duty of all Muslims and must be waged until eight objectives are met: ending persecution against Muslims, establishing Islam as the dominant way of life in the world, forcing infidels to pay jizya, fighting for the weak and feeble against oppressors, exacting revenge for killed Muslims, punishing enemies for violating oaths and treaties, defending all Muslim states, and recapturing occupied Muslim territory.

In the wake of the November 2008 Mumbai attacks, investigations of computer and email accounts revealed a list of 320 locations worldwide deemed as possible targets for attack. Only 20 of the targets were locations within India. Analysts believed that the list was a statement of intent rather than a list of locations where LeT cells had been established and were ready to strike.

In January 2009 the LeT publicly declared that it would pursue a peaceful resolution in the Kashmir issue and that it did not have global jihadist aims, but the group is still believed to be active in several other spheres of anti-Indian terrorism. Disclosures of Abu Jundal, who was extradited to India by the Saudi Arabian Government, however revealed that LeT is planning to revive militancy in Jammu & Kashmir and conduct major terror strikes in India.

Leadership

- Hafiz Muhammad Saeed – Living in Pakistan – Founder of Lashkar-e-Taiba and *amir* of its political arm, Jamaat-ud-Dawa (JuD).Shortly after the November 2008 Mumbai attacks Saeed denied any links between the two groups: "No Lashkar-e-Taiba man is in Jamaat-ud-Dawa and I have never been a chief of Lashkar-e-Taiba."

- Abdul Rehman Makki– Living in Pakistan – second in command of Lashkar-e-Taiba. He is the brother in law of Hafiz Muhammad Saeed. US has announced a reward of $2 million for information leading to the location of Makki.
- Zaki-ur-Rehman Lakhvi – In custody of Pakistan military – Senior member of LeT. Named as being one of the masterminds of the Mumbai attack.
- Yusuf Muzammil – Senior member of LeT. Named as a mastermind of the November 2008 Mumbai attacks by surviving gunman Ajmal Kasab.
- Zarrar Shah – in Pakistani custody – one of Lashkar-e-Taiba's primary liaisons to the ISI. An American official said that he was a "central character" in the planning behind the Mumbai attacks in 2008. Zarar Shah has boasted to Pakistani investigators about his role in the attacks.
- Muhammad Ashraf – LeT's top financial officer. Although not directly connected to the 2008 Mumbai plot, he was added to the U.N. list of people that sponsor terrorism after the attacks. However, Geo TV reported that six years earlier Ashraf became seriously ill while in custody and died at Civil Hospital on June 11, 2002.
- Mahmoud Mohamed Ahmed Bahaziq – The leader of LeT in Saudi Arabia and one of its financiers. Although not directly connected to the Mumbai plot, the U.N. added him to its list of individuals that sponsor terrorism after the 2008 Mumbai attacks.
- Nasr Javed – A Kashmiri senior operative, is on the list of individuals banned from entering the United Kingdom for "engaging in unacceptable behaviour by seeking to foment, justify or glorify terrorist violence in furtherance of particular beliefs."

HISTORY

Formation

In 1985, Hafiz Mohammed Saeed and Zafar Iqbal formed the *Jamaat-ud-Dawa* (Organization for Preaching, or JuD) as a small missionary group dedicated to promoting an Ahl-e-Hadith version of Islam.

In the next year, Zaki-ur Rehman Lakvi merged his group of anti-Soviet jihadists with the JuD to form the *Markaz-ud Dawa-wal-Irshad* (Center for Preaching and Guidance, or MDI). The MDI had 17 founders originally, and notable among them was Abdullah Azzam.

The LeT was formed in Afghanistan's Kunar province in 1990 and gained prominence in the early 1990s as a military offshoot of MDI. MDI's primary concerns were dawah and the LeT focused on jihad although the members did not distinguish between the two groups' functions.

According to Hafiz Saeed, "Islam propounds both dawa and jihad. Both are equally important and inseparable. Since our life revolves around Islam, therefore both dawa and jihad are essential; we cannot prefer one over the other."

Most of these training camps were located in North-West Frontier Province (NWFP) and many were shifted to Azad Kashmir for the sole purpose of training volunteers for the Kashmir Jihad.

From 1991 onwards, militancy surged in Indian Kashmir, as many Lashkar-e-Taiba volunteers were infiltrated into Indian Kashmir from Azad Kashmir with the help of the Pakistan Army and ISI. As of 2010, the degree of control that Pakistani intelligence retains over LeT's operations is not known.

Designation as Terrorist Group

Lashkar-e-Taiba had links to Jama'at-ud-Da'wah, however Jama'at-ud-Da'wah publicly retracted any association with them after theUnited States Department of State declared Lashkar-e-Taiba to be a terrorist organization.

On March 28, 2001, in Statutory Instrument 2001 No. 1261, British Home Secretary Jack Straw designated the group a Proscribed Terrorist Organization under the Terrorism Act 2000.

On December 5, 2001, the group was added to the Terrorist Exclusion List. In a notification dated December 26, 2001, United States Secretary of State Colin Powell, designated Lashkar-e-Taiba a Foreign Terrorist Organisation.

Lashkar-e-Taiba was banned in Pakistan on January 12, 2002.

It is banned in India as a designated terrorist group under the Unlawful Activities (Prevention) Act.

It was listed as a terrorist organisation in Australia under the Security Legislation Amendment (Terrorism) Act 2002 on 11 April 2003 and was re-listed 11 April 2005 and 31 March 2007.

On 2 May 2008 it was placed on the Consolidated List established and maintained by the Committee established by the United Nations Security Council Resolution 1267 as an entity associated with al-Qaeda. The report also proscribed Jamaat-ud-Dawa as a front group of the LeT. Bruce Riedel, an expert on terrorism believes that LeT with the support of its Pakistani backers, is probably more dangerous terror group than Al-Qaeda which has been substantially degraded.

The Aftermath of the November 2008 Mumbai Attacks

According to a media report, the U.S. accused JuD of being the front group for the prime suspects of the November 2008 Mumbai attacks, the Lashkar-e-Taiba, the organization that trained the 10 gunmen involved in these attacks.

On December 7, 2008, under pressure from USA and India, Pakistani army launched an operation against LeT and raided a *markaz*(centre) of the LeT at Shawai Nullah, 5 km from Muzaffarabad in Pakistan-controlled Azad Kashmir. The army arrested more than twenty members of the Lashkar-e-Taiba and Zaki-ur-Rehman Lakhvi, the alleged mastermind of the November 2008 Mumbai attacks. They are said to have sealed off the centre, which included a madrasah and a mosque alongside offices of the LeT according to the government of Pakistan.

On December 10, 2008 India formally requested the United Nations Security Council to designate JuD as a terrorist organization. Subsequently, Pakistan's ambassador to the United Nations Abdullah Hussain gave an undertaking, saying,

After the designation of Jamaat-ud-Dawah (JUD) under (resolution) 1267, the government on receiving communication from the Security Council shall proscribe the JUD and take other consequential actions, as required, including the freezing of assets.

A similar assurance was given by Pakistan in 2002 when it clamped down on the LeT; however, the LeT was covertly allowed to function under the guide of the JuD. While arrests have been made, the Pakistani Government has categorically refused to allow any foreign investigators access to Hafiz Saeed.

On December 11, 2008 the United Nations Security Council imposed sanctions on JuD, declaring it a global terrorist group. Hafiz Muhammad Saeed, the chief of JuD declared that his group will challenge the sanctions imposed on it in all forums. Pakistan's government also banned the JuD on the same day and issued an order to seal the JuD in all four provinces, as well as Pakistan-controlled Kashmir. Before the ban JuD ran a weekly newspaper named *Ghazwah,* two monthly magazines called *Majalla Tud Dawaa*and *Zarb e Taiba,* and a fortnightly magazine for children, *Nanhe Mujahid.*

The publications have since been banned by the Pakistani government. In addition to the prohibition of JuD's print publications, the organisation's websites were also shut down by the Pakistani government.

After the ban imposed by UNSC, Hindu minority groups in Pakistan came out in support of JuD. At protest marches in Hyderabad, Hindu groups said that JuD does charity work such as setting up water wells in desert regions and providing food to the poor.However, the credibility of the level of support during the protest is questionable.

Several protesters claim to have been under the impression they were protesting price rises. The BBC reported that protesters on their way to what they believed was a rally against price rises were handed signs in support of JuD. The organizations' banning has been met with heavy criticism in many Pakistani circles, which include many Christians and Hindus, as JuD was the first to react to the Kashmir earthquake and the Ziarat Earthquake. It also ran over 160 schools with thousands of students and provided aid in hospitals as well.

In January 2009 the JuD spokesperson, Abdullah Muntazir, stressed that the group did not have global jihadist aspirations and would welcome a peaceful resolution of the Kashmir issue.

He also publicly disowned LeT commanders Zaki-ur-Rehman Lakhvi and Zarrar Shah, who have both been accused of being the masterminds behind the November 2008 Mumbai attacks.

In response to the UN resolution and the government ban, the JuD reorganized itself under the name of Tehrik-e-Tahafuz Qibla Awal (TTQA).

Activities

The group conducts training camps and humanitarian work. Across Pakistan, the organization runs 16 Islamic institutions, 135 secondary schools, an ambulance service, mobile clinics, blood banks and seminaries according to the South Asia Terrorism Portal.

The group actively carried out attacks on Indian Armed Forces in Kashmir and Jammu.

Some breakaway Lashkar members have been accused of carrying out attacks in Pakistan, particularly in Karachi, to mark its opposition to the policies of former President Pervez Musharraf.

Training Camps

The Lashkar-e-Taiba training camps are presently located at a number of locations in Pakistan. These camps, which include its base camp, Markaz-e-Taiba in Muridke near Lahore and the one near Manshera, are used to impart training to militants. In these camps, the following trainings are imparted:

- the 21-day sectarian religious course (*Daura-e-Sufa*)
- the 21-day basic combat course (*Daura-e-Aam*)
- the three-months advanced combat course (*Daura-e-Khaas*)

26/11 mastermind, Zabiuddin Ansari alias, Abu Jundal arrested recently by Indian intelligece agences is reported to have disclosed that paragliding training was also included in the training curriculum of LeT cadres at is camps in Muzaffarabad. These camps have long been tolerated by the Pakistan's powerful Inter-Services Intelligence (ISI) agency because of their usefulness against India and in Afghanistan although they have been instructed not to mount any operations for now.

A French anti-terrorism expert, Jean-Louis Bruguière, in his *Some Things that I Wasn't Able to Say* has stated that the regular Pakistani army officers trained the militants in the LeT training camps until recently. He reached this conclusion after interrogating a French militant, Willy Brigitte, who had been trained by the LeT and arrested in Australia in 2003.

Markaz-e-Taiba

The LeT base camp Markaz-e-Taiba in Muridke, about 30 km from Lahore, was established in 1988. It is spread over 200 acres (0.81 km) of land and contains a madrassa, hospital, market, residences, a fish farm and agricultural tracts. The initial sectarian religious training, *Daura-e-Sufa* is imparted here to the militants. Markaz-e-Taiba is now under direct control of Punjab govt after Mumbai attacks. Khaqan babur is appointed administrator of Markaz-e-Taiba by provincial govt.

Other Training Camps

In 1987, LeT established two training camps in Afghanistan. The first one was the Muaskar-e-Taiba at Jaji in Paktia Province and the second one was the Muaskar-e-Aqsa in Kunar Province. American intelligence analysts justify the extrajudicial detention of at least one Guantanamo detainees because they allege he attended a Lashkar-e-Taiba training camp in Afghanistan. A memorandum summarizing the factors for and against the continued detention of Bader Al Bakri Al Samiri asserts that he attended a Lashkar-e-Taibatraining camp.

Mariam Abou Zahab and Olivier Roy in their *Islamist Networks: The Afghan-Pakistan Connection* (London: C. Hurst & Co., 2004) mentioned about three training camps in Pakistan-administered Kashmir, the principal one is the Umm-al-Qura training camp atMuzaffarabad. Every month five hundred militants are trained in these camps. Muhammad Amir Rana in his *A to Z of Jehadi Organizations in Pakistan* (Lahore: Mashal, 2004) listed five training camps. Four of them, the Muaskar-e-Taiba, the Muaskar-e-Aqsa, the Muaskar Umm-al-Qura and the Muaskar Abdullah bin Masood are in Pakistan-administered Kashmir and the Markaz Mohammed bin Qasim training camp is in Sanghar District of Sindh. Ten thousand militants had been trained in these camps till 2004.

Funding

Pakistan began to fund the LeT during the early 1990s and by around 1995 the funding had grown considerably. During this time the army and the ISI helped establish the LeT's military structure with the specific intent to use the militant group against India. The LeT also obtained funds through efforts of the MDI's Department of Finance. Until 2002 the group collected funds through public fundraising events usually using charity boxes in shops and mosques. The group also received money through donations at MDI offices, through personal donations collected at public celebrations of an operative's martyrdom, and through its website. The outfit also collected donations from the Pakistani immigrant community in the Persian Gulfand United Kingdom, Islamic Non-Governmental Organisations, and Pakistani and Kashmiri businessmen. Lashkar-e-Taiba operatives have also been apprehended in India, where they had been obtaining funds from sections of the Muslim Community.

Although many of the funds collected went towards legitimate uses, e.g. factories and other businesses, a significant portion was dedicated to military activities. According to U.S. intelligence, the LeT had a military budget of more than $5 million by 2009.

USE OF CHARITY AID TO FUND OPERATIONS

LeT assisted victims after the 2005 Kashmir earthquake. In many instances, they were the first on the scene, arriving before the army or other civilians.

A large amount of funds collected among the Pakistani expatriate community in Britain to aid victims of the earthquake were funneled for the activities of Lashkar-e-Taiba although the donors were unaware. About £5 million were collected, but more than half of the funds were directed towards LeT rather than towards relief efforts. Intelligence officials stated that some of the funds were used to prepare foran attack that would have detonated explosives on board transatlantic airflights. Other investigations also indicated the aid given for earthquake victims was directly involved to expand Lashkar-e-Taiba's activities within India.

Notable Incidents

- 1998 Wandhama massacre: 23 Kashmiri pandits were murdered on 25 January 1998.
- In March 2000, Lashkar-e-Taiba militants are claimed to have been involved in the Chittisinghpura massacre, where 35 Sikhs in the town of Chittisinghpura in Kashmir were killed. An 18-year-old male, who was arrested in December of that year, admitted in an interview with a *New York Times* correspondent to the involvement of the group and expressed no regret in perpetrating the anti-Sikh massacre. In a separate interview with the same correspondent, Hafiz Muhammad Saeed denied knowing the young man and dismissed any possible involvement of LeT. In 2010, the Lashkar-e-Taiba (LeT) associate David Headley, who was arrested in connection with the 2008 Mumbai attacks, reportedly confessed to the National Investigation Agency that the LeT carried out the Chittisinghpura massacre. He is said to have identified an LeT militant named Muzzamil as part of the group which carried out the killings apparently to create communal tension just before Clinton's visit.
- The LeT was also held responsible by the government for the December 23, 2000 attack in Red Fort, New Delhi. LeT confirmed its participation in the Red Fort attack.
- LeT claimed responsibility for an attack on the Srinagar Airport that left five Indians and six militants dead.

- The group claimed responsibility for an attack on Indian security forces along the border.
- The Indian government blamed LeT, in coordination with Jaish-e-Mohammed, for a December 13, 2001 assault on parliament in Delhi.
- 2002 Kaluchak massacre 31 killed May 14, 2002. Australian government attributed this massacre to Lashkar-e-Taiba when it designated it as a terrorist organization.
- 2003 Nadimarg Massacre 24 Kashmiri pandits gunned down on the night of March 23, 2003.
- 2005 Delhi bombings: During Diwali, Lashkar-e-Taiba bombed crowded festive Delhi markets killing 60 civilians and maiming 527.
- 2006 Varanasi bombings: Lashkar-e-Taiba was involved in serial blasts in Varanasi in the state of Uttar Pradesh. 37 people died and 89 were seriously injured.
- 2006 Doda massacre 34 Hindus were killed in Kashmir on April 30, 2006.
- 2006 Mumbai train bombings: The investigation launched by Indian forces and US officials have pointed to the involvement of Lashkar-e-Taiba in Mumbai serial blasts on 11 July 2006. The Mumbai serial blasts on 11 July claimed 211 lives and maimed about 407 people and seriously injured another 768.
- On September 12, 2006 the propaganda arm of the Lashkar-e-Taiba issued a fatwa against Pope Benedict XVI demanding that Muslims assassinate him for his controversial statements about the prophet Muhammad.
- On September 16, 2006, a top Lashkar-e-Taiba militant, Abu Saad, was killed by the troops of 9-Rashtriya Rifles in Nandi Marg forest in Kulgam. Saad belongs to Lahore in Pakistan and also oversaw LeT operations for the past three years in Gul Gulabhgash as the outfit's area commander. Apart from a large quantity of arms and ammunition, high denomination Indian and Pakistani currencies were also recovered from the slain militant.

- 2008 Mumbai attacks In November 2008, Lashkar-e-Taiba was the primary suspect behind the Mumbai attacks but denied any part. The lone surviving gunman, Ajmal Amir Kasab, captured by Indian authorities admitted the attacks were planned and executed by the organization. United States intelligence sources confirmed that their evidence suggested Lashkar-e-Taiba is behind the attacks. A July 2009 report from Pakistani investigators confirmed that LeT was behind the attack.
- On 7 December 2008, under pressure from USA and India, the Pakistan Army launched an operation against LeT and Jamat-ud-Dawa to arrest people suspected of 26/11 Mumbai attacks.
- In August 2009, LeT issued an ultimatum to impose Islamic dress code in all colleges in Jammu and Kashmir, sparking fresh fears in the tense region.
- In September and October 2009, Israeli and Indian intelligence agencies issued alerts warning that LeT is planning to attack Jewish religious places in Pune, India and other locations visited by Western and Israeli tourists in India. The gunmen who attacked the Mumbai headquarters of the Chabad Lubavitch movement during the November 2008 attacks were reportedly instructed that "Every person you kill where you are is worth 50 of the ones killed elsewhere."
- News sources have reported that members of LeT were planning to attack the U.S. and Indian embassies in Dhaka, Bangladesh, on November 26, 2009, to coincide with the one-year anniversary of the November 2008 Mumbai attacks. At least seven men have been arrested in connection to the plot, including a senior member of LeT.
- Two Chicago residents, David Coleman Headley and Tahawwur Hussain Rana, were allegedly working with LeT in planning an attack against the offices and employees of Jyllands-Posten, a Danish newspaper that published controversial cartoons of the Prophet Muhammad. Indian news sources have also implicated

the men in the November 2008 Mumbai attacks and in LeT's Fall 2009 plans to attack the U.S. and Indian embassies in Bangladesh.

EXTERNAL RELATIONSHIPS

Role in India-Pakistan Relations

LeT attacks have increased tensions in the already contentious relationship between India and Pakistan. Part of the LeT strategy may be to deflect the attention of Pakistan's military away from the tribal areas and towards its border with India. Attacks in India also aim to exacerbate tensions between India's Hindu and Muslim communities and help LeT recruitment strategies in India.

LeT cadres have also been arrested in different cities of India. On May 27, a LeT militant was arrested from Hajipur in Gujarat. On August 15, 2001, a LeT militant was arrested from Bhatinda in Punjab.

Mumbai police's interrogation of LeT operative, Abu Jindal revealed that LeT has planned 10 more terror attacks across India and he had agreed to participate in these attacks. A top US Counter terrorism official, Daniel Benjamin, in a news conference on 31 July 2012, told that LeT was a threat to the stability in South Asia urging Pakistan to take strong action against the terror outfit.

Inter-Services Intelligence Involvement

The ISI have provided financial and material support to the group. According to the declaration of LeT operatives, the Pakistan Armyfrom its 12th Infantry Division based in Azad Kashmir aids members of the outfit in their infiltration, extraction and clashes with Indian security forces around the Line of Control (LoC) by providing covering fire.

The LeT was also reported to have been directed by theInter-Services Intelligence (ISI) to widen its network in the Jammu region where a considerable section of the populace comprised Punjabis.

The LeT has a large number of activists who hail from Pakistani Punjab and can thus effectively penetrate into Jammu society. A

December 13, 2001 news report cited a LeT spokesperson as saying that the outfit wanted to avoid a clash with the Pakistani government.

He claimed a clash was possible because of the suddenly conflicting interests of the government and of the militant outfits active in Jammu and Kashmir even though the government had been an ardent supporter of Muslim freedom movements, particularly that of Kashmir.

Pakistan denies giving orders to Lashkar-e-Taiba's activities. However, the Indian government and many non-governmental think-tanks allege that the Pakistani ISI is involved with the group. The situation with LeT causes considerable strain in Indo-Pakistani relations, which are already mired in suspicion and mutual distrust.

Role in Afghanistan

The Lashkar-e-Taiba was created to participate in the Mujahideen conflict against the Najibullah regime in Afghanistan. In the process, the outfit developed deep linkages with Afghanistan and has several Afghan nationals in its cadre.

The outfit had also cultivated links with the former Taliban regime in Afghanistan and also with Osama bin Laden and his Al Qaeda network. Even while refraining from openly displaying these links, the LeT office in Muridke was reportedly used as a transit camp for third country recruits heading for Afghanistan.

Guantanamo detainee Khalid Bin Abdullah Mishal Thamer Al Hameydani's Combatant Status Review Tribunal said that he had received training via Lashkar-e-Taiba. The Combatant Status Review Tribunals of Taj Mohammed and Rafiq Bin Bashir Bin Jalud Al Hami, and the Administrative Review Board hearing of Abdullah Mujahid and Zia Ul Shah allege that they too were members or former members of Lashkar-e-Taiba.

LINKS WITH OTHER MILITANT GROUPS

While the primary focus for the Lashkar is the operations in Indian Kashmir, it has frequently provided support to other international terrorist groups. Primary among these is the Al-Qaeda Network in Afghanistan. LeT members also have been reported to have engaged in conflicts in the Philippines, Bosnia, the Middle East and Chechnya. There are also allegations that members of the Liberation Tigers of Tamil Eelam conducted arms transfers and made deals with LeT in the early 1990s

Al-Qaeda

- The Lashkar is claimed to have operated a military camp in post–September 11 Afghanistan, and extending support to the ousted Taliban regime. The outfit had claimed that it had assisted the Taliban militia and Osama bin Laden's Al-Qaeda network in Afghanistan during November and December 2002 in their fight against the US-aided Northern Alliance.
- A leading Al-Qaeda operative Abu Zubaydah, who became operational chief of Al-Qaeda after the death of Mohammed Atef, was caught in a Lashkar safehouse at Faislabad in Pakistan.
- A news report in the aftermath of the September 11 attacks in the U.S. has indicated that the outfit provides individuals for the outer circle of bin Laden's personal security.
- Other notable al-Qaeda operatives said to have received instruction and training in LeT camps include David Hicks, Richard Reid andDhiren Barot.

Jaish-e-Mohammed

News reports, citing security forces, said that the latter suspect that in the December 13, 2001 attack on India's Parliament in New Delhi, a joint group from the LeT and the Jaish-e-Mohammed (JeM) were involved.

The attack precipitated the 2001-2002 India-Pakistan standoff.

Hizb-ul-Mujahideen

The Lashkar is reported to have conducted several of its major operations in tandem with the Hizb-ul-Mujahideen.

Ties to attacks in the United States

- The Markaz campus at Muridke in Lahore, its headquarters, was used as a hide-out for both Ramzi Yousef, involved in the 1993 World Trade Centre bombing, and Mir Aimal Kansi, convicted and executed for the January 1993 killing of two Central Intelligence Agency officers outside the agency's headquarters in Langley, Virginia.
- A group of men dubbed the Virginia Jihad Network attended LeT training camps and were convicted in 2006 of conspiring to provide material support to the LeT. The leader of the group, Ali al-Timimi, urged the men to attend the LeT camps and to "go abroad to join the mujahideen engaged in jihad in Afghanistan." The men also trained with weapons in Virginia.
- Two U.S. citizens, Syed Haris Ahmed and Ehsanul Sadequee were arrested in 2006 for attempting to join LeT. Ahmed traveled to Pakistan in July 2005 to attend a terrorist training camp and join LeT. The men also shot videos of U.S. landmarks in the Washington, D.C. area for potential terrorist attacks. They were convicted in Atlanta during the summer of 2009 for conspiring toprovide material support to terrorists.
- U.S. citizen Ahmad Abousamra was indicted in November 2009 for providing material support to terrorists. He allegedly went to Pakistan in 2002 to join the Taliban and LeT, but failed.

ISLAMIST MILITANCY IN KASHMIR: THE CASE OF THE LASHKAR-I TAYYEBA

The emergence of radical Islamist groups in Kashmir over the last decade has added a new dimension to the ongoing conflict in the region. It has led to a rapid transformation in the terms of discourse in which the conflict is represented, by India, Pakistan and by many Kashmiris themselves.

The current stage in the Kashmir conflict can be dated to 1989, when the Jammu and Kashmir Liberation Front (JKLF) inaugurated an armed uprising against Indian rule. By the mid-1990s, however, the JKLF had been increasingly taken over by Pakistan-based Islamist groups.

The wiping out of many of its cadres in confrontation with the Indian armed forces, the withdrawal of Pakistani support and the growing realisation of the need for peaceful, as opposed to military, means for the eventual resolution of the Kashmir dispute, seem to be among the major reasons for the gradual decline of the JKLF as a military force in Kashmir, despite the fact that its goal of an independent Kashmir still commands the support of many Kashmiri Muslims. On the other hand, military and other forms of support from the Pakistani establishment, from private *jihad*ist groups in Pakistan and elsewhere, in addition to a passionate zeal for what is seen as a 'holy' cause, account, in large measure, for the gradual take-over of the armed struggle in Kashmir by militant Islamist groups, mainly based in Pakistan and led, for the most part, by Pakistani nationals.

Despite the active involvement of Islamist groups in the on-going struggle in Kashmir, little written has been written about them from a scholarly and detached point of view.

This article seeks to provide an account of the ideology, organization and development of one of the leading Islamist groups active in Kashmir today, the Lashkar-i Tayyeba. Of the several Pakistan-based Islamist groups active in Kashmir today, the Lashkar is, by far, the most well-organised, well-trained and heavily armed.

From the mid-1990s, this once little known group has emerged today as the most serious challenge to the Indian armed forces, being responsible for several attacks in Kashmir, killing a large number of Indian soldiers as well as civilians, both Hindu as well as Muslim.

This article looks at the emergence of the Lashkar as a key player in the present stage of the Kashmiri struggle. Owing to the relative paucity of published material, the article relies heavily on the official Internet web site of the Markaz Da'wat wa'l Irshad ('Centre for Invitation and Instruction'), of which the Lashkar is the armed wing.

This article is divided into three main sections. Part I looks at the origins of the Lashkar in the specific South Asian context, tracing its understanding of Islam and *jihad* to the emergence of the Ahl-i Hadith ('The People of the Prophetic Tradition'), an Islamic reformist movement, in the sub-continent.

We then look at the ideology of the Lashkar, seeing how it seeks to fashion armed *jihad* as a means for the 'liberation' of Muslims from what it sees as 'oppression' and to advance its own stated goal of establishing the 'supremacy' of Islam, as it understands it, as a global ideology. Part II examines the involvement of the Lashkar in Kashmir, seeing it as emerging out of a broader Islamist movement in the region, the roots of which go back to the early years of the twentieth century. The concluding section of the article looks briefly at how far the Lashkar has been able to actually establish itself among the Kashmiri Muslims. In assessing its ability to do so, a distinction is stressed between, on the one hand, its military engagements against the Indian armed forces, and, on the other, its ability to impose its own vision of Islam as the accepted version.

The Lashkar: Early Origins

The Lashkar is the military wing of the Markaz Da'wat wa'l Irshad, with its headquarters at the town of Muridke in the Gujranwala district in Pakistani Punjab. The Markaz was established in 1986 by two Pakistani university professors, Hafiz Muhammad Sa'eed and Zafar Iqbal.

They were assisted by the late 'Abdullah Azam' a close aide of Osama bin Laden, who was then associated with the International Islamic University, Islamabad. Funds for setting up the organization are said to have come from Pakistan's dreaded secret services agency, the Inter Services Intelligence (ISI).

The Markaz is affiliated to the Ahl-i Hadith school of thought, a reformist Islamic movement, which had its origins in early nineteenth century north India.

The founders of the Ahl-i Hadith, men such as Maulana Nazir Husain (1805-1902), Nawab Siddiq Hasan Khan Bhopali (d1832-90) and Maulana Sanaullah Amritsari (1870-1943), believed that they were charged with the divine responsibility of purging popular Muslim practice of what they saw as 'un-Islamic' accretions and borrowings from their Hindu neighbours, regarding these as 'unlawful innovations' (*bida'at*), and as akin to *shirk*, the sin of associating anything with God.

They insisted that Muslims must go back to the original sources of their faith, the Qur'an and the Hadith, the Traditions of the Prophet, and abandon all beliefs and practices not sanctioned therein. They called for Muslims to abide strictly by the Islamic law (*shari'ah*) and to abandon 'imitation' (*taqlid*) of the traditional schools of Islamic jurisprudence (*mazhab*. pl. *mazahib*), attempting to refashion the worldwide Muslim community in the mould of the Companions of the Prophet.

The *'ulama*of the Hanafi *mazhab*, representing the vast majority of the Muslims of South Asia, entered into bitter conflict with the Ahl-i Hadith on the matter of *taqlid*. The latter defended their opposition to *taqlid* on the grounds that the schools of jurisprudence had developed more than two hundred years after the death of the Prophet, and that, therefore, the Companions of the Prophet did not follow *taqlid*.

Since, they argued, Muslims should follow the model of the Companions, there was no need for them to 'blindly follow' the schools of jurisprudence, for this would be tantamount to 'personality worship' of the founders of the *mazahib*, a heinous sin. Further, they claimed, the Hanafis had fabricated numerous *hadith* to prove the claims of their *mazhab*, and quoted a *hadith* to the effect that 'he who fabricates *hadith* shall be thrown into hell-fire'.

Besides attacking the Hanafi *'ulama*, the Ahl-i Hadith directed their attention to bitterly critiquing Sufism, which they saw as a 'wrongful innovation', for, they argued, it had no sanction in the practice of the Prophet and his Companions. Every 'wrongful innovation', they insisted, was a heinous sin, the punishment for which was damnation in hell. They stiffly opposed the adoration of the Prophet as a superhuman being as well as the devotion to the saints and the cults centred on their shrines that are an integral part of popular Sufi tradition in South Asia, seeing this as a deviation from the practice of the Prophet and the early Muslims.

Faith in the powers of Sufi preceptors and the widespread belief in the Sufi saints as intermediaries with God were condemned as akin to polytheism. So, too, was the belief in the supernatural powers of the Prophet and of his being ever-present and all-seeing.

Given the immense popularity of the Sufi traditions and the influence of the Hanafi 8*ulama* among the Muslims of South Asia, it was hardly surprising that the Ahl-i Hadith faced stiffed opposition, being banned from worship at mosques and condemned as apostates and enemies of Islam. For their part, the Ahl-i Hadith appeared to have revelled in controversy, not losing any opportunity of attacking their Muslim opponents for what they branded as their 'un-Islamic' ways.

Engaged in constant conflict with other Muslims, drawing clear lines of division between themselves as the only truly Muslim group and the rest, seems to have played a crucial role in the development of a separate Ahl-i Hadith identity.

Confrontation with other Muslim groups created an atmosphere conducive to militancy, and the Ahl-i Hadith saw themselves as carrying on in the long tradition of *jihad*, which they accused other Muslims as having abandoned.

The founders of the Ahl-i Hadith claimed the legacy of the early nineteenth century jihad movement led by Sayyed Ahmad Barelvi and Isma'il Shahid against the Sikhs in the Punjab.

In the failed revolt of 1857 against the British, several Muslim *ulama* associated with Ahl-i Hadith-style activism played a role in leading uprisings at some places.

After 1857, while some Ahl-i Hadith leaders accommodated themselves to British rule and devoted themselves to peaceful preaching, others continued to carry on violent struggles against the British in the North-West Frontier Province, till they were finally crushed by the end of the nineteenth century.

Although from the early twentieth century onwards the Ahl-i Hadith, as a whole, gave up the path of violence in the face of British arms, an Ahl-i Hadith scholar writes that they 'refused to accept the supremacy of the British and the Hindus', and vowed to carry on the struggle through other means to 'convert India into an abode of Islam (*dar-ul islam*) through *jihad'*.

While they desisted from entering into violent confrontation with the British, their opposition to Sufism and to the Hanafis brought them into conflict with many traditional Muslims, which sometimes took violent forms. However, they were doomed to a marginal existence owing to their vehement opposition to popular Muslim practice, and hence were not able to emerge as a mass movement. Rather, they remained an elitist group, characterised, as Barbara Metcalf writes, by a sense of 'moral superiority' and 'self-righteousness', tinged with 'a certain harshness', and with a small following among urban Muslims, particularly in north India.

Bibliography

Alam, Aftab : *US Policy Towards South Asia: Special Reference to Indo-Pak Relations,* Raj, Delhi, 1998.

Arif. S.M.: *Islamic Fundamentalism and Jihad,* MD Pub, Delhi, 2010.

Benjamin, Joseph : *Indo-Pak Relations : Prospect and Retrospect,* Reference Press, Delhi, 2004.

Bernard Wood: *Development Dimension of Conflict Prevention and Peace-building,* New York: UNDP,. 2003.

Bruce, Hoffman: *Inside Terrorism,* New York: Columbia University Press, 1998.

Choueiri, Y.M. : *Islamic Fundamentalism,* London: Pinter Publishers; Delhi, 1990.

Das. P.K.: *Jihad : Terrorist Strategies Against the West,* Sumit Enterprises, Delhi, 2009.

Graham, Allison: *Nuclear Terrorism: The Ultimate Preventable Catastrophe,* New York: Times Books, 2004.

Greene, Mott : *Natural Knowledge in Preclassical Antiquity,* Baltimore, Johns Hopkins University Press, 1992.

Hiro, Dilip : *Holy Wars: The Rise of Islamic Fundamentalism* New York: Routledge, Chapman and Hall, Inc., 1989.

Howard T. : *Environment, Power and Society,* New York, Wiley-Interscience, 1971.

Laquer, Walter, *The New Terrorism: Fanaticism and the Arms of Mass Destruction,* Oxford: Oxford University Press, 1999.

Multani, R K P : *Islamic Fundamentalism in South Asia* : Sumit Enterprises, Delhi, 2007.

Noorani, A.G.: *Islam and Jihad,* Leftword, Delhi, 2002.

Sharma, Rajeev: *Global Jihad : Current Patterns and Future Trends,* Kaveri Books, Delhi, 2006.

Thomas Arnold: *The Spread of Islam in the World, A History of Peaceful Preaching,* Goodword Books, 2001.

Index

A

Abu Nidal organization, 53.
Abu Sayyaf Group, 54, 120, 121, 168.
Al Qaeda, 13, 17, 18, 19, 28, 29, 30, 37, 41, 42, 43, 48, 49, 63, 128, 133, 138, 139, 140, 141, 171, 172, 173, 175, 178, 179, 180, 181, 186, 187, 213, 215, 216, 217, 218, 219, 221, 222, 235, 236, 237, 239, 240, 247, 248, 249, 251, 252, 256, 257, 258, 259, 260, 261, 262, 263, 264, 265, 286.
Al-Aqsa Martyrs Brigade, 55.
Armed Islamic Group, 18, 42, 70, 166.
Army of Islam, 57, 207.

C

Combating Homegrown Terrorism, 222.
Counter Suicide Attacks, 31.

D

Diplomacy, 34, 35, 125, 128, 129, 130, 140.

E

External Relationships, 285.

F

Fluid Organization, 241.

I

Indian Mujahedeen, 80.
Islamic Fundamentalism, 42, 45, 50, 133, 183.
Islamic Jihad Union, 65, 85, 160.
Islamic Movement of Uzbekistan, 62, 65, 85, 160, 242.
Islamic Terrorism, 142, 143, 144, 147, 148, 152, 153, 166, 169.
Islamic Terrorist Organizations, 53.
Islamist Militancy, 288.
Islamist Movement, 161, 250, 253, 290.
Islamist Terrorist Groups, 41.

J

Jailhouse Jihadism, 187.
Jihadist Organizations, 1, 184, 206.

L

Leadership, 26, 27, 54, 56, 65, 71, 77, 86, 97, 98, 99, 100, 101, 102, 106, 107, 115, 116, 131, 167,